The Scie
HAIRDR

RUTH BENNETT
B.Sc., Dip.Ed.
Lecturer in Hairdressing Science,
Coventry Technical College

EDWARD ARNOLD

First published 1975
by Edward Arnold (Publishers) Limited,
25 Hill Street, London, W1X 8LL
Reprinted 1977

ISBN: 0 7131 1866 0

To my Mother and Father

Answers to the multiple choice questions in this book are contained in a leaflet which is available, free of charge, to bona fide teachers on request to the publishers. Please send your request with a stamped addressed envelope to The Education Department, Edward Arnold (Publishers) Ltd., Woodlands Park Avenue, Woodlands Park, Maidenhead, Berks., England.

Printed in Great Britain by T. & A. Constable Ltd., Edinburgh

Preface

by the Author

This book is intended for students taking courses in Hairdressing Science, who are preparing for the examinations of the City and Guilds of London Institute Craft Courses 760-1 (Basic) and 760-2 (Advanced), and for the Qualifying Examination of the Hairdressing Council.

The content of the book is as up-to-date as possible, and in some cases the information is so recent at the time of writing, that it may be considered controversial. The emphasis is on relating the scientific principles directly to the craft, so that the book is built round a framework provided by the procedures carried out in the salon.

The practical work included is a personal selection from a very large number of suitable experiments. All the experiments are regularly carried out by students studying hairdressing science, and have been found to be particularly helpful in aiding the learning process at this level.

The multiple choice questions placed at the end of each chapter should give the student experience in dealing with the type of question they will encounter in the City and Guilds examination in science, and give them the confidence to deal successfully with that paper.

Foreword

by G. N. Jackson, J.P.

National Chairman of the Hairdressing Industry Apprenticeship Council

The art of hairdressing is a combination of a natural flair in artistic fields, acquired skill, and technical knowledge of human hair and the chemicals and chemical processes used and applied to the human being. Each hairdresser must seek to interpret the combined knowledge of these in a manner that creates a unique way and style that belongs to him or her only.

In this book, Mrs. Bennett comprehensively gives the fullest explanations required in the day to day work of a hairdresser, and embraces all the scientific information necessary for examinations.

I congratulate her on the meticulously careful and adequately illustrated preparation of this book *The Science of Hairdressing*, which will help fill a long felt want and will greatly help students who are training for the craft of hairdressing and assist those responsible for training, in a practical and easily readable way.

Acknowledgements

I wish to thank my colleagues in the science and hairdressing sections at Coventry Technical College who have given information and advice during the preparation of this book, particularly Mrs. Hilary Robinson, Mrs. Elsie Milne, and Messrs. Jim Hendry Eric Johnson, John Main, and Tony Thomas. I am also grateful for specialist advice from Dr. Joan Ashley, and Mr. Claude Diamond, B.Sc., F.R.I.C., and for the photographs of experiments supplied by Mr. Frank Barlow.

I am indebted to Mr. D. J. Bale of the College of Food Technology and Commerce, Cardiff, for his careful reading of the manuscript, and constructive criticism.

The publishers would like to thank the following for permission to reproduce photographs in the book:
Dr. J. Almeida (159); Avery Ltd (19); A-Z Collection (90); Belling & Co Ltd (144); 'Blanche', Tachbrook Road, Leamington Spa (138); CEGB (108); Chubb Fire Security Ltd (184); Gene Cox Microcolour Ltd (159, 175); Electricity Council (57); Derek Ellis, University College Hospital (136); GEC-Xpelair Ltd (152); Hair Plan Ltd (104); Hurseal (Sales) Ltd (144); ICI Fibres Ltd (166); IMI Santon Ltd (155); Institute of Dermatology (100, 101, 171, 172); L'Oreal Ltd (1); Noeline Kelly (11, 12, 29, 44, 51, 52, 54, 62, 75, 83, 84, 86, 89, 91, 98, 103, 107, 110, 112, 113, 118, 121, 158, 168, 182, 183, 185); John Laing & Son (29); Lee Valley Water Co (30); Dr D. W. R. MacKenzie (158); The Permutit Co Ltd (35); Triton Instruments Ltd (159); Tube Investments Ltd (146); Unilever Films (37); Unilever Ltd (63, 180); M. I. Walker (7, 10, 130); Zoological Society of London (24).
The publishers would also like to thank Mrs R. E. Thomas of Isleworth Polytechnic School of Hairdressing for her help in allowing photographs to be taken at the college.

Contents

1 Structure of the Head

The head of the client is the hairdresser's main concern, and a knowledge of its structure is necessary if he or she is to handle the hair skilfully, and adapt the hairstyle to the shape of the head.

The skull

The framework of *bones* which supports and protects the other softer structures of the head, and to which the muscles are attached, is known as the *skull*. It is composed of two regions; the *cranium*, surrounding the brain and forming the top, back and sides of the skull, and the *face*, forming its front portion. The cranium is made up from eight curved, plate-like bones, which fit tightly together like the pieces of a jigsaw puzzle. These interlocking joints are *sutures*. The names and positions of the bones forming the cranium are given on the diagrams. The *mastoid* area which lies below the temporal bone just behind the angle of the jaw, surrounds and protects the internal part of the ear. The fourteen bones which make up the face are also joined at sutures, except for the *lower jaw* which is attached to the rest of the skull by a movable joint, so that the lower jaw can move up and down and from side to side when talking or chewing. Only the main bones giving shape to the face have been named in diagrams 1.1 and 1.2.

There are holes in the skull through which nerves and blood vessels pass. Above the cranium lies the tough membrane of the scalp, to the edges of which, muscles are attached which continue over the face or down into the neck.

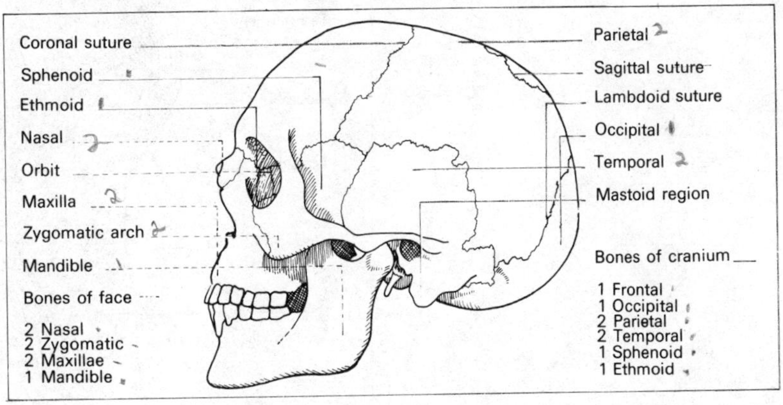

1.1 Side view of human skull

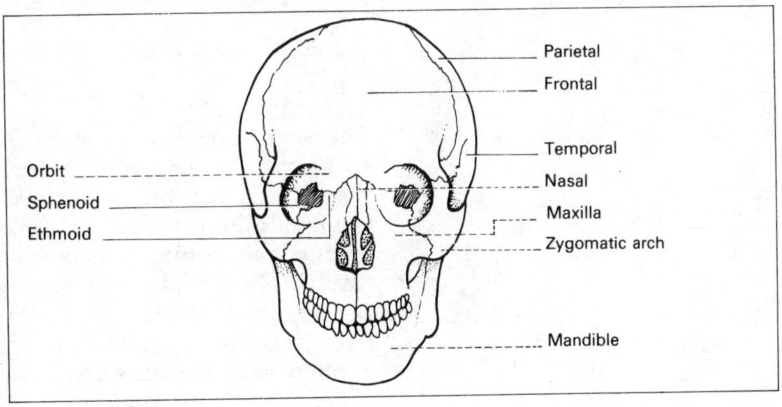

1.2 Front view of human skull

Muscles of the head

The *muscles* are blocks of fibres held together by a thin covering membrane, and form the flesh outside the skull. They bring about movements of the head in relation to the rest of the body, or move the individual parts of the head. The muscles cause movement by *contracting* in length. When not working they are *relaxed*. The *frontalis* muscle pulls the scalp forward, raises the eyebrows, and wrinkles the forehead. The *occipitalis* muscle moves the scalp at the back of the head. Frowning may therefore cause tension at the back of the neck. Both the eyes and the mouth are surrounded by circular *orbicularis* muscles, the orbicularis oculi closing the eyelids, and the orbicularis oris closing the lips. The *temporalis* muscle raises the lower jaw to shut the mouth, while the *masseter* muscle is used in chewing. The *radiating* muscles of facial expression lie between the eyes and mouth, and are used in the art of communication between the hairdresser and her client. The *trapezius* muscle tips the head backward, while the *sternomastoid* muscles bring the head forward on to the chest if they both contract together. Acting singly they turn the head to the opposite side. The *platysma* muscle moves the skin and maintains the shape of the neck. It also pulls down the corners of the mouth. The position of each of these muscles is shown in diagram 1.3.

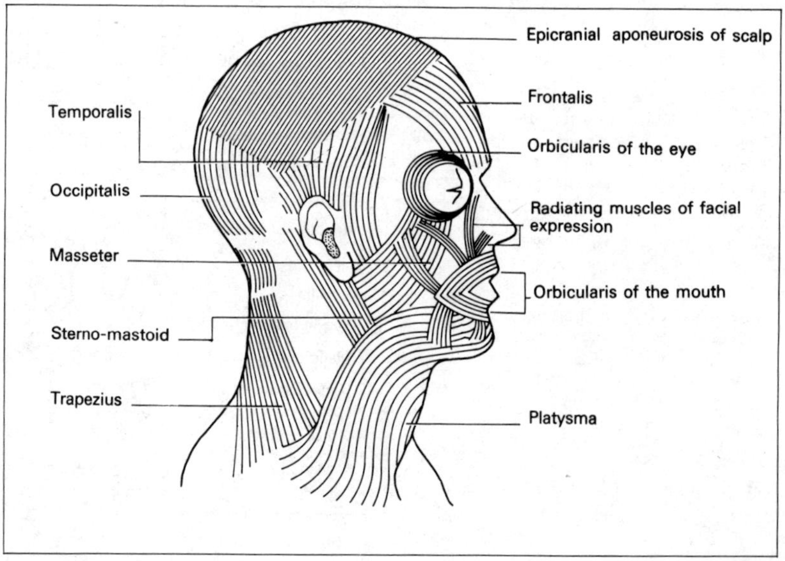

1.3 Some muscles of the head and neck

The scalp

The scalp consists of three layers of tissue lying outside the cranium. The innermost layer, which is only loosely attached to the underlying bone, is the *epicranial aponeurosis* tendon joining the frontalis/occipitalis muscle. This is moved over the cranium during shampooing, when the hairdresser massages the shampoo into the hair and scalp. (Scalp wounds gape widely because of retraction of the muscles attached round the edges of the aponeurosis, and continue to bleed for a long time.) Above the aponeurosis is a thin dense *fatty layer*, and outside this, a layer of *skin* producing the scalp hair. All these three layers are firmly joined together and move as one structure.

Nerves of the head

There are twelve pairs of *nerves* connected to the brain which control the movements of the head muscles, or carry information into the brain. The nerves mainly concerned with the face are the fifth and seventh pairs. The fifth or *trigeminal* nerve emerges from the skull in front of the ear. It controls the muscles used in chewing, and picks up skin sensations from the face and scalp. It has three branches. The seventh or *facial* nerve emerges below and behind the ear, and controls the muscles of facial expression. It has five branches. The names and distribution of each branch of the fifth and seventh nerves of the head are shown in diagram 1.4.

1.4 Side view of head showing fifth and seventh nerves

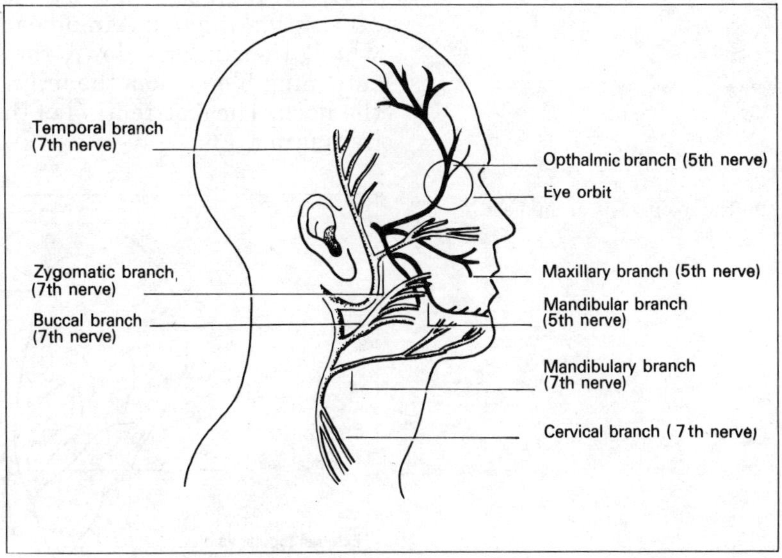

1.5 The main arteries of the head

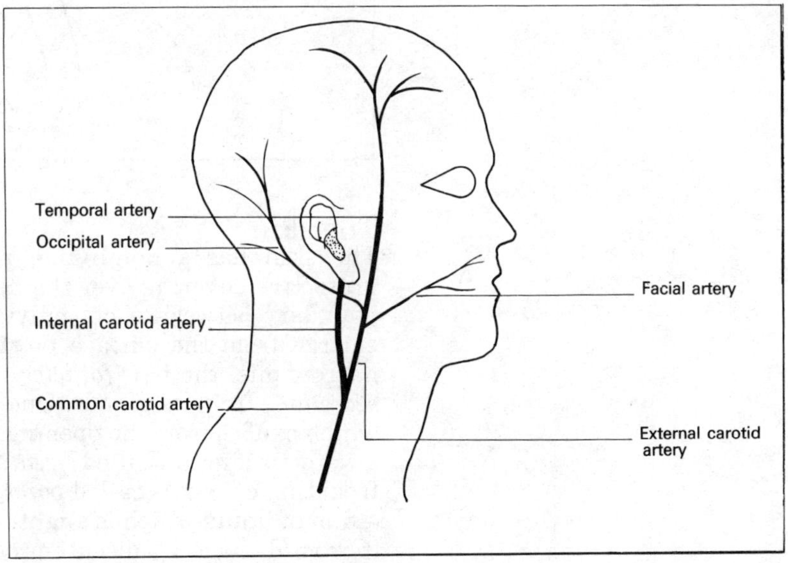

Blood vessels of the head

There are two types of larger blood vessels occurring in the head called *arteries* and *veins*. These are linked by networks of very fine vessels called *capillaries*. The arteries supply blood to the head, and the veins return blood from it. A *common carotid* artery passes up through the neck on each side bringing blood to the head. At the top of the neck it divides into two branches. One branch is the internal carotid artery which passes through the temporal bone taking blood to the brain. The other branch is the external carotid artery which remains outside the skull, and gives a branch to the *facial*, *temporal*, and *occipital* regions of the head. These three branches of the external carotid artery are shown on the diagram of the main arteries of the head. 1.5.

After passing from the arteries through capillary networks, the blood is collected up in *veins* from the facial, temporal, and occipital regions of the head. These three branches join to form an *external jugular* vein on each side, behind and below the ear, which then passes down the neck. An *internal jugular* vein returning blood from the brain also passes down on each side of the neck. The distribution of the main veins of the head is shown in diagram 1.6.

1.6 The main veins of the head

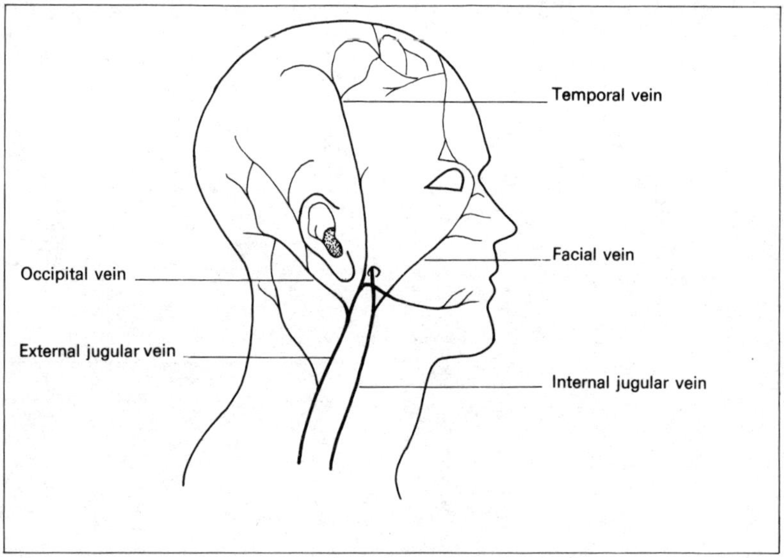

The skin

The skin has a non-living, ridged, outer surface, forming a protective covering over the head and rest of the body. It is the boundary between each individual and the environment. *Hairs* emerge from the surface of the skin at the openings of deep narrow pits, the hair *follicles.* The skin produces two liquids or *secretions* from its glands. One is a fatty secretion called *sebum,* which exudes from the openings of the hair follicles. The other is a watery secretion called *sweat,* which flows on to the skin surface from tiny openings called *pores.* The skin is therefore covered by a film of liquid which is slightly *acid,* and which helps to protect it from damage by disease-producing organisms. Any cosmetic which makes the skin *alkaline* for long periods is considered to be potentially harmful as it destroys the protective acid film. The average pH (see Chapter 2) of the skin of the face in women is 5·6 to 5·8.

The outer surface of the skin is constantly renewed from below as it is worn away by rubbing. The skin carries a large population of microscopic living organisms many of which are harmless.

Some are potentially dangerous as they may cause disease if they get into the deeper layers of the skin. The glandular secretions and flakes of dead skin at the surface provide the food for these micro-organisms. The skin is elastic and will stretch as the muscles below it cause movements. Strong sunlight and increasing age reduce the skin's elasticity so that it wrinkles after it has been stretched. The skin varies in thickness, being only 0·5 mm thick on the lips and eyelids, whereas it is 2·5 mm on the scalp.

Vertical sections through the skin show that there are two distinct layers, the outer *epidermis* and the inner thicker *dermis*. Sandwiched between the dermis and the muscles is a *fatty layer* which helps to prevent heat loss from within and gives rounded contours to the face.

THE EPIDERMIS

The epidermis is composed of several layers of very small *cells*. On the outer surface the cells are dead and compressed into flat scale-like flakes made of the horny material *keratin*. These dead flakes form the *cornified* (horny) layer of the epidermis, and prevent water loss from the skin, apart from that lost by sweating. If the cornified layer is stripped off, water loss increases up to twenty times. Next comes a *lucid* (clear) layer, followed by a *granular* layer where the keratin is formed in the epidermal cells. These two layers which are only clearly visible in the thick skin of the sole of the foot and palm of the hand, form the transition zone between the outer dead cornified layer and the inner living dividing cells which form the *germinating* layer (stratum germinativum; Malpighian layer). The germinating layer consists of several rows of *prickle* cells and a single lowermost row of *basal* cells. The basal cells divide, cutting off new cells to the outside. The growth rate is greatest between midnight and 4 a.m., which may explain the term 'beauty sleep'. These newly formed cells at first have fine threads connecting them to the cells around them, hence the name 'prickle' cells. As they are pushed towards the outside by new cells forming below, they become flatter.

1.7 Structure of the epidermis

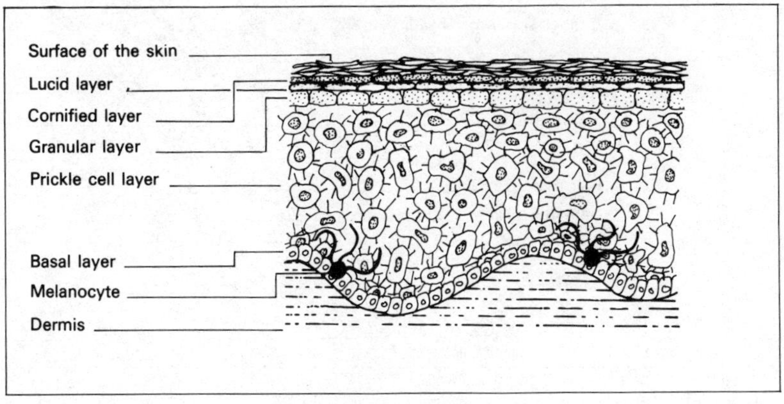

The germinating layer contains the dark pigment *melanin*. All races contain some melanin in their skin, the darker the skin the greater the amount of melanin. The dark pigment absorbs harmful *ultra-violet* rays present in sunlight. The melanin is produced by large branched cells called *melanocytes* which lie among the cells of the basal layer. *Freckles* are due to the occurrence of a few very active melanocytes forming small dark areas which increase on exposure to sunlight. *Moles* are congenital pigmented growths of the epidermis which do not contain blood capillaries. Hairy moles are common on the face. Moles must not be interfered with as they can become cancerous, and any increase in size of a mole should be reported to a doctor.

THE DERMIS

The outermost layer of the dermis pushes up into the epidermis as the *papillary* layer. These projections of the dermis into the epidermis are shallower in the skin of the scalp than elsewhere. The dermis contains a number of structures which have grown down from the epidermis. These are the *hair follicles* and hairs, *sebaceous glands*, and *sweat glands*. The dermis contains a regular network of *fibres* which give the skin its elasticity. It also contains networks of blood *capillaries* which are prominent in regions where growth or secretion occur, and where food and oxygen are thus being used up rapidly. Capillary networks occur just below the growing basal layer of the epidermis, and at the base of each hair follicle in the dermal *hair papilla*. They also lie over the sebaceous and sweat glands. Blood capillaries do not extend into the epidermis. The dermis contains *nerves*, some of which terminate in nerve endings just below the epidermis.

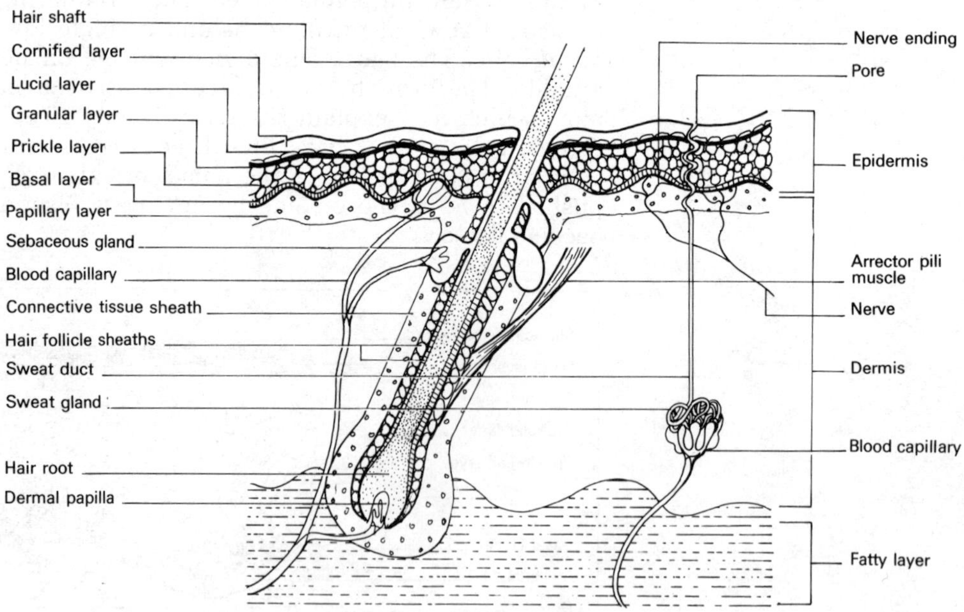

1.8 Section through the skin

Other nerves penetrate the hair follicle and hair, and some pass into the germinating layer of the epidermis. The *nerve endings* are sensitive to temperature changes, touch, or pain, and messages pass from the nerve endings along the nerve fibres to the brain, carrying information. The sweat glands and *arrector pili* muscles, attached to the hair follicles, have nerve endings which control their activity. The sebaceous glands which secrete the sebum have no nerve supply. *Eccrine* or small sweat glands are long fine tubes opening on a ridge at the skin surface at a *pore.* The pore is the opening of a spiral *duct* which passes inwards to a coiled *gland* which secretes sweat. *Sweat* is a watery fluid containing dissolved salts, mainly *sodium chloride* (common salt). *Sebaceous* glands lie over the hair follicle and open into it. From the glands the sebum passes into the follicle, coating the hair and spreading over the skin surface. On the face sebaceous glands may occur independently of hair follicles. Around six hundred sebaceous glands occur on every cm^2 of the scalp. They are most frequent on the skin of the forehead, and absent on the lower lip. Sebaceous activity is controlled by *hormones* (chemical messengers) in the blood. Activity of these glands is increased at puberty by the production of male sex hormones. It is reduced during pregnancy by changes in the balance of female sex hormones. *Sebum* is a fatty material similar to ear wax. It lubricates the hair and skin and helps to waterproof it.

1.9 Section through skin of scalp

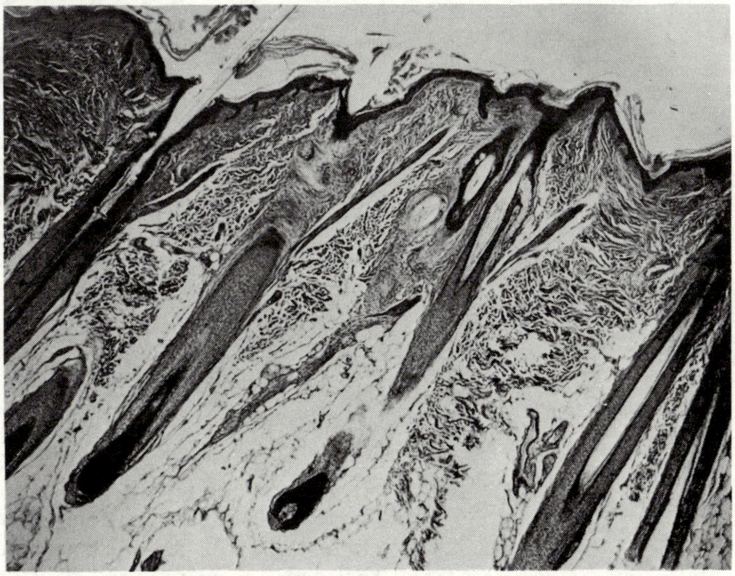

Structure of the hair follicle

Each hair grows from a follicle which is a narrow tube sunk into the dermis and formed by the epidermis. Around the epidermal hair follicle the papillary layer of the dermis forms a *connective tissue sheath.* At the base the follicle is pushed in like the bottom of a wine bottle, and the space produced is filled by dermal tissue containing a knot of blood capillaries, forming the *hair papilla.* This is attached to the connective tissue sheath, and supplies food and oxygen to the growing hair. The *sebaceous glands* open into the follicle about two-thirds of the way up. An *arrector pili* muscle is attached near the base of the follicle, and runs upwards ending just below the epidermis. The follicle slopes, and when the arrector muscle contracts it pulls the follicle upright, bunching up the skin at the surface to cause 'gooseflesh'. The wall of the follicle is double below the sebaceous gland openings, comprising inner and outer *root sheaths*. In the lower part of the follicle the *inner* root sheath is closely pressed against the growing hair, and grows up with it. Above the sebaceous gland openings the inner root sheath disappears, leaving a space into which hairdressing preparations, skin cosmetics, or germs can penetrate. The hair grows from the base of the follicle from a patch of dividing cells capping the dermal hair papilla, called the hair *bulb*. In the lower part of the bulb, the *matrix*, all the cells are dividing, and look alike. There is no pigment in the matrix but *melanocytes* occur at its outside border, and produce granules of melanin which colour the upper bulb. In the *upper bulb* the three layers of the hair shaft begin to develop as the hair grows upwards.

1.10 Structure of a hair follicle

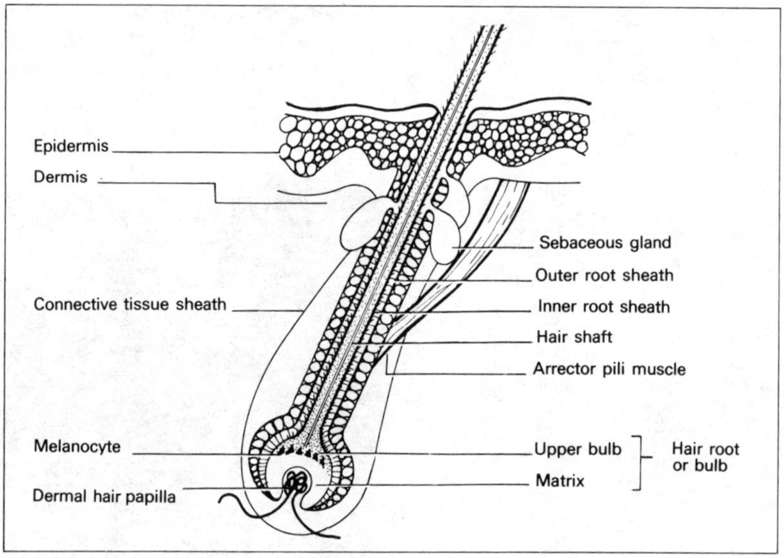

Structure of the hair

Two types of hair occur on the head. There is the *vellus* hair which consists of soft fair short hairs up to 2 cm long covering most of the face, except for the lips. Longer coarser *terminal* hairs occur on the scalp, eyebrows, eyelashes, and on the beard and moustache regions of the face in men. These terminal hairs vary in length from 1·25 cm in the eyebrows, to up to 100 cm on the scalp. Follicles which produce fine vellus hair up to the age of puberty, may then produce terminal hair. Follicles on the upper lips and chins of men do this. An average scalp contains 100,000 or so hairs, blond people having the most, and redheads the fewest. The part of the hair emerging from the skin is the hair *shaft* and is a completely dead structure composed of the hard horny protein *keratin*. The hair shaft gradually hardens during growth, but is not fully hardened until it has grown 1 cm above the skin surface. This, together with scalp heat, makes the action of chemicals more rapid on the hair roots than on the ends. The tip of the hair is pointed if it has never been cut. This is readily seen by looking at an eyelash.

Each hair is composed of three layers: the *cuticle* on the outside, then the *cortex*, with the *medulla* forming the centre of the hair. In fine terminal hairs and vellus hairs the medulla is usually absent. Until very recently, the nature of the internal structure of the hair shaft was based on information largely obtained by studying wool, i.e. sheep's hair. The *cuticle* was described as consisting of a single layer of overlapping flat scales arranged like the tiles on a roof, and having their free edges towards the tip of the hair. The cuticle layer is colourless and transparent. The *cortex* was said to consist of elongated spindle-shaped cells containing fibres of keratin, and the hair pigment melanin. These spindle-shaped cells, tapering at each end, were believed to be packed together to form a very dense tissue. The *medulla* was said to contain irregular loosely packed cells with large air spaces between them, forming a soft spongy tissue.

1.11 Structure of hair shaft (classical ideas)
Hair cut transversely (above)
Hair cut longitudinally (below)

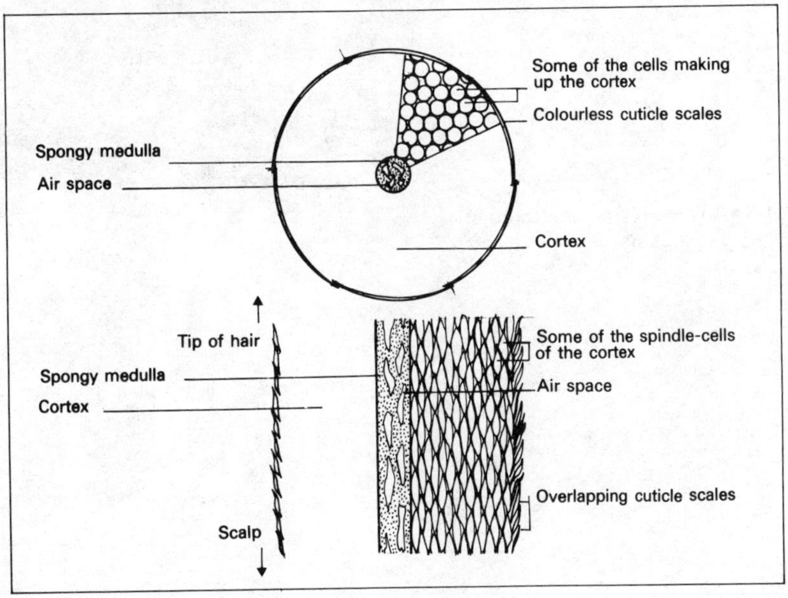

Recent work using the electron and stereo-scan microscopes suggests that some modification of these classical ideas on hair structure is needed. Instead of one layer of scales as in wool, the *cuticle* of the hair consists of several layers. There are between seven and ten irregular bands or rings of colourless rather brittle cuticular keratin extending completely or part-way round the hair. The free edge of each band is towards the tip of the hair, and they lift away from one another when the hair is stretched round a roller. Backbrushing and backcombing also lift up these cuticle bands. In number and thickness the cuticle bands are identical in fine and coarse hairs. Thus in coarse hair the cuticle forms around 20% of the total weight of the hair, but in fine hair it may account for as much as 40%.

The *cortex* is now said to have a fibrous structure consisting of very long *filaments* running parallel with the long axis of the hair shaft, and embedded in a *matrix*. The fibres of the cortex separate readily, and appear to be held together by the cuticle. The matrix has been described as a 'putty-like' material by some workers in this field. The melanin pigment granules which colour the hair occur in the matrix. No changes have been described in the structure of the *medulla*.

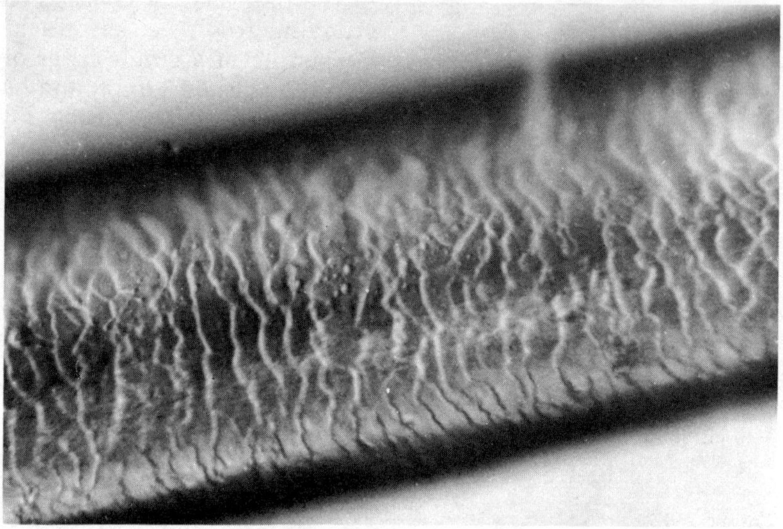

1.12 Hair showing cuticle rings

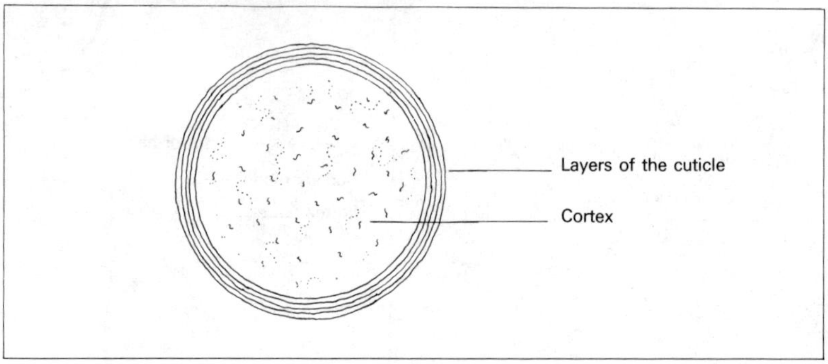

1.13 Transverse section through a fine human hair (recent studies)

Multiple choice questions

1 The part of the skull which is beneath the forehead is the
a temporal bone *b* frontal bone *c* occipital bone
d parietal bone

2 The dark pigment present in hair originates from the
a blood capillaries *b* sebaceous glands
c dermal papilla *d* melanocytes

3 The ring-shaped bands of muscle round the mouth and eyes are the
a orbicularis muscles *b* arrector muscles
c aponeurosis muscles *d* orbital muscles

4 The elasticity of the skin is due to
a shedding of the cornified layer *b* fibres in the dermis
c growth of the basal layer *d* the presence of melanin

5 Blood is supplied to the head by vessels known as
a jugular veins *b* cranial arteries *c* occipital veins
d carotid arteries

6 The cranial nerve activating the muscles of facial expression is the
a 12th *b* 7th *c* 5th *d* 3rd

7 The effect of sebum on the hair shaft is to
a increase its growth rate *b* supply extra keratin
c pull it erect *d* lubricate and waterproof it

8 The hair matrix is provided with food and oxygen for growth by the
a inner root sheath *b* dermal hair papilla
c connective tissue sheath *d* sebaceous glands

9 The skin layer in which the cells are actively dividing is the
a basal *b* cornified *c* granular *d* stratified

10 The main constituent of the hair shaft is a chemical called
a melanin *b* chitin *c* cystine *d* keratin

2 Hairdressing Preparations

Many hairdressing processes involve the application of preparations or reagents to the hair. The chemical substances contained in these preparations modify the properties of the hair either physically or chemically, i.e. produce physical or chemical changes.

Physical and chemical changes

Physical changes are easily reversed and do not form any new substances. *Examples* of physical changes to hair carried out during hairdressing are wetting, setting, conditioning, and colour-rinsing. All these processes are easily reversed, and the chemical structure of hair keratin is unaltered. Other physical changes are the change from liquid water to water vapour in the steamer and under the hairdryer, and the dissolving of substances in water.

Chemical changes are not easily reversed, so hairdressing processes involving chemical changes are usually permanent, e.g. permanent waving and tinting. The structure of chemical substances in the hair is altered by chemical changes. The dark pigment melanin is changed during bleaching to form a new substance which is not coloured. Many chemical changes give out heat and are said to be *exothermic*. A permanent waving chemical pad gives out heat because of the chemical change which occurs in it when it becomes wet. In some cases however, heat may have to be supplied to start the chemical change, but once it has started it produces more heat. This occurs during *burning*, when heat is needed to ignite the substance which then gives out more heat as it burns.

Elements and compounds

Substances are divided into two large groups. If a substance cannot be split up by any known chemical change it is an element. If it can be split up into two or more simpler substances it is a compound.

ELEMENTS are the basic parts from which all the substances occurring on the earth are built up. There are ninety-two different naturally occurring elements, a few of which are particularly important in hairdressing. *Examples* of elements are carbon (forming 44·3% of hair), oxygen, hydrogen, nitrogen, sulphur, phosphorus, fluorine, chlorine, and all the metals. Elements are divided into the two groups, metals and non-metals.

Metals are solids—with the exception of mercury. They have a characteristic *lustre* or shine. They are good *conductors* of heat and electricity, allowing both these forms of energy to pass through them. They are dense materials and can be hammered into sheets or drawn out into wire, and so are used to make much of the salon equipment. Most metals are attacked by *acids*, by which they undergo a chemical change to form a new substance called a *salt*. *Examples* of metals are gold, zinc, copper, nickel, iron, chromium, calcium, aluminium, magnesium, and sodium. Iron is used in electromagnets, copper is used in electrical wiring, chromium is used for plating iron so that it will not rust in a damp atmosphere, and magnesium is burnt as 'flash powder' when taking indoor photographs.

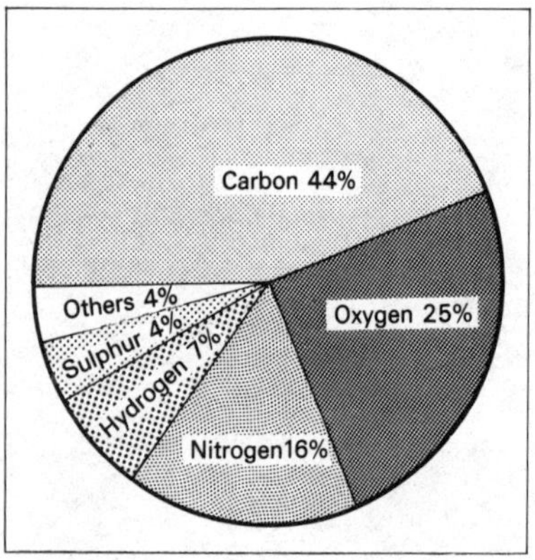

2.1 Elements from which hair is formed

Non-metals are all the rest of the elements which do not have the properties common to metals. Many non-metals are gases (hydrogen, oxygen, nitrogen, and chlorine), but some are solids (carbon and sulphur). They usually have a dull appearance, although carbon in the form of diamond is a notable exception. They are light in weight, and solid non-metals are usually *brittle*, snapping or crumbling readily like carbon in the form of charcoal. Because they are brittle they cannot be hammered into sheets or drawn into wire. Non-metals are poor conductors of heat, and all except carbon are poor electrical conductors also. They are not readily attacked by acids. On burning they form substances which are *acidic*, as they turn litmus solution red in colour. *Litmus* is a purple vegetable dye.

COMPOUNDS have a fixed composition, and their appearance and properties are usually quite different from those of the elements composing them. An enormous number of different compounds can be produced from the ninety-two elements. Some *examples* of compounds used in the salon are water, hydrogen peroxide, soap, and para-dye base. The main constituent of hair, keratin, is a compound, and so are most of the substances making up the body.

Organic compounds are the ones normally found in, or made by, living organisms. They all contain the element *carbon*, and are complex substances. *Examples* of organic compounds are keratin, melanin, proteins, fats, sugar, alcohol, and soap. *Inorganic* compounds are the rest of the compounds which are not organic. They may contain any of the elements, and are mostly simple compounds containing not more than three different elements. *Examples* of inorganic compounds are water (hydrogen and oxygen), salt (sodium and chlorine), and sulphuric acid (hydrogen, sulphur, and oxygen).

MIXTURES

Mixtures also contain two or more substances, which may be either elements or compounds. A mixture differs from a compound in that a chemical change is not involved in its formation. Its constituents can be separated by simple physical means such as dissolving one of them, attracting one with a magnet, or spinning them rapidly so that the heavier one sinks to the bottom of the container (centrifuging). Mixtures do not have a fixed composition, and their properties are an average of the properties of their components. A large number of the preparations used on hair and skin are mixtures, each component giving it certain of its properties. Air is a mixture of several gases, its composition varying only very slightly. Mixtures of metals (*alloys*) such as nichrome, brass, and fuse wire are produced for special purposes. Mixtures of mercury and other metals are known as *amalgams*, and are used in silvering mirrors and filling teeth. Steel consists of iron containing a small amount of carbon. Many cosmetic creams are mixtures of fatty materials and water.

Atoms and Molecules

The smallest particle into which an element can be subdivided without losing its identity is an atom. An atom is extremely small, only measurinq about a hundred millionth of a centimetre across. There are as many different types of atoms as there are elements, the atoms of any one element being all alike. Chemical changes do not destroy or create atoms, but during them, atoms will combine together to form molecules. If the elements iron and sulphur are heated together, each iron atom will combine with one sulphur atom to form one molecule of the compound iron sulphide.

2.2 Combination of atoms to form molecules

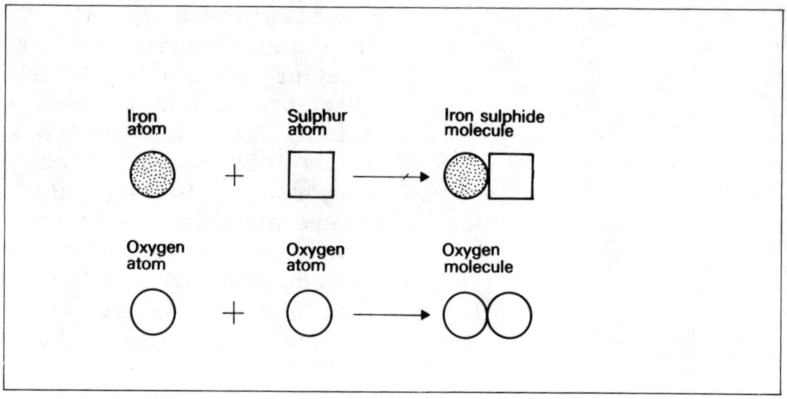

Under normal conditions elements which are gases rarely exist as single atoms. The atoms of these elements join together in pairs to form molecules.

Thus an *atom* is the smallest part of an element that can be involved in a chemical change. A *molecule* is the smallest part of an element or compound that can exist alone.

ATOMIC STRUCTURE

Atoms are made up of three smaller kinds of particle called *neutrons*, *protons*, and *electrons*. Neutrons and protons have the same weight, being 2000 times heavier than electrons. Protons and neutrons cluster together in the centre of the atom to form a nucleus, round which the electrons move. An electron moves

2.3 Hydrogen atom
Copper atom

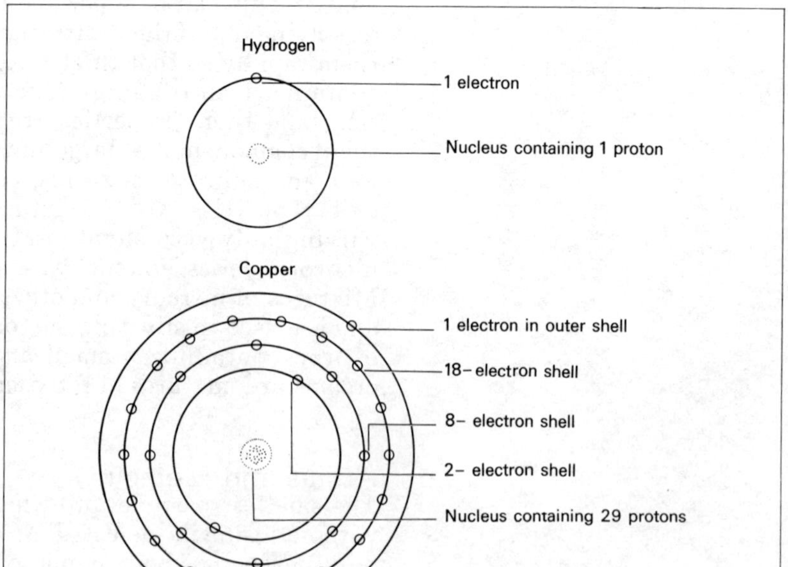

round the nucleus at a fixed distance from it, in a particular 'electron shell'. The numbers of neutrons, protons, and electrons are different in the atoms of different elements. A proton and an electron will attract one another and try to move closer together, while a proton repels other protons and an electron repels other electrons. Neutrons do not attract or repel the other types of particle, but only provide some of the weight of the atom. The forces of attraction and repulsion exerted by protons and electrons are *electrical* forces, protons being said to have a *positive*, and electrons a *negative*, charge. Neutrons have no electric charge. In each atom the positive and negative charges are balanced because there are the same number of protons and electrons. A *hydrogen* atom has one proton in the nucleus balancing one electron. A *copper* atom has twenty-nine protons in the nucleus balancing twenty-nine electrons which are arranged in four shells of two, eight, eighteen, and one electrons.

Because the negative and positive charges in the atom are equal it is said to be neutral. If electrons are removed from an atom it is left with an overall positive charge. If these electrons which have been removed are transferred to another atom, it will acquire an overall negative charge. By losing or gaining electrons atoms become *ions*.

States of matter

Matter may occur in three forms, or states, known as *solid*, *liquid*, and *gas*. If a solid becomes a liquid, or a liquid becomes a gas, or vice versa, this is a *change of state*.

GASES (the gaseous state)

In a gas the molecules are moving through space at very great speeds. They are continually colliding with each other and with the walls bounding the space they occupy, and on which they therefore exert a *pressure*. As the temperature of a gas is increased the molecules obtain more energy and so move faster. Thus an increase in temperature will increase the pressure of a gas, as more molecules will hit the retaining walls in a given time.

LIQUIDS

If the temperature of a gas is reduced the molecules will slow down until a point is reached when they become close enough to attract one another due to the electrical forces within the atoms. These attractive forces make the molecules stick together or *cohere*, although they still have some freedom of movement, and can slide over one another. As there is much less space between the molecules, liquids can be compressed very much less than gases.

SOLIDS

If the temperature of a liquid is decreased the molecules are drawn so close together by the molecular forces that at a particular temperature, the *freezing point*, the molecules take up definite positions in relation to one another. Each molecule may retain its identity (e.g. in ice and plastics), or a large number of atoms may group together to form 'giant' molecules (e.g. in diamond and metals). The molecules are arranged in regular patterns to form *crystals*. Most, though not all, solids are crystalline. The atoms are very tightly packed together and can move only very slightly.

Soluble and insoluble substances

When some substances are added to a liquid they *dissolve*, forming a *solution*. The substance which dissolves is the *solute*, and the liquid in which it dissolves is the *solvent*.

Solute + *solvent* = *solution*.

Examples of substances which are soluble in water are hydrogen peroxide, ammonia gas, washing soda, and common salt. Substances which will not dissolve in a particular liquid are *insoluble* in it. A substance may be insoluble in one liquid but soluble in another, e.g. fats are insoluble in water but soluble in carbon tetrachloride (dry-cleaning fluid). Other substances which are insoluble in water are chalk, talc, and waxes. Soluble and insoluble substances can be separated by dissolving one substance in a solvent and filtering off the insoluble one. The soluble substance can then be obtained by evaporating the filtrate.

Solutions

Many hairdressing preparations are solutions. The *solute* may be a solid, e.g. citric acid or cetrimide in conditioners, or a liquid, e.g. hydrogen peroxide in bleach, or a gas, e.g. formaldehyde in sterilizing fluid. Because dissolving is a physical change solutes can readily be obtained from a solution. Solid solutes will be left behind if the solution *evaporates*, and liquids or gases are obtained by *distillation* of the solution (see Chapter 3). Solutes cannot be removed from a solution by filtering. The solute molecules are evenly distributed in the solvent, so that a solution is a *homogeneous* mixture. A solution containing a large amount of solute is *concentrated*, while one containing very little is *dilute*. If a solution contains as much solute as it can hold it is *saturated*. As a solution is heated it may become able to hold more solute, so that more solute is required to form a saturated solution. Some substances therefore become more soluble as the temperature is increased. Gaseous solutes however become less soluble, and are driven off as a solution is heated, e.g. formaldehyde gas in a sterilizing cabinet (see Chapter 14).

Solvents can be separated from a solution by distillation. Water is the solvent most commonly used in hairdressing preparations. Other solvents used are ethanol (ethyl alcohol) in spirit preparations, isopropanol (isopropyl alcohol) in hair lacquer, acetone in nail varnish remover, and carbon tetrachloride.

Solutions are clear or transparent, although they may be coloured, e.g. salt solution is colourless; 'brilliant green' solution is coloured. The particles of solute in a solution are very small.

Suspensions

A suspension may form from an *insoluble* solid which remains homogeneously mixed with a liquid, instead of settling to the bottom or rising to the surface. On standing however, the solid slowly separates out from the liquid. Suspensions are produced when the solid and the liquid have nearly equal weight per unit volume. The solid particles are large enough to be visible, so the suspension is *cloudy*. The solid can be removed from the suspension by *filtering*. Magnesium oxide, zinc oxide, talc, and clay (mud pack), all form suspensions with water.

Colloids

Some substances, when mixed with a solvent, appear to form a solution, but the suspended particles are larger than the individual molecules of solute present in a solution. They are however smaller than the particles forming a suspension, as they are small enough to pass through a filter paper, and so cannot be removed by filtering. There are two classes of colloids; *suspensoids* where the individual suspended particles are solid, and *emulsoids* where the suspended particles are minute liquid droplets. Soap and starch are suspensoids and mix with water to form a colloid which is cloudy in appearance. If the colloid is very concentrated, a *gel* is produced, which is semi-solid. Emulsoid colloids are usually termed *emulsions* or creams.

Emulsions

An emulsion is thus a suspension of droplets of one liquid in another liquid in which it is insoluble, i.e. the two liquids are *immiscible*. If two such liquids are shaken up together, one liquid separates out into tiny droplets, and is termed the *disperse phase*. The other liquid is the *continuous phase*. On standing the two liquids settle out as two layers. If an *emulsifying agent* is added the two liquids do not settle out, and the emulsion is permanent.

2.4 Structure of an emulsion

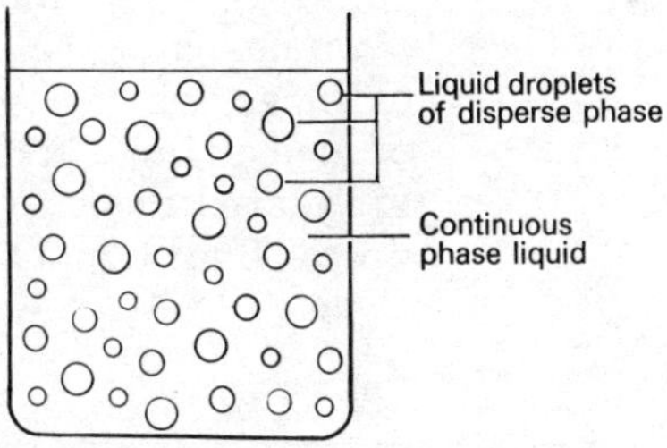

Emulsions are commonly prepared from oils and water. *Examples* of emulsions used in the salon are cream shampoo, hair conditioning cream, and barrier cream. In creams where oil forms the disperse phase, it is an *oil in water* (o/w) emulsion, e.g. handcream. Where water forms the disperse phase, it is a *water in oil* (w/o) emulsion, e.g. cold cream. Oil in water emulsions are less greasy, and can be rinsed away with water. Water in oil emulsions do not rinse away, but must be wiped away with a tissue, or removed by a detergent or fat-solvent (see Chapter 3). *Emulsifying agents* produce their effect because they are *surface-active* agents, lowering the surface tension of water (see Chapter

3). Substances which act as emulsifying agents are: detergents, quaternary ammonium compounds (cetrimide), beeswax, lanolin, synthetic emulsifying waxes (Lanette wax), egg yolk, and water softening salts (washing soda, borax). In preparing emulsions both phases must be warmed separately to 70°C before mixing, as emulsions form more readily at higher temperatures.

Units of measurement

When using preparations on the hair not only the nature of the chemicals they contain, but the quantity also, is important. Too small an amount means that the preparation will be ineffective, while too large an amount could make it damaging to the hair or skin. Thus the amounts of the substances used in making hairdressing preparations must be measured. The system of measurement used is called the *metric system*, in which two of the basic units are the *metre* for measuring length, and the *kilogramme* for measuring weight and mass. Larger or smaller quantities are derived by multiplying or dividing these units by multiples of ten.

MEASURING LENGTH

The metric unit of *length* is the *metre* (m) which is equal to 39·37 inches or 1·094 yards. Each metre is divided into 100 *centimetres* (cm) where 2·5 cm equal 1 inch. Length is measured by the *metre rule.*

MEASURING VOLUME

Volume is the amount of space occupied by matter. The usual metric unit of volume is the *litre* (l), and is the volume of 1000 *cubic centimetres* (cm^3). The litre can be divided into 1000 parts called *millilitres* (ml) so that 1 ml is equal to 1 cm^3. One litre is equal to 1·76 pints, and there are 28·4 ml (cm^3) in 1 fluid ounce. Volumes may be measured fairly accurately in a measuring cylinder, which is graduated in millilitres. A more accurate way of measuring a fixed volume of liquid is by using a pipette or a graduated flask. A burette can be used to measure any volume up to 50 ml (cm^3) accurately.

2.5 Apparatus used in measuring volume

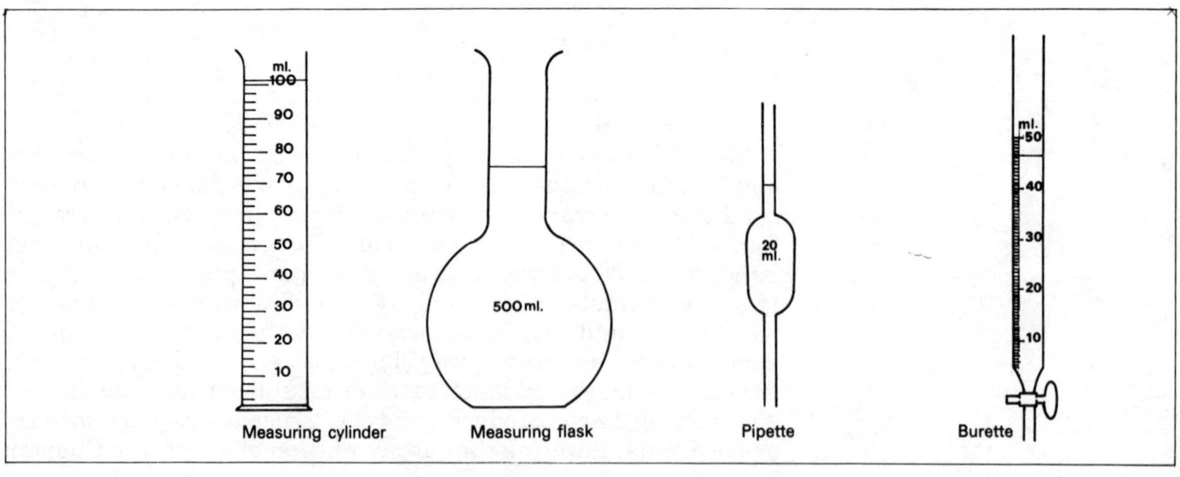

2.6 The meniscus produced by water

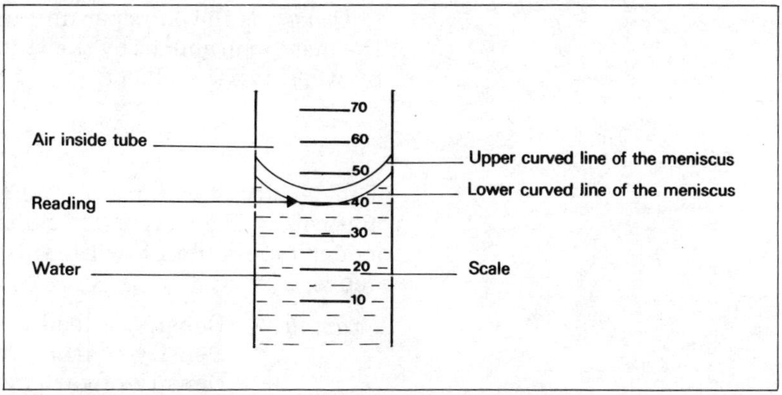

In a narrow tube a water surface appears as a double curved line dipping downwards called the *meniscus*. The lowest point of the lower line of the meniscus is compared with the scale when taking a reading, and the meniscus must be at eye level.

MEASURING WEIGHT AND MASS

Mass is the amount of matter contained in a known volume of substance, while *weight* is the pull of *gravity* on that mass. The mass of a body remains constant whereas its weight will vary if gravity becomes smaller or greater. Thus in space a body has mass but no weight; on earth its weight and mass are equal. The metric unit of weight and mass is the *kilogramme* (kg) which is equal to 2·2046 pounds. The kilogramme can be divided into 1000 smaller parts called *grammes* (g) where 28·34 g are equal to 1 ounce, and 453·6 g equal 1 pound. Weight is measured on a *balance*. In a *spring* balance the object compresses or extends a spring, which moves a pointer over a scale. In a *beam* balance the object is balanced against the weights placed at the opposite end of the beam, which see-saws on a central fulcrum.

2.7 Spring balance

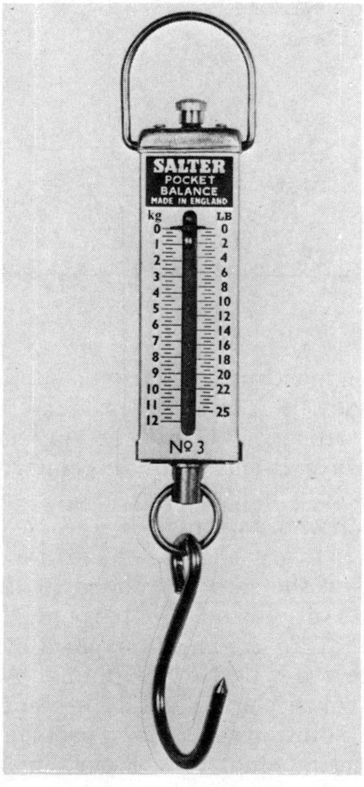

Beam balance

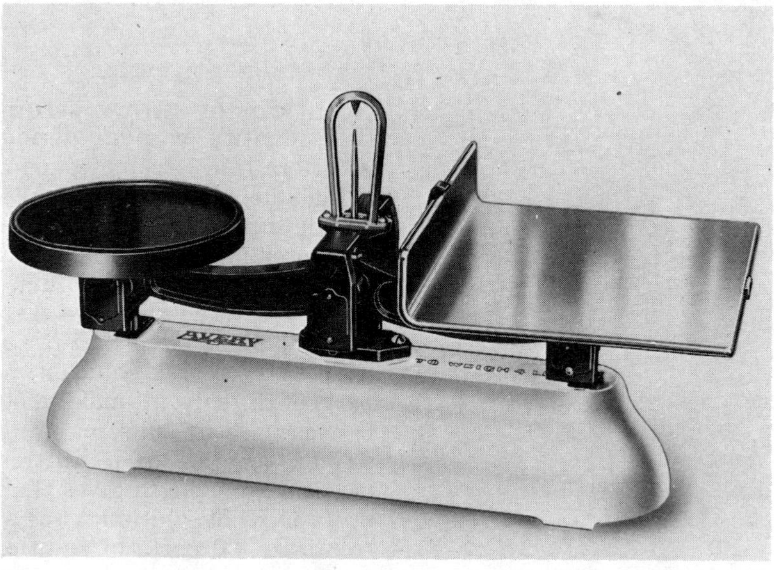

Density is the *mass* per unit *volume*, and is obtained by dividing the mass in grammes by the volume in ml (cm³). Mass is measured by weighing the object.

$$\text{Density} = \frac{\text{Mass (g)}}{\text{Volume (cm}^3)}$$

The density of water is 1 g/ml (cm³) as 1 ml (cm³) of water has a mass of 1 g and weighs 1 g. Substances which float on water have a density less than 1, while substances which sink have a density above 1.

Examples: Density of lead = 11·34 g/ml (cm³)
Density of iron = 7·87 g/ml (cm³)
Density of carbon tetrachloride = 1·6 g/ml (cm³)
Density of ethanol = 0·79 g/ml (cm³)

The relative density is the density of the substance divided by the density of water, which is 1. The relative density has the same numerical value as the density but no units, e.g. concentrated ammonium hydroxide solution has a density of 0·88 g/cm³ and a relative density of 0·88. The relative density of a liquid can be measured by using a *hydrometer*. This consists of a glass tube or stem marked with a scale and ending in a weighted bulb. The hydrometer is floated in the liquid and the depth to which it sinks is measured by taking a reading where the liquid surface comes on the scale. This reading gives the relative density.

2.8 Using a hydrometer

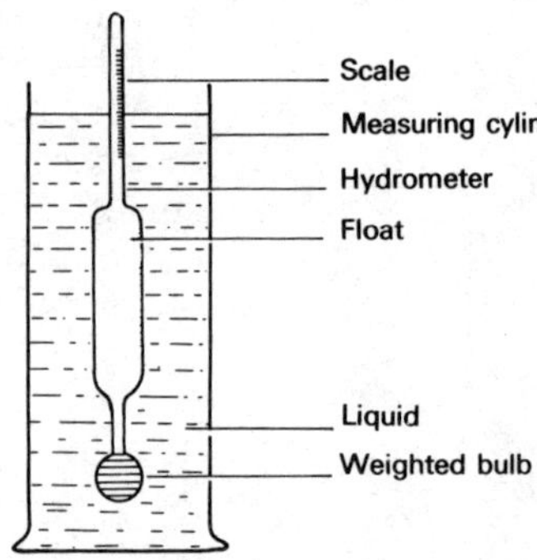

Solutions of known strength

The quantity of *solute* dissolved determines the *strength* of a solution. Hairdressing preparations must not vary from sample to sample, and their strength must be known to produce a standard product at all times. The strength of a solution may be expressed in a number of different ways. It may state the relative amounts, by weight or volume, of solute and solution, expressed as *parts*, or as a *percentage*. A solution whose strength is expressed as 1 part in 50 has 1 part of solute in every 50 parts of solution. To prepare such a solution, 1 part of the solute is added to 49 parts of the solvent, making 50 parts of solution. The parts must be measured in the same units, i.e. all in grammes for parts by weight, and all in millilitres (cm³) for parts by volume. A percentage strength gives the number of parts of solute present in 100 parts of solution. Thus a 20% solution contains 20 parts of solute in 100 parts of solution, and is equal to a 1 part in 5 solution. To prepare a 20% solution, 20 parts of solute are added to 80 parts of solvent to form 100 parts of solution, where the parts are all measured in the same unit.

Where a solution produces a gas, its strength may be measured in terms of *volume strength*, which is the number of ml (cm^3) of gas produced from 1 ml (cm^3) of the solution. Volume strength is used for hydrogen peroxide solutions (see Chapter 7). The *relative density* may also express the strength of a solution, as changes in concentration change the density. The strengths of ammonium hydroxide solutions are expressed as relative density. As this is a solution of a gas in water, the greater the amount of gas dissolved, the lower the density of the solution. The strongest available solution of ammonium hydroxide has a relative density of 0·88. As the solution gives off ammonia gas becoming more dilute, its relative density becomes nearer and nearer to 1, the density of pure water.

Chemical nature of substances

By studying their properties, chemical compounds may be arranged in a number of classes.

OXIDES

If elements are *burned* in air or oxygen they form compounds known as *oxides* since the element combines with *oxygen* during the chemical change. The oxides of metals are *basic* oxides, turning *litmus* solution *blue*. The oxides of non-metals are *acidic* oxides turning litmus solution *red*. An exception is the oxide formed on burning hydrogen. This oxide is water, which is *neutral* as it does not change the colour of litmus solution. Hydrogen and a few other substances will also form oxides containing more oxygen than the usual oxide. These compounds are called *peroxides*. Hydrogen peroxide is *acidic* turning litmus solution *red*.

ACIDS

Acidic oxides react with water to form acids. An *acid* is a substance containing *hydrogen* which can be replaced by a *metal* to form a *salt*:

e.g. carbon dioxide + water = carbonic acid
zinc + sulphuric acid = hydrogen gas + zinc salt.

There are two types of acids. Strong or *mineral* acids are inorganic compounds, e.g. sulphuric acid, phosphoric acid, hydrochloric acid. Weak or *organic* acids have a greater use in hairdressing, e.g. acetic acid (vinegar), citric acid (lemon), thioglycollic acid, salicylic acid, tartaric acid.

The *strength* of an acid is measured on the *pH scale*. This scale goes from 0 to 14. From 0 to 7 indicates decreasing acidity, pH 7 being neutral, so acid pHs are those below 7. pHs above 7 indicate basic properties. There are a number of substances which change colour in acidic and basic solutions. These substances are *indicators*, one of which is litmus which turns red in acidic solutions.

Phenolphthalein is another indicator, and is colourless in acidic solutions. Some indicators change colour at different pH values, and these are used to produce *pH paper*, where a colour chart shows the pH for each colour of the indicator. All acids

2.9 pH chart

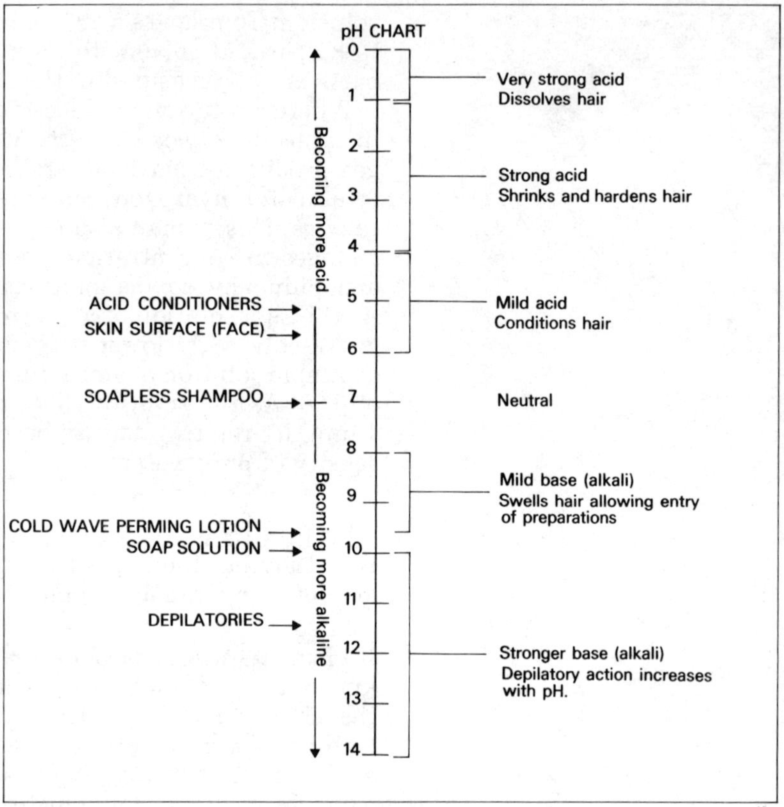

are *corrosive*, burning skin hair and fabric. Mineral acids are more corrosive than organic acids, and the more concentrated a solution of acid is, the greater its corrosive effect. In very dilute solutions acids have a *sour* taste. A stronger acid will take the place of a weaker acid in its salts. When most acids are added to *sodium carbonate* (a salt of the weak carbonic acid produced when carbon dioxide reacts with water) carbon dioxide gas is liberated, and the stronger acid forms a sodium salt.

Stronger acid + sodium carbonate → sodium salt of strong acid + carbonic acid

Carbonic acid → carbon dioxide gas + water.

INORGANIC BASES AND ALKALIS

The oxide of a metal is a *basic oxide*. Basic oxides may form basic *metal hydroxides* with water. Metal oxides and hydroxides are called *inorganic bases*. A few metal hydroxides are soluble in water and are called *alkalis*, e.g. sodium hydroxide (caustic soda), potassium hydroxide (caustic potash), and calcium hydroxide (limewater). Ammonium hydroxide, although not a metallic hydroxide, has properties like the other alkalis, and is included with them. Bases and alkalis have a pH above 7. They turn litmus solution blue, and phenolphthalein pink. They feel *soapy* and very dilute solutions have a *bitter* taste. They are *corrosive* (caustic), and will burn skin, hair and fabrics. They will react with an acid to form a salt and water only. This type of chemical change is *neutralization*:

acid + base or alkali → salt + water = neutralization.

ORGANIC BASES

Certain organic compounds will also react with acids to form *organic salts* and water. The two main groups of organic bases are the *alcohols* and the *amines*. *Alcohols* are *organic hydroxides* (containing a hydroxyl group). They are neutral having a pH of 7. When they react with organic acids the organic salts they form are called *esters*. *Examples* of alcohols are methanol (methyl alcohol), ethanol, isopropanol, cetyl alcohol and glycerol. *Amines* are organic substances related to ammonia, and have properties resembling those of the alkalis. They have a pH above 7, turn litmus solution blue, and feel soapy. *Examples* of amines are triethanolamine, diamines (para-dyes), and quaternary ammonium compounds such as cetrimide.

SALTS AND ESTERS

A *salt* is produced when the hydrogen of an acid is replaced by a metal or an ammonium group. Salts consist of a *metal* (or ammonium) and an *acid radicle*, which is what remains of the acid molecule after giving up its hydrogen.

Metal	**Acid Radicle**	**Acid from which it is produced**
Sodium	Carbonate	Carbonic
Sodium	Chloride	Hydrochloric
Calcium	Sulphate	Sulphuric
Ammonium	Thioglycollate	Thioglycollic

Examples of salts are sodium carbonate (washing soda), sodium chloride (common salt), and ammonium thioglycollate (in cold permanent waving solution). Most salts are neutral with a pH of 7.

An *ester* is produced when an organic acid is neutralized by an alcohol:

$$\text{organic acid} + \text{alcohol} \rightarrow \text{ester} + \text{water}.$$

Esters are neutral with a pH of 7, and many are liquids with a fruity smell.

Examples of esters are ethyl acetate, amyl acetate (peardrops), isopropyl myristate, nipagin, and animal and vegetable oils and fats.

Fats and *oils* differ in whether or not they are solid or liquid at room temperature; a fat is solid, an oil is liquid. The alcohol from which they form is always *glycerol*, which combines with three *fatty acid* molecules to form a *triglyceride* or fat. The fatty acids are commonly stearic, palmitic, oleic, or lauric acids. *Examples* of vegetable oils are almond, arachis (peanut), castor, olive, palm, and coconut oil. *Examples* of animal fats and oils are lard (pigs), tallow (sheep and beef), and turtle oil.

Essential oils are pleasant-smelling vegetable oils which, being *volatile*, evaporate readily. The heat from the body is sufficient to vaporize them. The essential oil comes from a particular part of the plant. Rose and lavender oil come from the flowers; bay from the leaves; orange and citron from the fruit; sandalwood from the wood. The oils are obtained from the plant material by distillation; dissolving them out with a solvent, e.g. ether; pressure; or absorption by cold fat (lard) to give pomade. When making *perfumes*, blends of essential oils are mixed with certain *animal secretions* which cause the essential oils to evaporate at equal rates so 'fixing' the overall odour of the perfume until it is all used. These animal secretions are *ambergris* from the whale, *musk* from the male musk deer and musk rat, *civet* from the civet cat, and *castor* from the beaver.

2.10a Musk deer

2.10b Civet cat

Waxes are esters of *fatty acids* and complex *fatty alcohols* such as cholesterol. *Examples* are lanolin (wool wax), beeswax, sebum, spermaceti (whale wax), and the synthetic Lanette wax.

HYDROCARBONS

These substances occur in *petroleum*, and are called *mineral* oils and waxes. They consist of long chains of *carbon* atoms to which *hydrogen* atoms are attached. When petroleum is distilled, a number of substances can be separated from it, e.g. petroleum gases such as *alkane*, used in making some soapless detergents; *petrol*; *liquid paraffin*; *petroleum jelly* (Vaseline); *paraffin wax*. Mineral oils are not absorbed by the skin, but form a protective covering layer. They are used in the preparation of protective and cleansing creams, and brilliantine.

Practical work

1 TO PREPARE A COMPOUND FROM ITS ELEMENTS

Take a piece of scrap paper and on it place a spoonful of *iron filings* and the same quantity of *sulphur*. Note the appearance of each of these two elements, then mix them together. Note the appearance of the mixture. Hold a *magnet* above the mixture and use it to separate the iron from the sulphur. Remix the two elements again and place them in a pyrex test-tube. Clamp the tube horizontally, and tap it to spread the mixture along the tube. Place a bunsen flame under the mixture half-way along the tube, and *heat* the mixture until a red glow develops. Remove the bunsen, and watch the red glow travel through the mixture to the end of the tube. Leave the test-tube to cool then knock out its contents on to the piece of scrap paper. Note the appearance of this substance, and hold a magnet above it to try to separate the iron filings from the sulphur. Although a few iron filings may be present the rest have joined with sulphur to form a new substance, the compound *iron sulphide*. The glow was due to heat being produced by the *chemical change*.

2 PROPERTIES OF METALS AND NON-METALS

(*a*) Note the appearance of as many metals and non-metals as are available, to see if they have lustre or are dull. Test them to see if they are hard or brittle.

(*b*) Take a thin stick of *charcoal* and a piece of *iron wire* of the same length and thickness. Hold one in each hand and put the last 1 cm of the other end into a bunsen flame. Notice which one becomes too hot to hold first. This will be the better conductor of heat.

(*c*) Take a small piece of *magnesium* ribbon in a deflagrating spoon, and ignite it at a bunsen flame. Immediately put the deflagrating spoon into a gas jar. When the flame goes out, knock the ash from the spoon into the jar. Drop pieces of wet red and blue *litmus* paper onto the ash and note any colour change. Wash out the apparatus thoroughly, then place a little *sulphur* onto the deflagrating spoon. Ignite the sulphur and allow it to burn inside the gas jar when fumes will form. Remove the deflagrating spoon and cover the gas jar with a glass plate. Drop in wet litmus papers as before. From your observations decide whether you have made a basic or an acidic oxide in each case.

From the results of these three experiments compare the properties of metals and non-metals.

3 TO FIND THE DENSITY OF A SUBSTANCE

(*a*) *Glass* Take a glass stopper and weigh it on a balance. Attach a length of cotton to it, and lower it into a 100 ml (cm^3) measuring cylinder which contains 50 ml (cm^3) of water. Note the increase in volume when the stopper is fully immersed. This increase is the volume of the stopper. Divide the weight of the stopper in grammes by its volume in ml (cm^3) to obtain the density of glass.

(*b*) *Water* Take a small beaker and weigh it on a chemical balance. Measure out 10 ml (cm^3) of water with a pipette and place it into the weighed beaker. Record the weight of the 10 ml (cm^3) of water you have added to the beaker, and divide this weight by the volume (10 ml (cm^3)) to give the density of water. Use this method to find the density of other liquids, e.g. ethanol, brine, vegetable oil.

4 TO TEST THE SOLUBILITY OF SUBSTANCES IN WATER

Prepare a table using column headings as shown below:

1. Name of substance	2. Soluble: forms a solution	3. Insoluble: forms a colloid	4. Insoluble: forms a suspension	5. Insoluble: settles out

List all the substances to be tested in column 1. Take a clean test-tube and put a very small amount of the first substance in it, then add half a test-tube of water. Shake the tube well then allow it to stand in a test-tube rack for a few moments. If the substance disappears and the water is clear, place a tick in column 2. If the substance clearly floats to the top or sinks to the bottom of the tube, place a tick in column 5. If the mixture looks cloudy pour it through a double filter paper. If the liquid comes through clear, place a tick in column 4. If the liquid comes through the filter paper still cloudy, filter it again to make sure that the filter paper was not damaged. If it is still cloudy it is probably a colloid, so place a tick in column 3. Test the solubility of the rest of the substances similarly. Suggested substances to test are: sodium sesquicarbonate, P.V.P. resin, hard soap, soft soap, cetrimide, olive oil, methylated spirit, glycerol, beeswax, zinc carbonate, magnesium carbonate, liquid paraffin, shellac, agar, sodium lauryl sulphate.

5 PREPARING SOLUTIONS OF KNOWN STRENGTH

(*a*) Prepare 20 ml (cm^3) of a 1 part in 5 solution of methylated spirit in distilled water, using a measuring cylinder.

(*b*) Prepare 50 g of a 10% solution by weight of triethanolamine lauryl sulphate in distilled water and place it in a beaker. This solution may be used as a soapless shampoo if it has been prepared correctly.

(*c*) Using a measuring flask prepare 500 g of a 2% solution by weight of copper sulphate in tap water.

Solutions (*a*) and (*c*) should appear identical in colour and volume to the solutions prepared by other students.

6 TESTS ON ACIDS AND BASES

Prepare a table using column headings as shown below:

Name of substance	Effect on litmus	Effect on phenol-phthalein	pH	Effect on metals	Effect on carbonate

Take a test-tube rack and place five test-tubes in it. Into each test-tube put 1 cm of the acid or base you are testing. Into the first tube put a few drops of *litmus* solution. Into the second put two drops of *phenolphthalein* indicator. Into the third tube put a piece of *pH paper* and compare its colour with the chart to obtain the pH of the substance. Into the fourth tube drop 1 cm of *magnesium* ribbon. Into the fifth drop some anhydrous *sodium carbonate* from the end of a splint. In every case write down in the table the name of the substance and the results of the tests. Carry out these five tests on each substance in turn. Substances to be tested are dilute solutions of: sulphuric acid, hydrochloric acid, acetic acid, citric acid, ammonium hydroxide, calcium hydroxide, sodium hydroxide, cetrimide, triethanolamine, ethanol and glycerol.

7 PREPARATION OF MASCARA USING THE ELEMENT CARBON

Animal charcoal (carbon)	1 g
Beeswax	3·5 g
Carnauba wax	1 g
Stearic acid	3 g
Triethanolamine	I ml (cm^3)

Weigh out each of the solid constituents in turn on a rough balance and place them in a small beaker. Measure the triethanolamine in a 10 ml (cm^3) measuring cylinder and pour it into the beaker. Place the beaker on a tripod and gauze over a bunsen flame and heat very gently until all the solids melt. Remove from the heat and mix very thoroughly with a glass rod. Reheat if the mixture begins to solidify. Take a small watch glass and rinse it under the tap to wet the surface. Allow the mascara to cool but not to set, then pour it onto the watch glass. Leave it to set hard then remove the cake of mascara by gently pressing from one side.

8 PREPARATION OF A W/O COSMETIC EMULSION: COLD CREAM

Beeswax	8 g
Liquid paraffin	25 g
Sodium borate (borax)	0·5 g
Distilled water	16 ml (cm^3)
Nipagin (preservative)	a pinch
Perfume	

Place the *beeswax* and *liquid paraffin* in one beaker, and the *sodium borate, Nipagin* and *distilled water* in another beaker. Put each beaker on a tripod and gauze over a bunsen flame. Heat each beaker until the contents reach 75°C, stirring with a glass rod to mix them thoroughly. Pour the water into the waxes steadily stirring all the time, and continue to stir as the emulsion cools. Add perfume when the beaker becomes cool enough to hold, and pour the cream into a wide-necked container (an empty Yoghurt container is suitable).

Multiple choice questions

1 Sodium hydroxide is soluble in water, and in solution it forms
a an emulsion *b* a colloid *c* an alcohol *d* an alkali

2 The number of grammes equivalent to 1 ounce is approximately
a 2·5 *b* 28 *c* 100 *d* 453

3 Which of the following hairdressing processes causes a physical change in the hair?
a bleaching *b* conditioning *c* permanent tinting
d brightening

4 The element which all acids contain and which can be replaced by a metal is
a oxygen *b* carbon *c* hydrogen *d* sulphur

5 The smallest particle of a compound that can exist alone is
a a molecule *b* an electron *c* an atom *d* an element

6 8 g of soapless detergent paste dissolved in distilled water to form 80 g of shampoo gives a solution having a strength of
a 0·8% *b* 8% *c* 10% *d* 11%

7 20 ml (cm^3) of a non-poisonous liquid may be measured out very accurately by using a
a measuring cylinder *b* conical flask *c* beaker
d pipette

8 When an organic acid reacts with an alcohol the products are water and
a an ester *b* an amine *c* a base *d* an oxide

9 To prepare a 1 part in 25 solution of citric acid in water as an acid rinse 2 g of citric acid must be dissolved in
a 24 g of water *b* 25 g of water *c* 48 g of water
d 50 g of water

10 A suspension of tiny droplets of one liquid in another liquid is
a a precipitate *b* an emulsion *c* a filtrate
d a suspensoid

3 Washing Hair

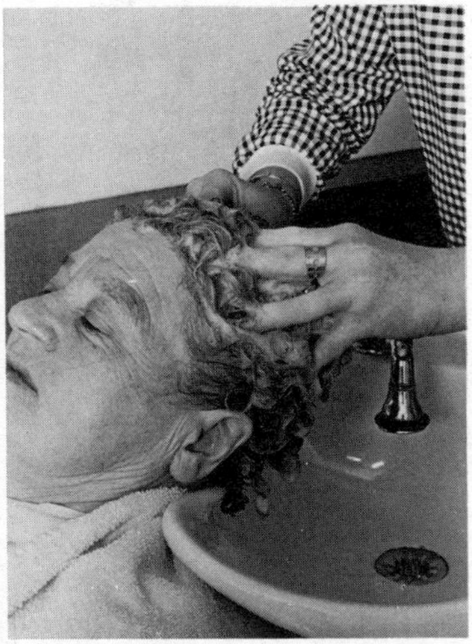

Water is the commonest of all substances on the earth, forming more than two-thirds of its surface, and up to three-quarters of the body weight of each person. Water, because of its high *surface tension*, is not very efficient at washing hair. Its ability to remove grease and dirt needs to be improved by dissolving other substances in it. These are the substances which we apply as *shampoo*.

The water supply to the salon

Water authorities are required to supply water which is free from visible suspended particles, disease-producing organisms, and chemical substances injurious to health (pollutants). The original source of all water supplies is rainfall, which is part of the *natural water cycle* on the earth.

Water vapour precipitates from the clouds as *rain*, some of which runs as *surface* water over the ground, entering streams and rivers, and ultimately reaching the sea. The rest of the rain sinks through the ground as *soil* water. This may be trapped by a layer of impervious rock to form *wells* or *springs*, or may sink down to the *water table*. Water evaporates from the rivers and sea into the air, forming *clouds*. Some soil water is absorbed by plants, and given off from their leaves by *transpiration*. Water vapour is also given out by people as they *breathe* and *perspire*.

Streams and rivers are dammed to form *reservoirs*, usually in hilly districts. From here water is conveyed through large pipes to smaller service reservoirs near the towns, or water may be pumped from a river. Reservoirs are placed at a higher level than the town, so that water *pressure* will drive the water into the salon. Water pressure is caused by the weight of water acting on unit area of surface. The deeper the water, the greater its weight, and the greater the pressure. The vertical distance between the top of the water in the service reservoir and the salon is known as the *head of water*. The greater the head of water, the greater the water pressure. *Water towers* are used in flat districts to obtain the necessary head of water. The water has to be pumped up to the top of the tower.

The local water authority treats the water in various ways, e.g. by adding *chlorine*, and the purified water is then passed into the *mains* below the street. A *service pipe* takes water into the salon. A *stop valve* to control the flow of water through the pipe is fitted outside the premises under a small cover, so that water can be turned off at this point. An additional stop valve is often provided inside the premises near the point of entry of the service pipe. Know where the stop valves are in your salon, and see that they are easily turned on and off.

3.1 Reservoir

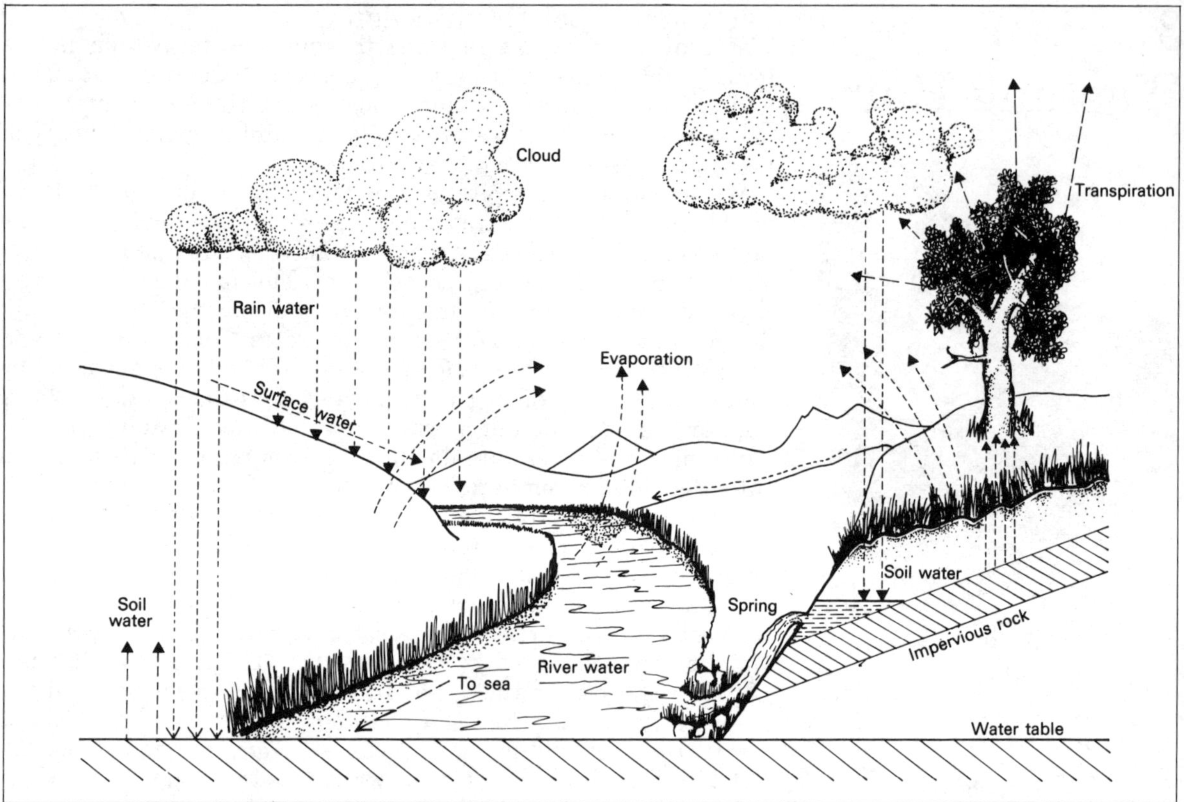

3.2 The water cycle

3.3 Water tower

The service pipe usually supplies at least one cold tap directly, and this should be used for *drinking* water. The other taps are supplied from a cold water *storage tank* in the roof space to provide a head of water above the taps.

A *water tap* is a *valve* at which water can be drawn off. Water is forced out of an open tap by water pressure. When a tap is turned off, a spindle rotates downwards inside the tap, pressing a *jumper* and *washer* down on to a *seating*, to close the gap. In most cold water taps the jumper is separate and can be lifted out. In other taps, the jumper is fixed to the spindle. When turning the tap on, the spindle rotates upwards and lifts the jumper if it is fixed, otherwise the jumper and washer are forced up by water pressure. Washers made of *leather* or *composition* (usually black) are used in cold water taps; *red composition* washers in hot water taps.

If the tap drips when turned off, or makes hammering or singing noises, a new washer is required. If changing a washer, turn off the main stop valve first then turn on the tap until the water stops running. For hot taps this will empty the salon hot-water system. Unscrew the cover to expose the nut. Unscrew the nut with a spanner, and remove the head of the tap. Unscrew the nut below the washer, change the washer, then reassemble the tap. (*See Fig.* 3.5)

Water

Water is a compound of the elements *hydrogen* and *oxygen*, which are gases. It can be split up into its components by means of an

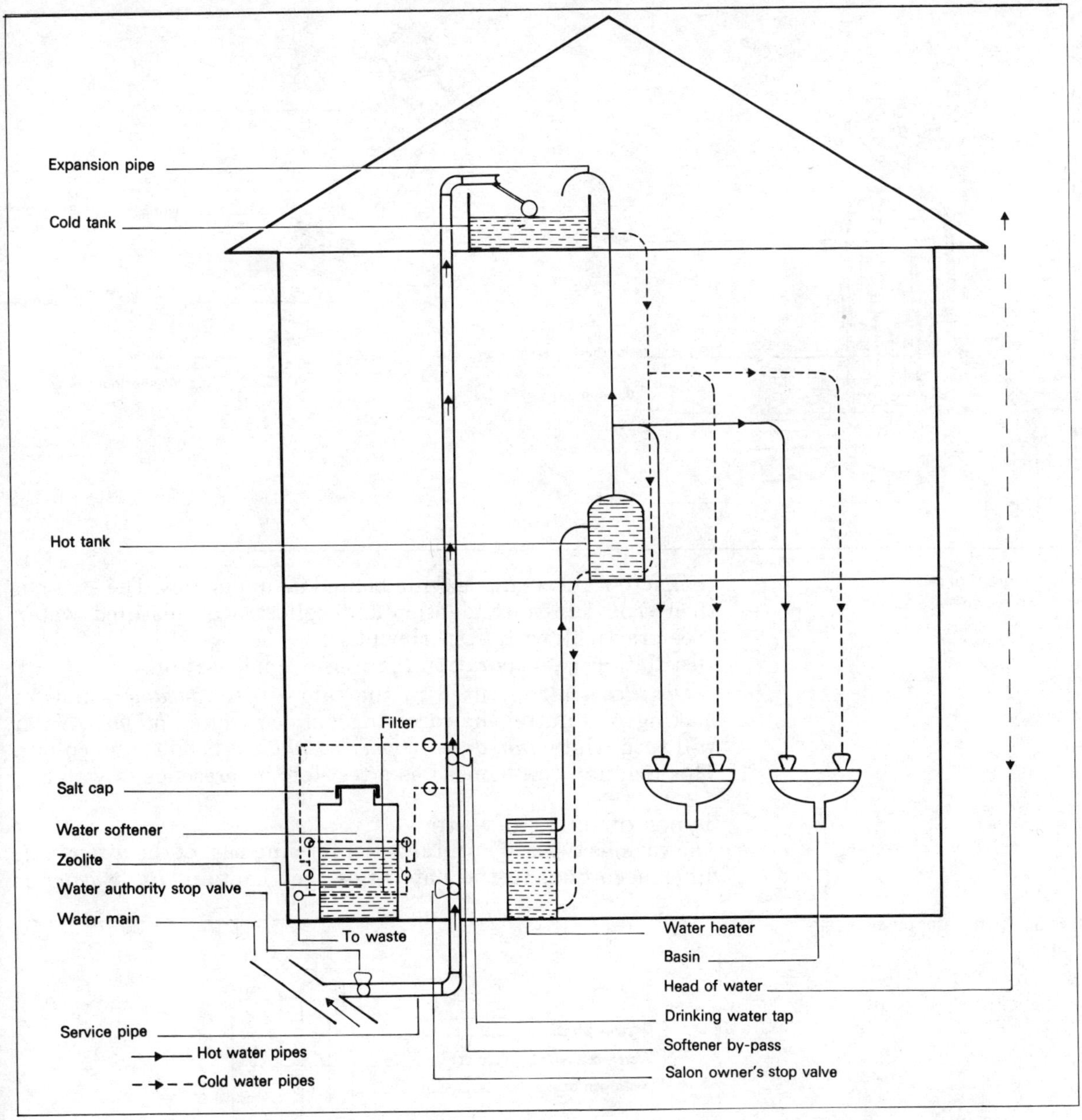

3.4 Salon water supply

electric current when the volume of hydrogen obtained is twice that of oxygen. This splitting up occurs very slowly if pure water is used, but the process can be speeded up by adding a little acid to carry the current.

Water is the *neutral oxide* of hydrogen. It is a colourless liquid without smell or taste. It boils at 100°C (212°F) and freezes at 0°C (32°F). Because it is a neutral substance, being neither acidic nor basic (pH 7), it does not damage skin or hair. There are very few substances which do not dissolve in it, at least slightly, so that water is sometimes referred to as a '*universal solvent*'. For this reason water is very difficult to obtain in the pure state.

Fairly pure water can be obtained by *distillation* of tap water. In this process, the tap water is first heated so that it *evaporates*

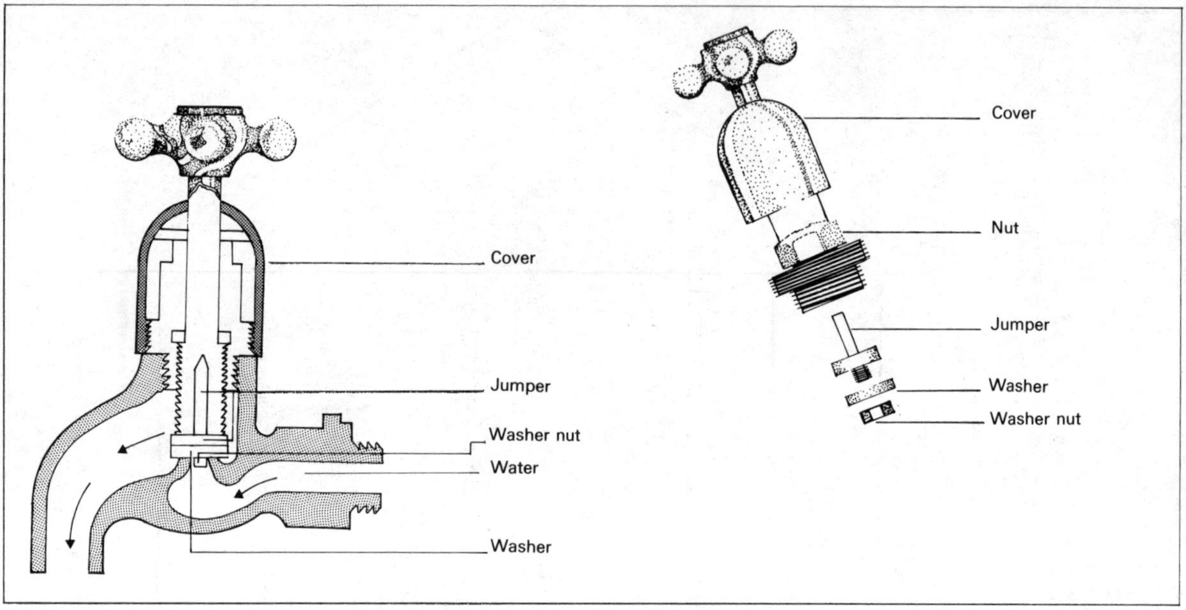

3.5 Diagram of tap
How to rewasher a tap

(boils) to form steam, leaving behind its impurities. The steam is then *cooled* in a condenser, and collected as distilled water. (See practical work, Experiment 1).
Distillation = evaporation (boiling) + condensation.

Distilled water is used in the salon in the *steamer*, and for making or diluting hairdressing and cosmetic *lotions*. Water will turn white *anhydrous copper sulphate* a bright blue colour. This reaction can be used as a test for the presence of water.

Types of natural water

The various types of natural water forming part of the *water cycle* differ according to the impurities they contain. *Rain water* is

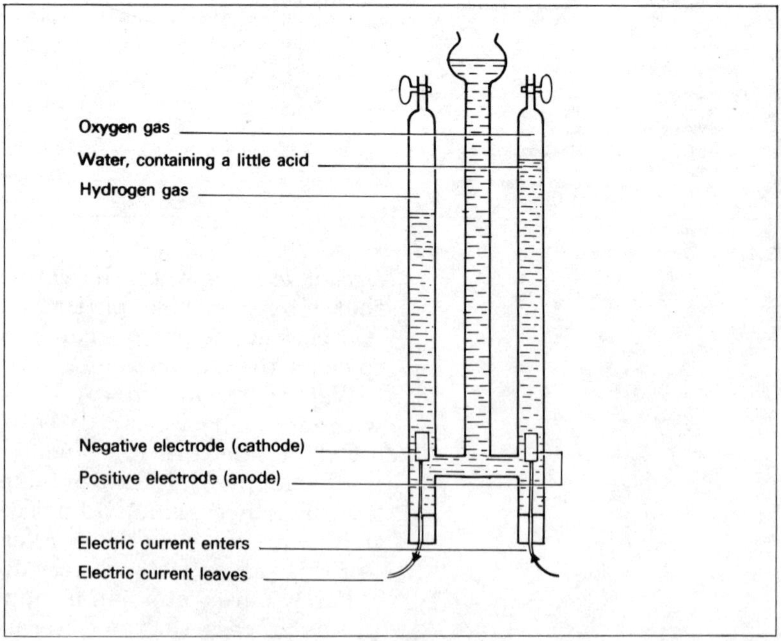

3.6 Splitting water by an electric current

the purest, and closely resembles distilled water. It contains only dissolved gases from the air, but no dissolved solids, at least in clean-air districts. It is good for washing hair. *River water*, which provides most of our tap water, contains dissolved gases from the air, and usually some dissolved solids, the amount and type varying with the rocks and soil over which the river flows. River water contains suspended solids also, making it look muddy. *Spring* and *well water* has percolated through the soil, during which time most of the suspended matter has been filtered out, leaving it clear and sparkling. It does, however, contain dissolved gases and solids, and may also be contaminated by disease-causing organisms, which make it unsafe to drink unless tested and approved by the water authority. *Sea water* contains the largest amount of dissolved solid impurities (3·6%), mainly *sodium chloride* (common salt). Sea water should always be rinsed out of the hair, or the salt will be left as a deposit on the hairs when the water evaporates. Salt is *hygroscopic*, absorbing water vapour from damp air, and forms a stickly layer over each hair, giving it a lank appearance.

Hard and soft water

Some of the dissolved solid impurities in tap water make it *hard*, preventing it from readily forming a *lather* with soap. Water which does not contain these dissolved solid impurities, and thus lathers readily with soap, is *soft*. The impurities making water hard are the following salts: *calcium sulphate*, *magnesium sulphate*, *calcium bicarbonate*, and *magnesium bicarbonate*. One or several of these impurities may be present in any one sample of hard tap water. Hardness due to the presence of the *bicarbonates* is said to be *temporary*, as it is removed by boiling the water. The dissolved bicarbonates are changed into insoluble *carbonates* which are deposited as '*scale*' or 'fur', leaving the water soft.

$$\underset{\text{(dissolved impurity)}}{\text{Calcium bicarbonate}} \xrightarrow{\text{boil}} \underset{\text{(scale)}}{\text{calcium carbonate}} + \underset{\text{dioxide}}{\text{carbon}} + \text{water.}$$

Hardness due to the *sulphates* is said to be *permanent*. Sulphates are not changed chemically by boiling, but remain dissolved in the water.

Hard water usually has a slight taste from the dissolved salts it contains, which makes it pleasant to drink. The calcium salts are also needed for the hardening of bones and teeth. However, in the salon it has disadvantages because of the way it reacts with soap, and its effect on hot water appliances and pipes. With hard water soap undergoes a chemical change with the dissolved calcium salts to form insoluble calcium soaps or '*scum*', usually *calcium stearate*. The soap is used up in producing scum, and is not available for cleansing until all the impurity has been converted into scum. Soap is thus wasted, unless the impurities are removed from hard water by some softening method before adding soap. The scum is deposited on the skin, hair, or fabric being washed, as a grey film. Hot water pipes and appliances such as the steamer, kettles, and boilers become coated with *scale* left behind as the water evaporates. A build up of scale will block water pipes, reduce the volume of water present so that overheating occurs, and lower the efficiency of electrical heating elements.

3.7 Scale blocking hot water pipes

Softening hard water

Boiling will soften water having *temporary* hardness. It will not soften permanently hard water. The addition of certain chemicals to water may cause a chemical change to occur between them and the dissolved salts, which removes the hardness.

Sodium carbonate (washing soda) reacts chemically with the impurities forming *calcium carbonate* (chalk).

Sodium carbonate (softener)	+ calcium bicarbonate (impurity)	= calcium carbonate (insoluble)	+ sodium bicarbonate.

The calcium carbonate formed is insoluble, and cannot form scum with dissolved soap, so the water is now soft. *Bath salts* consist of large coloured sodium carbonate crystals, or the smaller feathery crystals of *sodium sesquicarbonate*, and are used as water softeners. *Sodium borate* (borax) also reacts with the impurities in hard water to form insoluble *calcium borate.*

Sodium borate (softener)	+ calcium sulphate (impurity)	→ calcium borate (insoluble)	→ + sodium sulphate.

Borax is less harsh on the skin than washing soda because it is less alkaline.

Sodium hexametaphosphate also reacts with the dissolved impurities of hard water. The calcium hexametaphosphate formed is soluble in water, but does not react with soap, so the water is soft. The advantage here is that no small solid particles are deposited on the hair or fabric being washed. Sodium hexametaphosphate can be used as a water-softening *Calgon rinse* to remove traces of scum and hard water salts from the hair, and to increase the sheen.

Boiling, or the addition of chemicals, are only suitable softening methods for small volumes of water. For softening the entire salon water supply an *ion* or *base exchange* method is used, by percolation through *zeolite.* The water flows down through zeolite, which is a sand-like material, packed in a cylinder. Zeolite is a complex sodium compound. As the hard water passes, the calcium impurities are removed by a chemical change

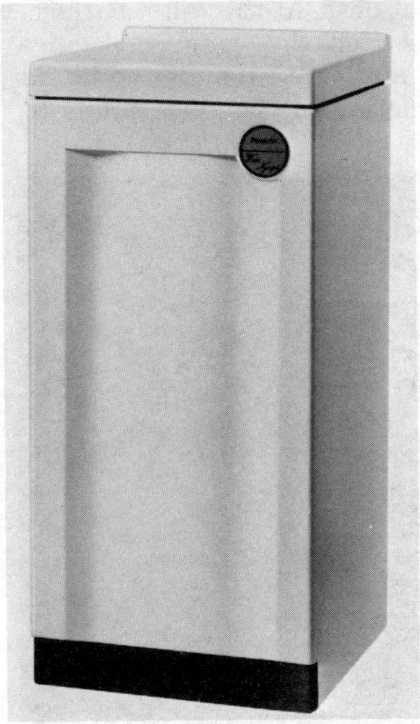

3.8 Domestic mains water softener

between the impurities and the zeolite.

Calcium sulphate (impurity) + sodium zeolite (in cylinder) → calcium zeolite (in cylinder) + sodium sulphate (in softened water).

After a certain volume of hard water has passed through the cylinder, all the sodium zeolite has been changed into calcium zeolite, and it will no longer soften the water. To change the calcium zeolite back again to sodium zeolite, sodium chloride (common salt) is flushed through the cylinder, and a chemical change occurs.

Calcium zeolite (in cylinder) + sodium chloride (salt) → sodium zeolite (in cylinder) + calcium chloride (washed away).

This is known as the Permutit method of water softening.

Resin columns containing sodium ions which can be exchanged for the calcium ions in the hard water can be used instead of zeolite. The calcium ions are present because when salts dissolve in water they split up to form positive and negative electrically charged groups.

Surface tension of water

In a beaker of water, the molecules all attract one another so that they remain together in the liquid. At the surface, although the attractive force between the molecules acts sideways and inwards, there is no force acting outwards into the air. Thus there is an overall *inward* pull, causing contraction of the surface, which is known as the *surface tension*. This has the effect of producing a '*skin*' at the surface, on which a needle will float. It is this 'skin' which causes a drop of water placed on hair or fabric to remain as a spherical drop, and not to penetrate, or wet the material. Thus water is a poor *wetting agent* because of its high surface tension.

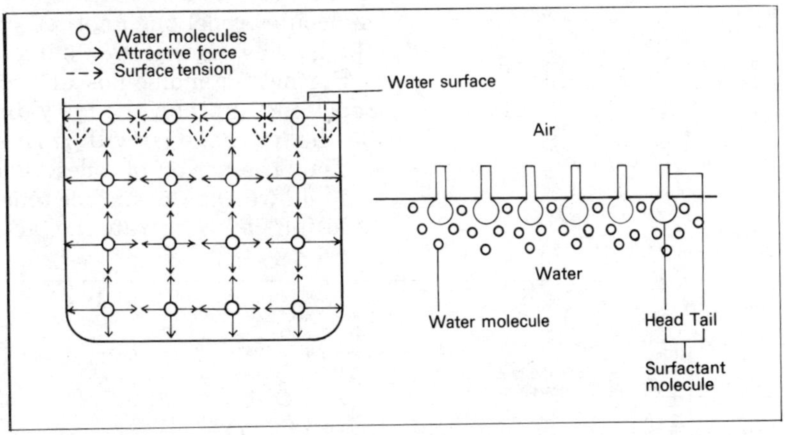

3.9 Surface tension (left)
Surfactant at water surface (right)

Certain substances will arrange themselves at the surface of water because of their particular molecular structure, and in doing so, will lower the surface tension. Such substances are known as *surface active agents* or *surfactants*. Surfactant molecules have two parts, a water-loving (hydrophilic) '*head*' and a water-hating (hydrophobic) '*tail*', so that the molecules can be thought of as tadpole-shaped structures which stick their heads in the water, and keep their tails out of it. At the water surface, the surfactant molecules push between the water molecules with their tails sticking up in the air. This expands the liquid surface and counteracts the contraction of the surface due to surface tension.

3.10 Floating a 2 Fr coin

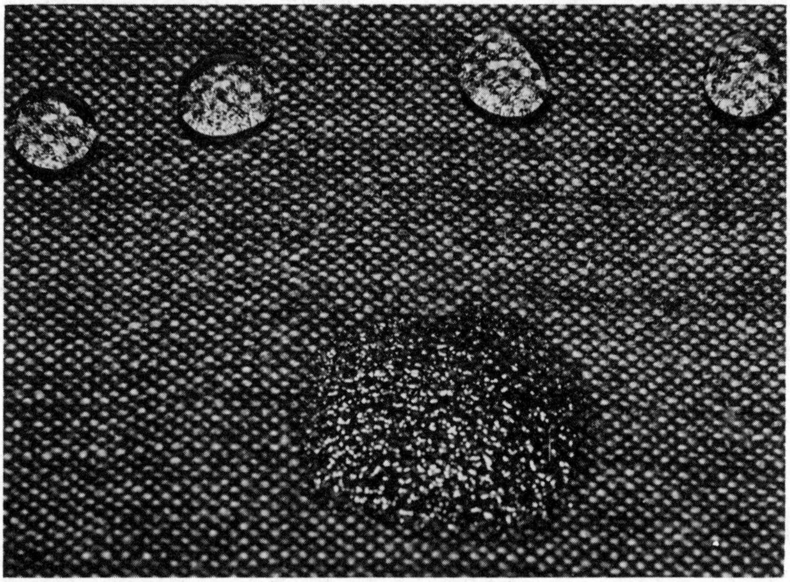

3.11 Cloth with water drop and detergent water stain

Detergency

A *detergent* is a substance which removes dirt from surfaces. On the hair, the *dirt* usually has two components, *greasy* dirt and *particulate* dirt, the solid dirt particles being held in the grease film from the sebum present. Surfactant molecules, when present in water, will bury their hydrophobic 'tails' in the greasy dirt to get them out of the water. The hydrophilic 'heads' of the molecules repel one another, and the fatty dirt is separated from the hair as a small drop surrounded by surfactant molecules.

Surfactant molecules also coat the hair, and as the 'heads' repel one another, the fatty dirt is prevented from settling back on the hair, and so will be rinsed away.

Thus the action of a detergent involves three stages:

1 Lowering the surface tension of water, so that the detergent solution can penetrate, i.e. acting as a *wetting agent.*

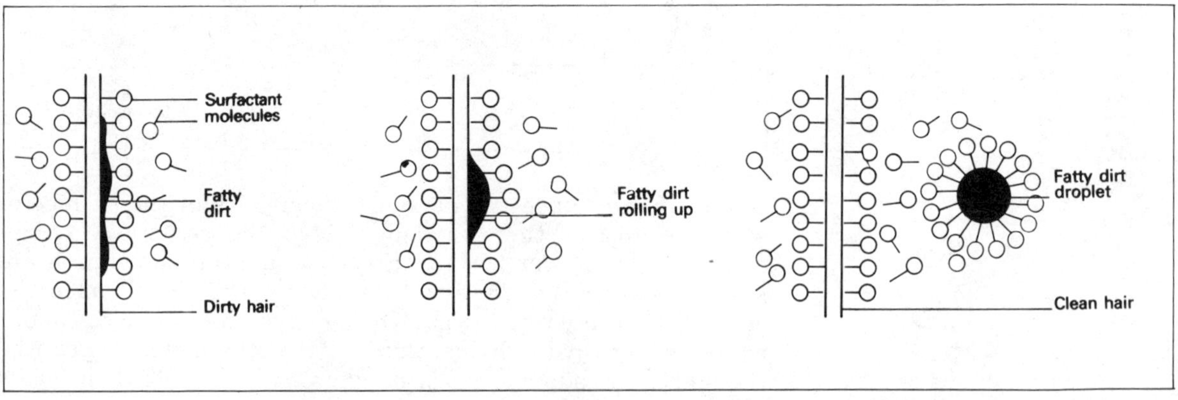

3.12 Detergent action

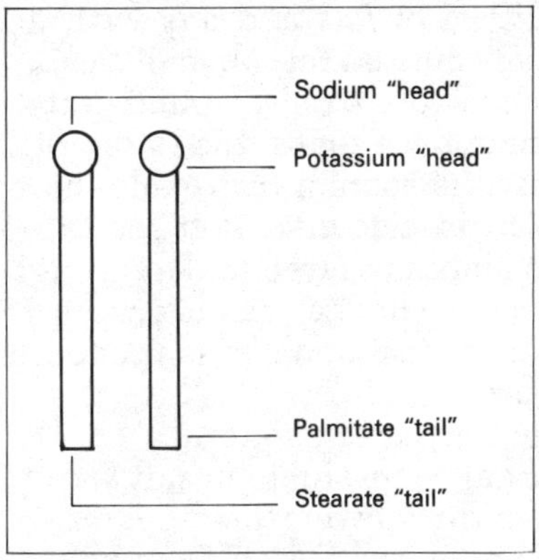

3.13 Soap molecules

2 Attaching itself to the fatty dirt, so that it is freed from the hair, and suspended in the water, i.e. acting as an *emulsifying agent*.

3 Coating both hair and fatty dirt droplets, so that *repelling* forces prevent dirt resettling on the hair.

The detergent action is helped by *heat*, as emulsions form more readily in hot water. It is also assisted by *agitation*, moving both the hair and the water, as in shampooing.

N.B.—Detergent solutions do not dissolve fatty dirt, they emulsify it.

DETERGENTS

Two kinds of detergents are used with water for removing dirt from skin and hair. These are the *soaps*, and the *soapless detergents* of the *lauryl sulphate* type. Both have the tadpole-shaped molecule characteristic of surface active agents.

SOAPS

Soap is the *sodium* or *potassium salt* of a *fatty* acid. *Sodium stearate* is the sodium salt of stearic acid, and is a solid, or *hard* soap. *Potassium palmitate* is the potassium salt of palmitic acid, and is a jelly-like or *soft* soap.

3.14 Ripe palm fruit
Cross section of coconut

Soap is made by heating a mixture of *fats* and *oils* with an *alkali*. The fats and oils used include mutton fat, olive oil, palm-kernel oil, coconut oil, and arachis oil (from ground nuts). The more solid fats are used to make hard soaps, the liquid oils to make soft soap. If the alkali used is sodium hydroxide, hard soap will be produced. Potassium hydroxide gives soft soap.

The mixture of fats and alkali is placed in large tanks through which steam is passed. The chemical change which occurs is called *saponification*. *Glycerol* from the fats and oils is produced as a by-product of soap manufacture.

$$\text{Fat or oil} + \text{alkali} \rightarrow \text{soap} + \text{glycerol} + \text{water.}$$

Water and *salt* are then added. Soap is insoluble in salt water, and floats to the top of the tank as a thick layer, thus separating from the soluble glycerol which can be drained off from below. This process is known as *salting out*, but can only be used for hard soap. The glycerol remains mixed with soft soap. Hard soap is used in toilet soap, and in soap washing powders. Soft soap is used in liquid soap shampoo and shaving soap.

Soaps have the disadvantage of forming a *scum* of calcium stearate with hard water. They only dissolve readily in hot water, and are insoluble in salty water. They form an alkaline solution in water, and are destroyed by acid solutions.

3.15 Two beakers of hard water, one with soap and one with surfactant

3.16 Lauryl sulphate molecule

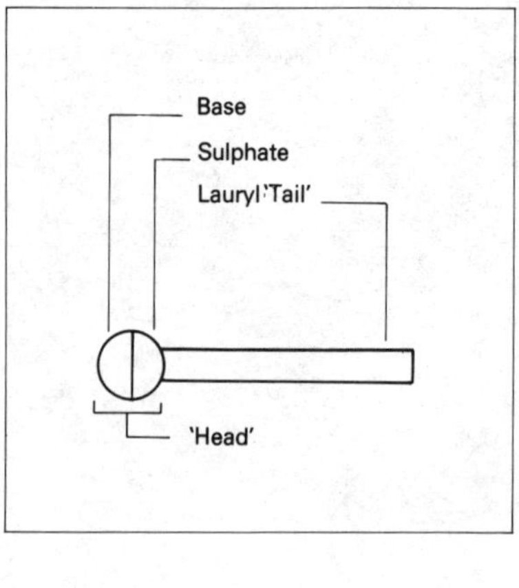

SOAPLESS DETERGENTS

Few soapless detergents are suitable for shampoos. They must be readily soluble in water, and easily rinsed out of the hair. They must produce a rich lather of small bubbles. They must leave the hair easily manageable, and not irritate the scalp. The *lauryl sulphates* have these properties and are usually used in soapless shampoo. They are *organic salts*, the lauryl group forming the 'tail' of the molecule.

Lauryl sulphates are manufactured from *vegetable oils* such as olive oil, castor oil, and coconut oil, which are *sulphonated* by treating them with *sulphuric acid*. The sulphonated oils are then *neutralized* by a *base*, either *sodium hydroxide*, or the organic base *triethanolamine*. Varying the base affects the solubility of the detergent. *Sodium lauryl sulphate* has limited solubility in water, and tends to be harsh to the hair. It is a white powder or paste. *Triethanolamine lauryl sulphate* has good solubility and is mild to the hair. It is a thin colourless liquid, and used at strengths between 10% and 20% is the basis of most good soapless shampoos.

Shampoos often contain materials in addition to the detergent. *Foam stabilizers* may be added to maintain the foam. Although foam has no effect on detergency, because people who previously used soap as a detergent expected foam to be present, it was thought necessary to produce soapless detergents which foamed equally well. *Alkylolamide* is usually added as a foam stabilizer. *Medicating agents* may be added to increase the antiseptic properties of the shampoo. Among the antiseptics used are *coal tar*, *zinc pyrithione*, and 0·1% *hexachlorophene*. The use of hexachlorophene as a medicating agent has been prohibited in products used for babies, as concentrated solutions have been found to damage babies' brains. *Conditioners* to make the hair more manageable may be added. They also reduce the eye-irritancy of the shampoo. Soluble *lanolin* compounds are used, or synthetic *resins*, e.g. P.V.P. resin. *Thickeners* which increase the viscosity, or thickness, of the shampoo are often added. Common *salt* (sodium chloride), *borax* (sodium borate), or *soap* are used for this purpose. A shampoo which is thick is not necessarily concentrated. *Protein* is added to about 10% of the shampoos on the market, the manufacturers claiming that the protein helps to repair splits in the end of the hair shafts. However, as the hair shaft is a dead structure, and as independent tests have been unable to prove that this repair of split ends does take place, the inclusion of protein in shampoo would appear to be without value in this respect.

Soapless detergents have advantages over soaps, which is why they have largely replaced them in shampoos. Lauryl sulphates dissolve readily in cold water as well as in hot water, and they do not form a scum in hard water which makes them more economical. They are soluble in salt solutions, so will wash salt water out of the hair. They are neutral, so are not caustic to the skin, although they will damage skin and hair by removing too much sebum if used at too high a concentration. They are not destroyed by acid solutions.

Acid rinses

These are weak solutions (4%) of either *acetic* or *citric* acid, which neutralize traces of soap left on the hair after using a soap shampoo, and remove scum, so that the hair is less dull-looking.

Acetic acid, when pure, is a colourless rather oily liquid with a very strong smell, known as *glacial* acetic acid. *Vinegar* is a weak impure solution of acetic acid, made by dripping stale beer or wine through beech shavings carrying a mould which causes fermentation. *Fermentation* is a process by which the mould obtains energy by changing substances present in the beer or wine into acetic acid.

Citric acid consists of white crystals, and is obtained from lemon juice, or by fermenting sugar cane.

Like all acids, acetic and citric acid are *corrosive*, burning the skin if used at concentrations greater than 4%. Acetic acid rinse will also increase the redness of a henna dye. Malt vinegar rinses should be used on dark hair, and white vinegar rinses on fair hair.

Beer rinse

If beer is put on to the hair in the final rinse after shampooing, it makes the hair easier to set.

Practical work

1 PREPARATION OF DISTILLED WATER

Assemble the Quickfit distillation apparatus, after half-filling the distilling flask with tap water. Place a small beaker at the lower end of the condenser to collect the distilled water produced. Watch the top of the condenser carefully when the condensation of steam begins.

Note the surface tension film round the large water drops as they run down the condenser. Note the solids left behind in the flask. Place a little anhydrous copper sulphate on a watch-glass, and pour a drop of the distilled water you have collected onto it. Notice the colour change.

3.17 Distillation of water apparatus

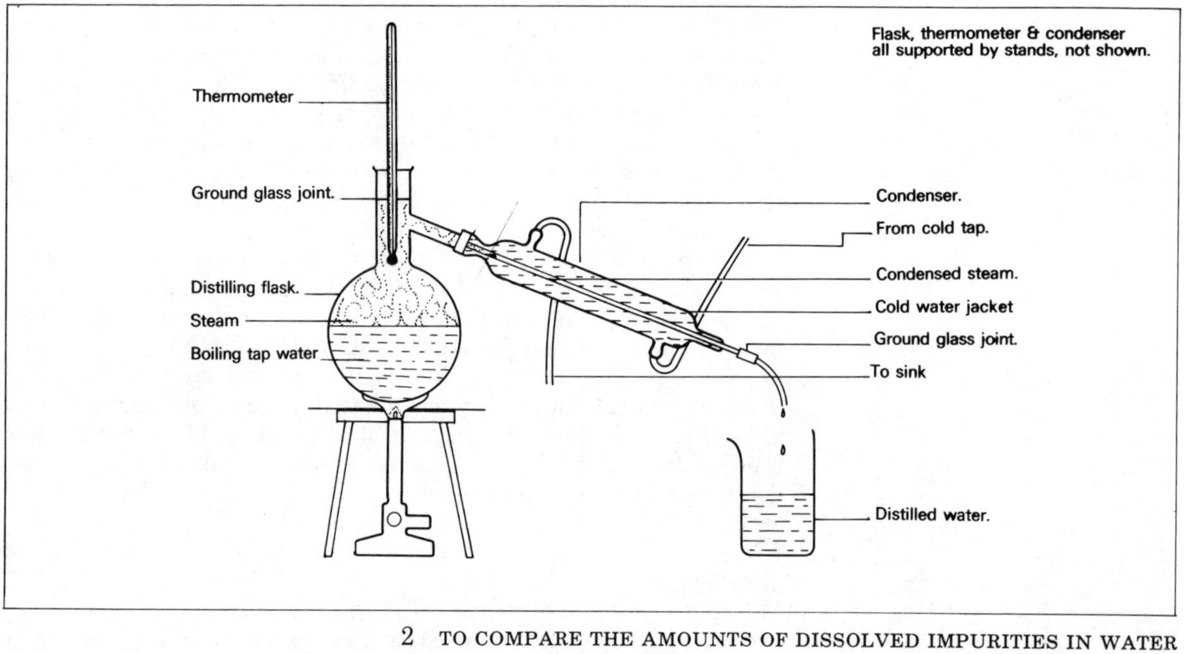

2 TO COMPARE THE AMOUNTS OF DISSOLVED IMPURITIES IN WATER SAMPLES

Take a large watch-glass which must be cleaned and polished. Into it pour a little of one of the water types listed: distilled water, rain water, tap water, sea water (or 2% sodium chloride solution). Work in groups of four, so that each type of water will be tested, and your results can be shared. Place the watch-glass over a beaker of boiling water, and leave it to evaporate the water sample. When cool, test any solid left on the watch-glass for a salty or a chalky taste.

3 SOAP TITRATIONS OF WATER SAMPLES

Fill a burette with soap solution, and ensure that the level on the scale gives a reading of 0 ml (cm^3). Using a pipette, transfer 20 ml (cm^3) of distilled water into a conical flask. Place 20 ml (cm^3) of tap water into each of three other conical flasks. If the tap water is not hard in your district, it can be made harder by dissolving a little calcium hydroxide in the tap water. Leave one of the three flasks unaltered, and add a little Calgon water softener to another. Boil the tap water in the third flask for one minute, then cool it thoroughly. Run soap solution from the burette 1 ml (cm^3) at a time into each conical flask in turn, starting with the flask containing distilled water, and finishing with the boiled tap water flask. After each addition of 1 ml (cm^3) of soap, shake the conical flask to see if a lather is formed which does not quickly disappear again. Once a persistent lather is obtained, stop adding soap and note the number of ml (cm^3) of soap already added. Compare the amounts of soap needed to produce a lather, and explain your results in terms of hardness of the water samples.

4 LOWERING THE SURFACE TENSION OF WATER

(*a*) Take a large evaporating dish, and add water to within 1 cm of the top. Place a fine needle, or a very light coin, e.g. a 2 franc piece, horizontally on the surface of the water, so that it remains floating. Add liquid shampoo from a dropper pipette onto the water surface, and note that the object sinks as the surface tension is lowered by the detergent.

(*b*) Sprinkle some powdered sulphur on top of some water in a beaker. Stir with a glass rod, and note that the sulphur remains at the surface. With a dropper pipette place two or three drops of liquid shampoo on the centre of the water surface when, owing to the lowering of the surface tension, the sulphur sinks to the bottom.

(*c*) Take a clean dropper pipette and two small beakers, one containing a little distilled water, and the other containing water to which a little soapless shampoo has been added. Take a piece of fabric with a close weave and, using the pipette, place two drops of distilled water on the fabric about 5 cm apart. Then place one drop of shampoo solution on the fabric 5 cm from the other drops. Add a second drop of shampoo solution to one of the distilled water drops. Note the wetting effect of the shampoo.

5 PREPARATION OF SOFT SOAP

Measure out 20 ml (cm^3) olive oil and 5 g coconut oil into a beaker and warm them gently to melt the coconut oil. In a second beaker place 25 ml (cm^3) distilled water and add 5 g potassium hydroxide pellets. Stir with a glass rod to dissolve the pellets, remembering that they are caustic. Then add 5 ml (cm^3) ethanol (I.M.S.) to act as a catalyst. Pour the contents of the second beaker into the oils, stir well, then add 50 ml (cm^3) distilled water. Warm the contents of the beaker to 90°C and stir for thirty minutes, during which time the two layers stop separating out, the mixture thickens, and a foam develops. Leave to cool. Test a small quantity on your wet hands to see if it lathers and feels soapy, then thoroughly rinse your hands. It is inadvisable to apply this preparation to the hair as a shampoo, as it may be sufficiently alkaline to damage the scalp.

6 PREPARATION OF A SOAPLESS CREAM SHAMPOO
Weigh out 8 g lanette wax and 2 g lanolin and place them in a beaker, then warm them gently to 75°C. Separately heat 30 ml distilled water to 75°C and dissolve 20 g sodium lauryl sulphate in the water. Pour the waxes into the water and stir continuously as the mixture cools, to form a cream. Then add a few drops of brilliant green solution as a colourant, and perfume.

7 TO DEMONSTRATE THE DIFFERENCES BETWEEN SOAP AND SOAPLESS DETERGENTS
(*a*) Make up 50 ml (cm^3) soap solution by dissolving a teaspoonful of soap flakes in hot distilled water. Make up 50 ml (cm^3) soapless detergent solution in the same way using sodium lauryl sulphate in place of the soap flakes. Using 1 cm samples of each solution in separate test-tubes, carry out the following tests on the soap and soapless detergent solutions:

(1) Add a few drops of phenolphthalein.
(2) Add a piece of pH paper and determine the pH from the colour chart.
(3) Add a little hard water and look for scum formation.
(4) Add a little 2% sodium chloride solution to see if salting-out occurs.
(5) Add a little 4% acetic acid solution (acid rinse) and note any effect.

(*b*) Take 2 beakers each containing 2 cm of cold distilled water. Add a small quantity of soap flakes to one beaker, and the same amount of sodium lauryl sulphate to the other. Compare their solubility in cold water.

Multiple choice questions

1 The term 'head of water' is used to indicate
a density *b* pressure *c* lather *d* volume

2 Distilled water should be used in the steamer instead of tap water to prevent
a too high a temperature *b* too rapid cooling
c scale being deposited *d* reduced pressure

3 The smallest amount of dissolved solids is found in
a rain water *b* sea water *c* tap water *d* limewater

4 When dissolved in water, the sulphates of calcium and magnesium produce the type of hardness called
a temporary *b* semi-permanent *c* partial
d permanent

5 Calcium salts in hard water form a scum with toilet soap. The chemical name of this scum is calcium
a sulphate *b* acetate
c stearate *d* carbonate

6 Which of the following is used as a water softening agent?
a sodium hexametaphosphate
b calcium hydrogen carbonate
c potassium aluminium sulphate
d calcium thioglycollate

7 The surface tension of water is lowered by adding
a an indicator *b* a surfactant *c* a neutralizer
d a catalyst

8 During shampooing, greasy dirt is removed from the hair by
a the dissolving action of the detergent
b the foam stabilizer in the shampoo
c the emulsifying action of the detergent
d an increase in surface tension

9 Soap is formed by a chemical change due to the action of steam on
a an alcohol and an alkali
b an alkali and a fat
c a salt and an alkali *d* a fat and an alcohol

10 Triethanolamine lauryl sulphate is the substance used as the basis of
a vinegar rinse *b* depilatory creams
c bath crystals *d* soapless shampoo

4 Setting Hair

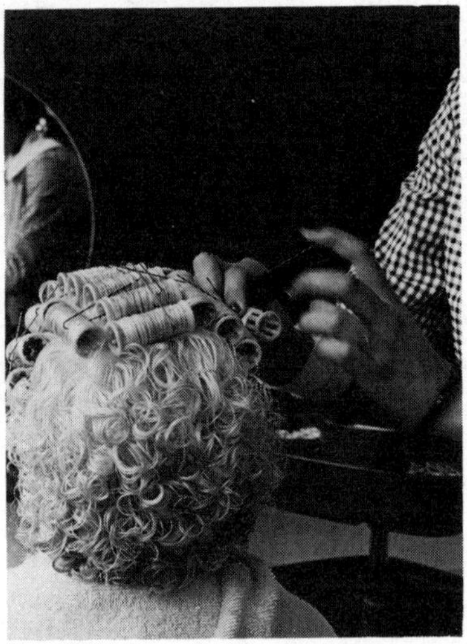

It is the chemical structure of the keratin molecules which makes it possible to set hair. The shape of the keratin molecule is physically changed by the wetting and stretching processes involved in the set.

Chemical structure of hair keratin

Keratin, since it contains the element carbon, is an *organic* compound. The other elements it contains are hydrogen, oxygen, nitrogen, and sulphur (see diagram 2.1). Like other *proteins* keratin consists of large numbers of smaller units, called *amino-acids*, which are linked together in a long chain by *peptide bonds*. Each amino-acid unit has a basic (amino) part and an acidic part. A peptide bond is formed by joining the basic (amino) part of one amino-acid to the acidic part of another. When a large number of amino-acids are linked together by peptide bonds, the resulting molecule is a *polypeptide* chain.

There are eighteen different amino-acids present in the polypeptide chains of keratin. The proportions of the various amino-acids in keratin result in an excess of acidic negative groups over basic positive groups. This causes keratin to *attract* chemical groups which have lost negative electrons, and so have a positive electrical charge. Such groups are known as positively charged *ions*, and by being attracted, are said to be *substantive* to the negatively charged hair. Many substances used as *conditioners* (e.g. cetrimide) have positively charged ions and so are attracted to the hair.

The polypeptide chains of the cortex keratin are coiled into a spiral shape called an *α-helix*, and so have a regular (crystalline) structure. The α-helix is stabilized by cross-links called *hydrogen bonds*, which form between an amino-acid unit of the polypeptide chain and one 3 units along, which lies just above or below it in the next turn of the spiral. The hydrogen bonds form between a *hydrogen* atom in one amino-acid and an *oxygen* atom in the other.

Hydrogen bonds are extensible and rather weak but, as they occur in large numbers, they keep the α-helix fairly rigid. Hydrogen bonds also occur between adjacent polypeptide chains. There is less hydrogen bonding in the keratin of the *cuticle*, where an α-helix structure is not thought to predominate.

Disulphide bonds occur as cross-links between two adjacent polypeptide chains which are thus held together in a network. The disulphide bonds occur in one of the amino-acids called *cystine* which forms 10% of keratin, and contains the element *sulphur*. Part of each cystine molecule occurs in one polypeptide chain, while the other part occurs in a different chain, the two parts being linked through two sulphur atoms. These disulphide bonds are strong, and can only be broken by a *chemical change*. Disulphide bonds are particularly frequent in the keratin of the *cuticle*.

Salt bonds also form cross-links between the acidic part of an amino-acid unit in one polypeptide chain and the basic (amino) part of an amino-acid in another chain. These bonds are weak, and break when the hair is wet.

In a *dry unstretched* condition, the protein of hair is known as *α-keratin*, and the cortical fibres contain the α-helix arrangement in bundles (protofibrils). If the hair is *stretched* when *wet* the spiral α-helix is straightened out, like a pulled spring, to form a randomly folded chain known as *β-keratin*. When the stretching force is removed the molecules return to the α-keratin form.

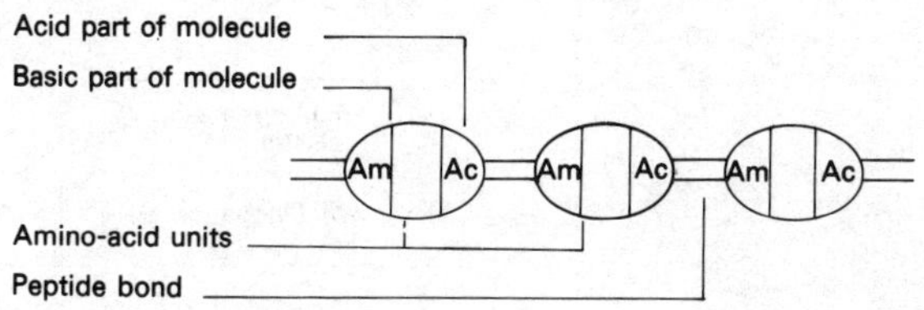

4.1 Peptide bonds in a polypeptide chain

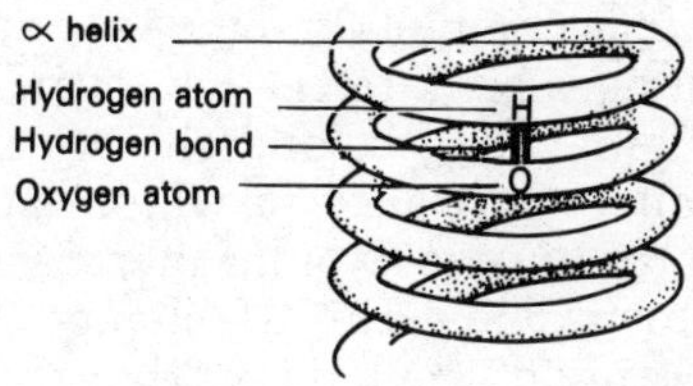

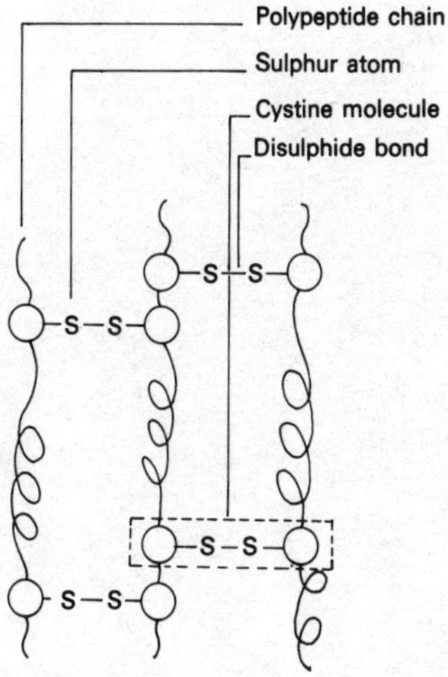

4.2 Hydrogen bond in an α-helix (bottom left)

4.3 Disulphide bonds in polypeptide network (bottom right)

Elasticity of hair

The *cross-linkages* in keratin, particularly the hydrogen bonds, prevent hair from breaking up in water, and also give it *elasticity*. Elasticity is the property which enables hair to increase in length when pulled, and return to its original length when the stretching force is removed. The *elastic limit* is reached when the hair does not return completely to its original length when the stretching force is removed. When the elastic limit is exceeded, hair will continue to increase in length until it suddenly *breaks*. In experiments, the usual stretching force applied to hair is produced by a *weight* suspended from the hair, i.e. *grammes force*. The increase in length of the hair on stretching is expressed as % *elongation*. Hair has a greater *tensile strength* when dry than when wet, so dry hair will support a greater weight before breaking. Wet hair stretches more readily and much further than dry hair, having greater elasticity. *Steamed* hair has even greater elasticity as it can be reversibly stretched to twice its original length.

The set

To produce a set the hair is first made *wet*, and then *stretched* over rollers. The rollers change the shape of the hair, making it bend or curl. Wetting and stretching the hair change the α-keratin to β-keratin. Care must be taken when stretching the hair over the roller that the pull on the hair does not reach the hair's *elastic limit*. The hair is then dried in the stretched condition. This causes the keratin to remain in the β-keratin

4.4 Elasticity data table for hair (average values)

	Wet hair	Dry hair
Force reaching elastic limit	21 gf.	42 gf.
% Elongation at elastic limit	30%	15%
Breaking force	90 gf.	150 gf.
% Elongation as hair breaks	52%	44%

condition even when the stretching force is removed, once the hair is completely dry. As soon as the hair becomes wet again it changes back to the α-keratin condition, the hair shortens to its original length, and the set is lost. Hair is a *hygroscopic* substance, as it absorbs water vapour from the air, and will take in water until its weight increases by 30%. This absorption of water allows β-keratin to change back to α-keratin without total wetting of the hair, so that the set is gradually lost. Because the change from α to β-keratin is easily reversed by wetting the hair, a set is a *physical* change.

Conditioners

Shampoos remove the oily film of *sebum* surrounding the hair, so conditioners are applied before setting the hair to counteract the effects of de-greasing. Conditioners make the hair more manageable, elastic, and glossy, and help to *preserve* the *set*. Some conditioners contain an *oil* or *wax* to put back a film of lubricant round the hair. An oil-in-water *emulsion* is the simplest type, or a lanolin-in-water emulsion may be used. Both these types of conditioners must be used sparingly, or the hair will be too greasy. Synthetic mixtures of *fatty acids* having a similar composition to sebum can be applied. *Organic acids* such as citric, lactic, or tartaric acid, are used in conditioning creams. They neutralize excess alkali on the hair, and prevent the continuation of oxidation after bleaching and tinting. *Protein* conditioners ('fillers') which are allowed to dry on the hair, will leave a coating of protein round each hair fibre. This will improve the appearance of porous hair, but does not increase its strength or elasticity. These conditioners can be applied before tinting or perming the hair. They readily go mouldy and are difficult to preserve. *Cetrimide* conditioners are either 1·5–2% solutions in water, or the cetrimide is added to an oil-in-water emulsion. As they foam on wet hair they must be rinsed away before setting the hair. However their effect remains after rinsing away.

Setting lotions

Setting lotions are applied to the wet hair, and are intended to make a set last longer by coating each hair with a flexible clear film, which will prevent the hair absorbing atmospheric water vapour and rapidly returning to the α-keratin condition. The substances used to produce the film on the hair are natural *gums*, or synthetic *resins*. Gums are organic substances, being plastic solids which form slimy solutions. Gum *Tragacanth* is a white powder obtained from the bark of a shrub growing in Turkey. *Karaya* is an Indian gum which is less expensive than Tragacanth. To form a setting lotion, the gum is ground up with a little alcohol, and then water is added. Gum setting lotions readily go mouldy, and require a preservative. *Plastic setting lotions* usually contain *synthetic resins* (see Chapter 6) dissolved in a 50 : 50 mixture of ethanol and water.

Practical work

1 TO TEST FOR SOME OF THE ELEMENTS PRESENT IN KERATIN

(*a*) *Carbon* (1) Burn some hair on a gauze, when a black deposit of carbon is left.

(2) Chop up some hair and place it in an ignition tube with a little copper oxide, and heat the tube strongly. The carbon from keratin is oxidized to carbon dioxide, which is given off as a gas. Dip a glass rod in limewater, and hold it so that the drop of limewater is opposite the opening of the tube. Any carbon dioxide produced will turn the limewater milky.

4.5 Testing hair for the presence of carbon

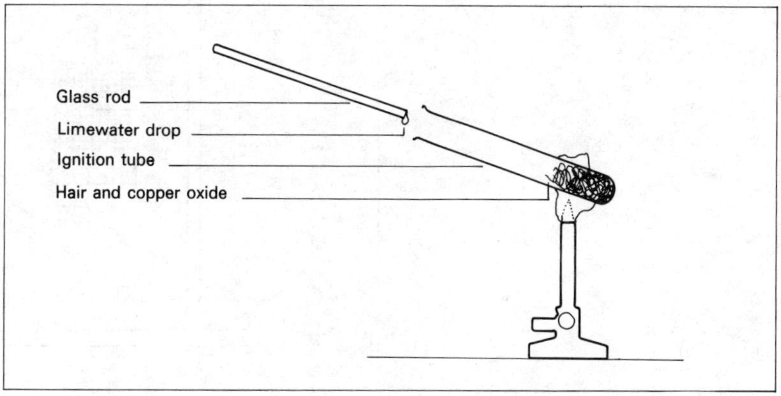

(*b*) *Hydrogen* Chop up some hair, dry it, then place it in an ignition tube with copper oxide, then heat the tube. The hydrogen from keratin will be oxidized by the copper oxide to form water, which will condense as droplets at the top of the tube.

(*c*) *Sulphur* Heat some chopped hair with soda-lime in an ignition tube, when hydrogen sulphide gas is formed from the keratin sulphur. Dip a piece of filter paper in lead acetate solution, and hold it across the opening of the tube. The paper will turn black if hydrogen sulphide is produced. CARE. Lead acetate is highly poisonous. Wash your hands after touching the paper soaked in it.

2 ELASTICITY OF HAIR AND BREAKING FORCE

Obtain a single long hair, and attach one end to a support. Tie the other end of the hair to a piece of stiff gauze, and measure the length of the hair (in cm) between the two fixed points, using a metre rule. Make a paper weight-holder, and attach it by cotton to the gauze. Place a 5 g weight on the weight-holder, wait for five minutes for the hair to elongate, then measure the length of the hair. Replace the 5 g weight by a 10 g weight, and repeat the procedure as before. Continue increasing the weight by 5 g each time, noting the elongation of the hair, until it breaks. Write down your measurements as a table:

weight (gf)	0	5	10	15	etc.
hair length					

(gf = grammes force)

State the force which causes the hair to break. Calculate the % increase in length of the hair at the breaking point from the expression below:

$$\frac{\text{Final length} - \text{Original length}}{\text{Original length}} \times 100.$$

4.6 Testing the elasticity of a hair

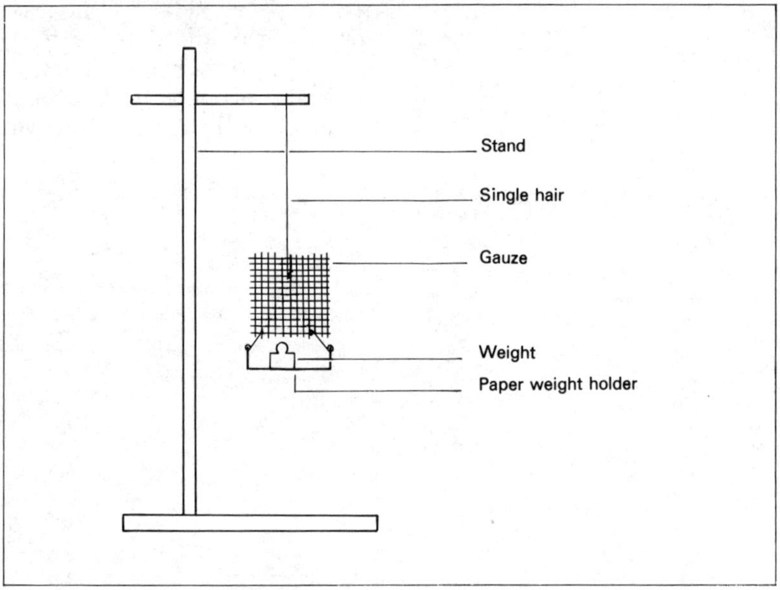

3 TO FIND THE ELASTIC LIMIT OF A HAIR
Using the apparatus used in experiment 2, measure the length of the hair, and place a 10 g weight on the weight-holder. Leave the weight in place for five minutes and measure the length of the hair after stretching. Remove the weight, and leave for a further five minutes, then remeasure the hair to see if it has regained its original length. Continue to increase the weight by 5 g additions checking the length of the hair each time to see if it shortens to its original length. The first weight at which the hair fails to shorten completely represents the force just exceeding the elastic limit of the hair.

4 PREPARATION OF HAIR CONDITIONERS
(*a*) *Lanolin type*
Lanette wax 15 g
Lanolin 4 g
Citric acid 1 g
Distilled water 90 ml (cm^3)
Place the lanette wax and the lanolin in a small beaker, and warm to 75°C. Do not overheat. (A water-bath may be used if preferred.) Warm the distilled water to 75°C, and dissolve the citric acid in

the water. Steadily pour the waxes into the water, stirring all the time, to form an emulsion.

(*b*) *Organic acid type*

Lanette wax	16 g
Lactic acid	1 g
Distilled water	100 ml (cm^3)

Heat the lanette wax in one beaker, and the water and lactic acid in another beaker, using the method as in *a*), to form an emulsion.

(*c*) *Cetrimide type*

Cetrimide	1·5 g
Cetyl alcohol	5 g
Lanolin	3 g
Distilled water	90 ml (cm^3)
Rose water (perfume)	0·5 ml (cm^3)

Place the lanolin and cetyl alcohol in a 250 ml (cm^3) beaker and warm them together gently to 75°C. Warm the distilled water in another beaker to 75°C, and dissolve the cetrimide in the water. Pour the water mixture into the lanolin and cetyl alcohol, stirring all the time. Continue stirring as the mixture cools, then add the rosewater.

5 PREPARATION OF SETTING LOTIONS

(*a*) *Gum setting lotion*

Gum Tragacanth (powdered)	2 g
Isopropanol	5 ml (cm^3)
Distilled water	80 ml (cm^3)

Place the gum in a mortar, and add the isopropanol. Grind the two together with a pestle, adding some of the water. Pour the mixture into a small bottle, and add the rest of the water. Shake the mixture thoroughly as the gum does not dissolve easily.

(*b*) *Plastic setting lotion*

P.V.P./V.A. 60/40	2 g
Industrial methylated spirit	65 ml (cm^3)
Distilled water	50 ml (cm^3)
Perfume	

Dissolve the synthetic resins in the water/alcohol mixture in a beaker, then add perfume.

Multiple choice questions

1 Hair is a hygroscopic structure because it will
a fall out readily *b* absorb atmospheric moisture
c dry rapidly *d* fade in strong light

2 Synthetic resins are one of the components of
a barrier creams *b* lanolin conditioners
c β-keratin *d* plastic setting lotions

3 Because keratin is a protein it is formed from smaller units of
a lactic acid *b* amino-acid *c* citric acid *d* acetic acid

4 The element which forms the cystine cross-links in keratin is
a sulphur *b* carbon *c* hydrogen *d* oxygen

5 The spirally twisted long chains in a keratin molecule are
a amino-acids *b* polypeptides *c* polyvinyls
d polysulphides

6 The protein molecules of the hair are changed to β-keratin from α-keratin when the hair is being
a conditioned *b* shampooed *c* set *d* dried

7 The elasticity of a hair fibre is largely due to
a electrostatic bonds *b* disulphide bonds
c polypeptide chains *d* cystine links

8 The force which reaches the elastic limit of an average dry hair to cause overstretching would be
a 0·4 gf *b* 4 gf *c* 40 gf *d* 400 gf

9 A preparation for conditioning the hair containing cetrimide must be rinsed away before setting because it
a is an oily substance *b* breaks the disulphide bonds
c stings the scalp *d* foams on wet hair

10 Before reaching its elastic limit, a wet hair will increase its length by
a 5% *b* 30% *c* 50% *d* 100%

5 Drying Hair

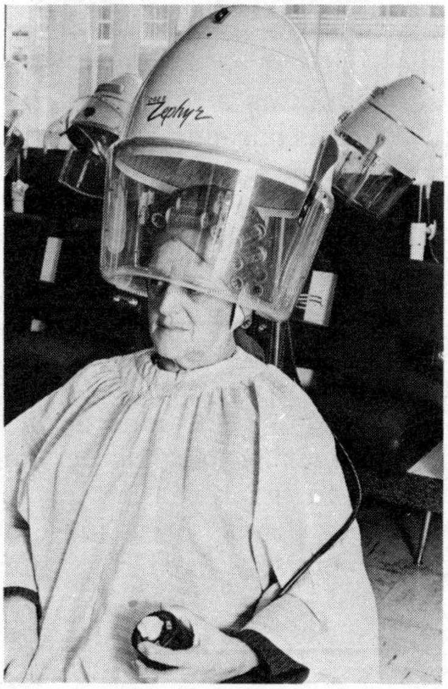

To remove the water from wet hair it is first towel-dried, being rubbed or blotted with an absorptive material which removes water in the *liquid* state. This is usually carried out before setting the hair and removes only a small part of the water present. The rest of the water is removed in the *gaseous* state by *evaporation*, either during blow-drying or, after setting, under the usual type of salon dryer.

5.1 Capillarity in glass tubes

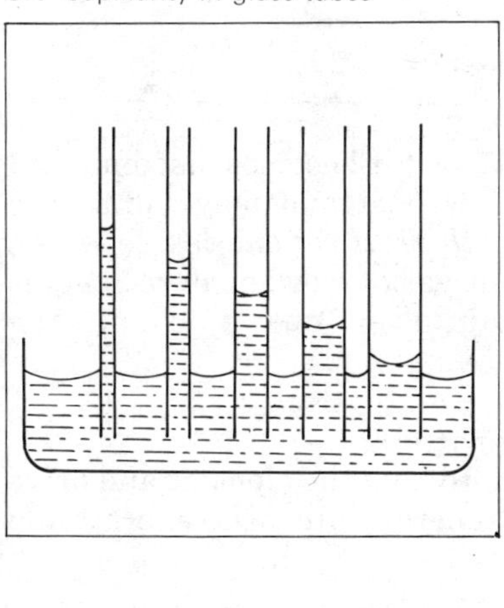

Towel drying

A towel is composed of cotton threads woven together to form a fabric. Between the threads are very narrow *air spaces*. If a fine glass tube with a very narrow central air space, called a capillary tube, stands upright in a shallow dish of water, the level of the water rises inside the tube to a greater height than the water level in the dish. The narrower the glass tube the higher the water will rise.

This effect is called *capillarity*, and is due to the surface tension of water tending to make the surface contract. Water molecules are attracted to a glass surface so the water curves upwards against the glass. The very narrow *air spaces* between the fibres in the towel behave like the narrow glass tubes, so that water passes from the hair through these spaces by *capillarity*. Cotton *fibres* will also *absorb* water from the air spaces and hair, until both fibres and air spaces are saturated with water.

Evaporation of water from the hair

When water becomes invisible water vapour, it *changes its state* from a liquid to a gas. This change of state is called *evaporation* and it requires heat to be supplied while it is taking place. The heat absorbed when a liquid changes its state becoming a gas is *latent heat*. The molecules in a liquid move with varying speeds. If a faster one comes to the surface it may have enough *energy* to overcome the attractive forces between the molecules and escape from the liquid. The *heat* supplied by a hairdryer gives more molecules this extra energy that they need to escape from the liquid, so the dryer provides latent heat. If no outside heat is supplied, water molecules from wet hair absorb the latent heat from the scalp, making the person's head cooler. This is the *cooling effect* of evaporation, and is also produced during *sweating* and when *after-shave* lotions or *Cologne-sticks* are used on the skin. Evaporation of water from wet hair takes place at all temperatures but it occurs much more rapidly at higher ones. It is an invisible process; you need to feel the hair to find out if it is completely dry. Water will only evaporate if the surrounding air is able to hold more water vapour. As soon as the air round a wet head becomes *saturated* with water vapour, no more water can evaporate. Thus *air movements* which remove the layers of saturated air from around the wet head will cause evaporation to occur faster. Hairdryers are therefore designed to supply *heat* and *movement of air*, to speed up evaporation. They contain a *heating element*, and a *fan* to move the air which would otherwise be trapped under the hood of the dryer.

When the wet hair is *blow-dried* it is brushed as this separates the strands of hair. As a greater *surface area* of wet hair is exposed to the air, the rate of evaporation is further increased.

The salon hairdryer

A salon hairdryer consists of a *hood* mounted on a *stand* so that its height can be adjusted. At the back of the hood is a *fan* driven by an *electric motor*, and round the rim is a *heating element* held on porcelain supports. The client is protected from contact with the heating element by a *shield*. The heater is controlled by an adjustable switch, and a thermostat. The *thermostat* is a device

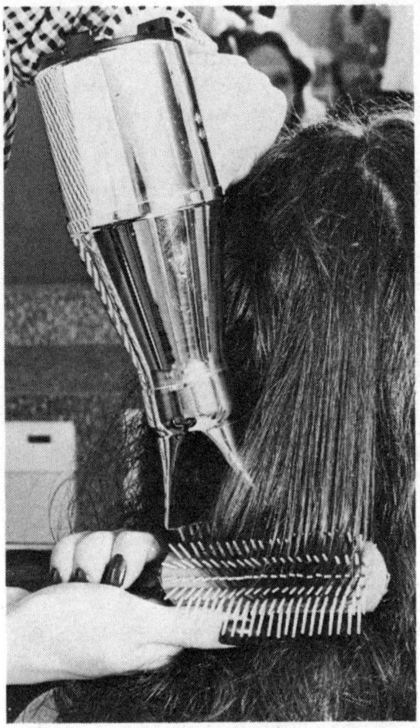

5.2 Blow-drying hair

for controlling the temperature under the hood automatically. It acts by cutting off the electric current to the heating element once it reaches a selected temperature which is set on a dial. When the temperature under the hood falls the electric current heats the element again. The thermostat may operate a small light on the dryer which lights up when the element is being heated, and goes out when the electricity stops flowing. The simplest type of electrical thermostat contains a *bimetal strip*. The scientific principle on which its action is based is that different metals *expand* by different amounts for the same temperature rise. Most solids *expand* on heating and *contract* on cooling, although the change in length is small. The metal *brass* behaves in this way. The metal *invar* which is a mixture, or *alloy*, of steel and nickel, hardly expands at all on heating. If a strip of brass and a strip of invar are joined together to form a bimetal strip and heated, the brass expands more than the invar, and the strip *bends*. As the strip cools down it will straighten out again as the brass contracts to its original length. In the thermostat the electricity flows through a bimetal strip to reach the heater at first, but as it becomes hotter the strip bends, breaking an electrical connection and preventing electricity from reaching the heating element.

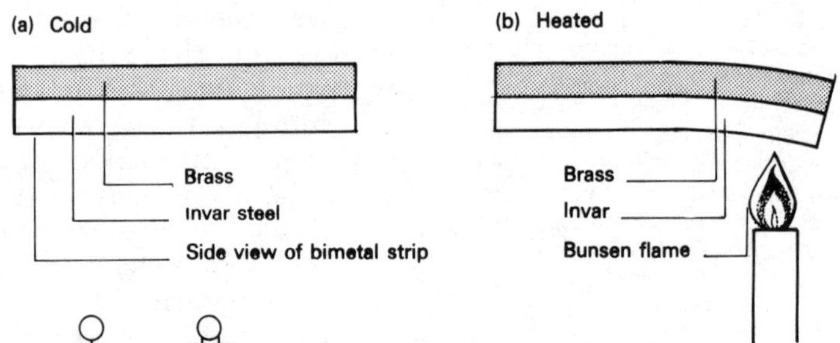

5.3 Action of heat on a bimetal strip

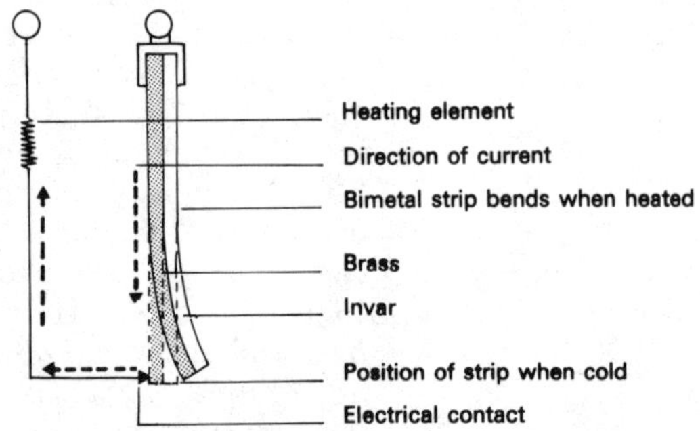

5.4 An electric thermostat

If the *fan* in the dryer hood jams or if it becomes disconnected from the motor, the dryer will overheat and may burst into flames. It should therefore have a *thermal cut-out* device which will switch off the heating element as soon as the dryer begins to overheat. The dryer must remain out of operation until the fault has been repaired.

How the salon hairdryer operates

A hairdryer uses an *electric current* to heat the element and drive the fan, by converting *electrical* energy into *heat* energy and

5.5 Hood of hairdryer

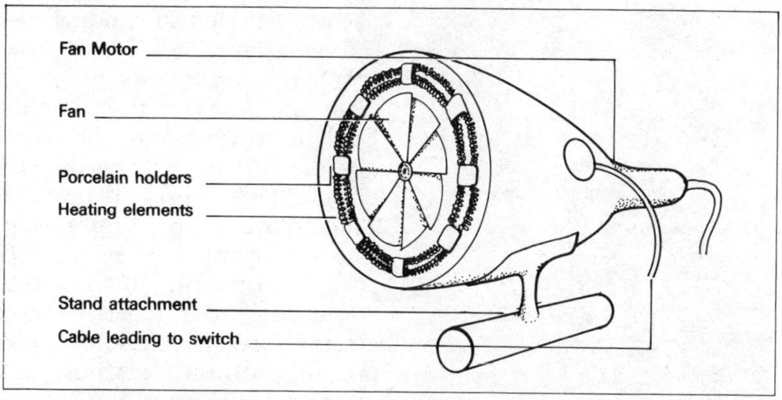

mechanical energy respectively. An electric current is produced because of the special structure of atoms. In some substances the outer *electrons* (see Chapter 2) are continually moving in a random manner from atom to atom. Such substances will allow an electric current to pass through them and are therefore *conductors*. The electric current passes when the free electrons move in the same direction. Most *metals* have atoms which provide free electrons and therefore will conduct electricity.

5.6 Movement of electrons in copper wire

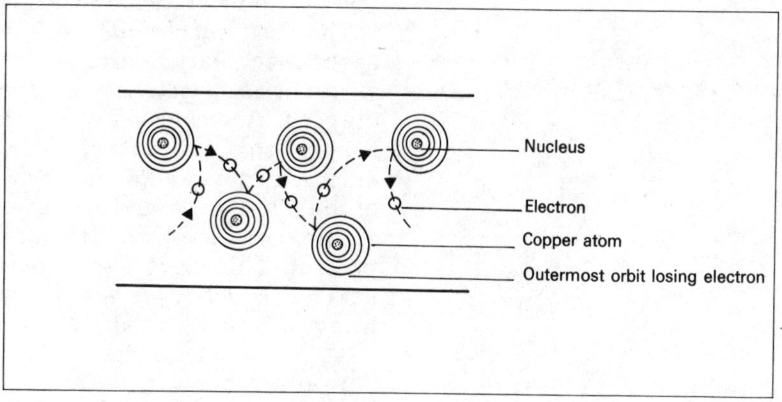

Substances which do not provide free electrons and through which an electric current will not pass are called electrical *insulators*. Rubber, plastic, porcelain, and dry air are examples of insulators. In a hairdryer the copper wires in the flex are *conductors*, the plastic parts of the dryer, the rubber and plastic coverings to the wires in the flex, the plastic covers to the plug and switch, and the porcelain holders for the heating element, are all *insulators*. Some hairdryers are *all-insulated* the outside being made entirely of an insulating material, i.e. plastic, and having no metal exposed. Even when electricity passes through conductors it meets some resistance, as the free electrons do not move very readily. The energy used in overcoming this resistance produces heat and light. The *nichrome* wire used in the heating element in the hairdryer is a *high resistance conductor* and therefore gets red hot when an electric current passes through it. Nichrome wire is a mixture of the metals *nickel* and *chromium*. The electrical resistance in copper wires is very low so they do not get hot when an electric current passes, and can safely be

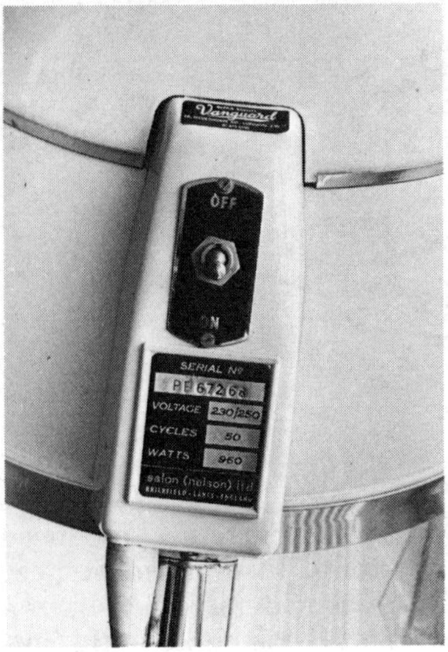

5.7 Wattage plate of hairdryer

used in the flex to conduct electricity from the mains supply to the hairdryer.

When a *continuous* closed path is provided for electrons to go from one place to another this path is called an *electric circuit*. Each hairdryer must be part of an electric circuit if it is to operate. A *force* is needed to drive the electrons round this circuit. This is provided by the mains supply, and is the *voltage*. The *electrical* force or *pressure* is measured in units called *volts*. The mains supply is usually 240 volts. The number of electrons passing any point in the circuit in each second determines the *strength* of the electric *current*. The unit of *rate of flow* of electric current is the *ampere*, or amp. Approximately 6 million, million, million electrons passing each second gives a current of one amp. The ability of a conductor to *resist* the flow of electric current is measured in units called *ohms*. 1 volt of electrical pressure keeps a current of 1 amp flowing through a circuit with a resistance of 1 ohm.

The amount of heat and fan movement that the electric current can produce in one second in the hairdryer is the electric *power* or *wattage*, and depends on both the voltage and rate of flow of the current. The unit of *electric power* is the *watt*, where: 1 watt = 1 amp × 1 volt. A salon hairdryer usually has a power of 800 to 1000 watts; a hand-held hairdryer, 500 watts. The voltage and wattage are marked on a plate fixed to the hairdryer.

The *electrical circuit* into which the hairdryer is plugged begins at the Electricity Board's meter and *main switch*. A *live conductor* wire carries electricity to the *socket* into which the dryer is plugged. A second wire the *neutral conductor* goes back to the supply from the socket. These conducting wires are usually enclosed in *conduits*, metal or plastic tubing, below the plaster of the salon walls, and are covered with thick insulating material. A third conductor which leads from the socket to the earth is also present. This *earth wire* provides a path of low resistance, and acts as a *safety device*, carrying electric current harmlessly away into the ground.

The electric plug

The *plug* attached to the *flex* from the dryer must be suitable for the socket and must have *three pins* so that the *earth* wire can be connected. Plugs are usually of two kinds, square-pinned and round-pinned. To ensure safety, any square-pinned plug should conform to the British Standard BS/1363, and any round-pinned plug to BS 546. These letters and numbers should be stamped on the plugs you use. The flex must be connected to the plug so that the three wires of the flex are attached to the correct *terminals*, or attaching screws, inside the plug.

The *brown* covered wire (red on older flex) must be connected to the terminal marked *Live* or L.

The *blue* covered wire (black on older flex) must be connected to the terminal marked *Neutral* or N.

The *green and yellow* covered wire (green on older flex) must be connected to the terminal marked *Earth* or E.

Since July 1970 the colour of insulation in flex must conform to the *international colour code* described above. All electrical appliances sold in this country must by Law have flex conforming to this colour code.

5.8 Connections between plug and flex

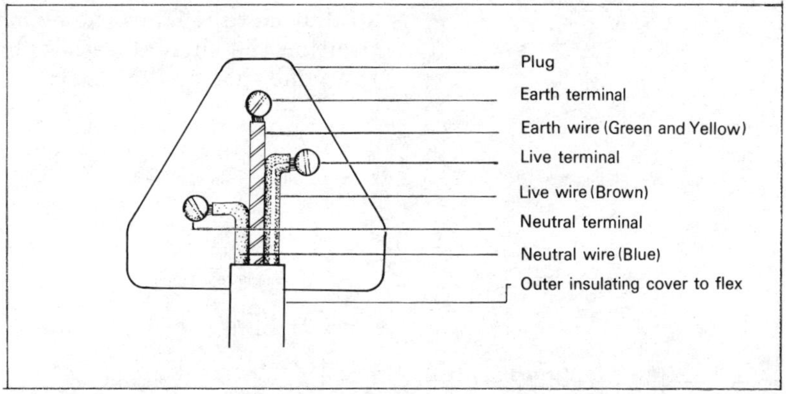

Connecting the earth wire to the live terminal would make metal parts of the hairdryer 'alive' and very dangerous. Crossing the live and neutral connections would mean that the switch would not cut off the live conductor. The *earth pin* on the plug is longer than the other two pins and will make contact in the socket first. Most modern sockets are *shuttered*, so that the holes close when the plug is withdrawn. When the plug is put into the socket the long earth pin moves the shutter to open the holes for the live and neutral pins. This makes it safer when putting in and removing the plug. When the plug is pushed into the socket the pins make contact with terminals behind the socket plate, and electricity can pass through the plug and flex to operate the dryer. The earth wire in the flex is connected to the outer *casing* of the dryer, so that if any metal parts come in contact with the live wire the earth wire conducts this electricity away, preventing the user from getting an *electric shock*.

A further safety device is also present in the plug. This is the *cartridge fuse*, which lies over the live terminal. This fuse is the weakest part of the circuit, being a *high resistance wire* made of a mixture of copper, tin, and lead which is wound on a procelain cylinder with metal caps at each end.

If the current passing is too large for the circuit the fuse wire becomes hot and melts thus *breaking* the circuit and stopping the electric current. A 3 amp fuse should be used for a dryer with a wattage below 720 watts, and a 13 amp fuse for dryers exceeding this wattage.

5.9 3 amp and 13 amp cartridge fuses

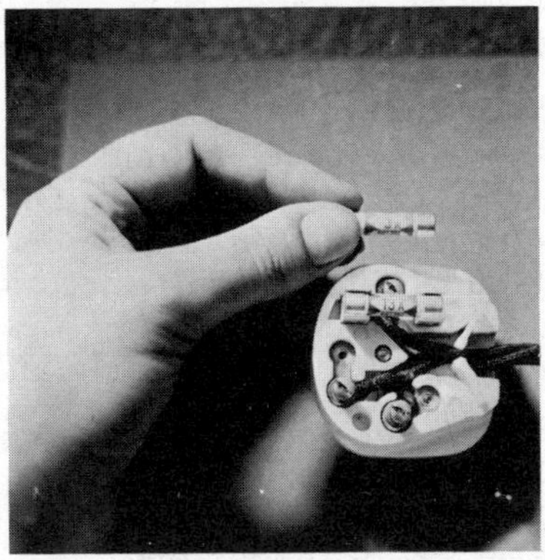

Dry air is a good insulator so if an air gap occurs in a circuit the flow of electricity will stop. An *air gap* is introduced into the circuit by means of an *on-off switch*, so that a hairdryer need not operate continuously. With the switch *off* the air gap is present. On switching on, a metal *bridge* is moved to cross the air gap and complete the circuit. This type of switch is often present in the socket. Many hairdryers are fitted with a *three-heat switch* which is under the user's control. This type of switch can be moved to any one of four positions namely: off, low, medium, and high. The low, medium, and high positions determine how hot the *heating element* becomes by controlling the amount of electricity that reaches the element. In the *low* position the electric current must pass through two *resistances* one after the other so that only a little current reaches the element. In the *medium* position the electric current needs to pass through one resistance only so that more reaches the element, making it hotter. In the *high* position the current passes through two parallel resistances at the same time so that even more current reaches the element.

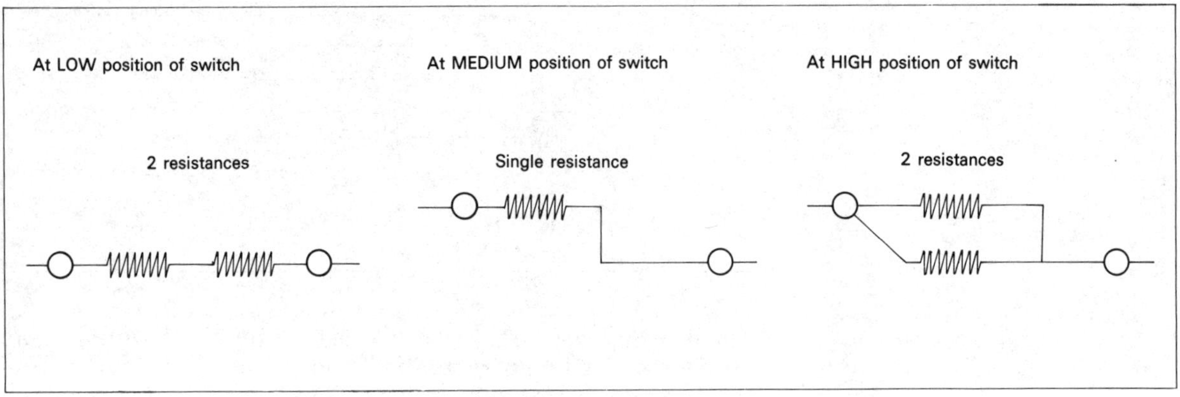

5.10 Three-heat switch

The ring circuit

The best method of supplying electric power for several electric appliances such as a row of hairdryers, is the *ring circuit.* One length of cable travels right round the salon and back to the mains supply. The cable carries live and neutral wires, with a connection from each wire to every power socket. There is also a third earth wire connected to each socket as a safety device to prevent electric shock.

5.11 Ring circuit

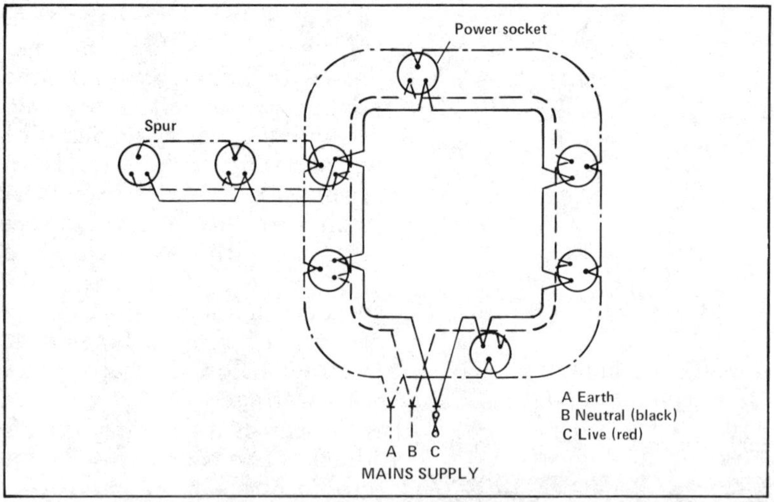

The live wire of the ring circuit passes through a 30 amp *fuse* which will 'blow' if the circuit becomes *overloaded.* A miniature *circuit-breaker* can be installed instead of the 30 amp fuse. The circuit-breaker has a switch which turns itself off, and so disconnects the circuit from the mains supply, if overloading occurs due to a fault developing in an appliance, or too many appliances being connected. After unplugging the appliances the circuit can be made operable again by pressing the circuit-breaker switch.

The ring circuit has a number of advantages over the older methods of wiring, where there is a separate circuit from the

5.12 Miniature circuit breaker

main supply for each power point. Less cable is used so it is cheaper to install. Sockets can be connected to the ring at any required point, and further sockets added cheaply at a later date. Each socket is of the *same size* and type, taking a 13 amp three-pin plug, so that any appliance can be plugged into any socket. Each plug carries its own *fuse* which will 'blow' if the appliance is faulty without affecting any other socket in the ring circuit. Each socket will supply a *maximum* number of *watts* of electric power. This number is obtained by multiplying the number of *amps* by the mains *voltage*:

Example: 13 amps × 250 volts = 3250 watts.

If the maximum wattage is *exceeded* by connecting several hairdryers to one power point by means of an adaptor, the circuit will become *overloaded* and the fuse will 'blow'.

Cost of operating a hairdryer

The amount of electricity used by an electrical appliance such as a hairdryer depends on its *power* (wattage) and the length of *time* it is operating. The unit of electrical energy is the *kilowatt-hour*, i.e. the electricity consumed when an appliance having a power of 1 kilowatt (1000 watts) operates for 1 hour. As most salon hairdryers have a wattage of slightly less than 1 kilowatt, they will operate for more than 1 hour before they have used 1 unit of electricity. To calculate the number of hours an appliance will operate for 1 unit of electricity divide 1000 by the wattage of the appliance.

Examples: (1) A 500 watt hairdryer operates for $\frac{1000}{500} = 2$ hours, using 1 unit.

(2) An 800 watt hairdryer operates for $\frac{1000}{800} = 1{\cdot}25$ hours, using 1 unit.

If a hairdryer operates for several hours the total number of units used is obtained by multiplying the $\frac{\text{wattage}}{1000}$ by the number of hours it is in use.

Example: if a hairdryer is used for 8 hours each day for 6 days (a total of 48 hours), and has a wattage of 800, the number of units used is

$$\frac{800}{1000} \times 48 = 38{\cdot}4 \text{ units.}$$

If five hairdryers operate for the same number of hours the number of units used will then be

$$5 \times \frac{800}{1000} \times 48 = 192 \text{ units.}$$

The *number of units* of electricity used in the salon is measured by the Electricity Board's *meter*. Recently installed meters display the number of units used. Older meters record the units on a series of four large *dials*, each having a pointer whose position must be read. The dials should be read from left to right. Where the pointer lies between two numbers the smaller number should be taken, except between 9 and 0, where 0 represents 10, and where 9 is the number to be taken.

5.13 Electricity meter dials

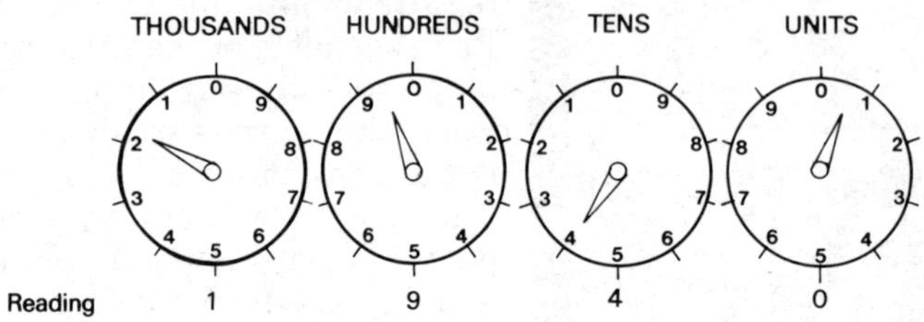

To obtain the number of units used in a given period, e.g. a week, the meter should be read at the beginning and at the end of that period. The first reading is then subtracted from the second reading.

Example: First reading at beginning of week: 1940 units
Second reading at end of week: 2185 units
Units used in the week $= 2185 - 1940 = 245$ units

The rate charged per unit is then employed to obtain the cost of the electricity used. If each unit costs 1 p, then the cost of the 245 units used in the example above would be 245 p or £2·45. Thus the cost of operating a hairdryer, or a group of these appliances, is obtained from the following formula:

$$\text{Cost} = \frac{\text{Total wattage}}{1000} \times \text{hours used} \times \text{cost per unit.}$$

Practical work

1 CAPILLARITY EXPERIMENTS

(*a*) Take a petri dish and almost fill it with water which has been coloured with water-soluble dye. Take six glass capillary tubes with holes of varying size (ignore the thickness of the glass), and stand them upright in the dish in order of increasing diameter of the hole. Once the liquid has stopped rising in all the tubes, measure the height of liquid in each tube in millimetres. Compare the height to which the liquid will rise with the diameter of the hole in the tube.

(*b*) By means of drawing-pins fasten 2 cm wide strips of equal length of a number of different materials to a ruler. Suitable materials would be: cotton sheeting, towelling, muslin, white or clear plastic, paper towel, and file paper. Support the ruler horizontally by means of a stand and clamp over a shallow dish of water coloured with a water-soluble dye. Lower the ruler so that the bottom 1 cm of each material is in the water. Measure the height to which the coloured water has risen up each strip after a suitable time. Use the process of capillarity to explain your results.

2 EVAPORATION EXPERIMENTS

(*a*) *Effect of temperature* on the rate of evaporation. Take 4 small evaporating dishes and, using 10 ml (cm³) measuring cylinders, place 1 ml (cm³) of one of the following liquids in each dish: water, ether, acetone, methylated spirit. Place each evaporating dish on the bench over a named piece of paper to identify each liquid. Time how long it takes for each liquid to evaporate and write down this time on the paper. Using a Celsius thermometer take the laboratory temperature. Repeat the experiment preparing the 4 evaporating dishes as before, but float them on hot water in a large trough or bowl, again noting the time each liquid takes to evaporate. Take the temperature of the hot water just before placing the evaporating dishes into it. You should find that increasing the temperature increases the rate of evaporation of each liquid.

(*b*) *Cooling effect of evaporation.* Take a copper calorimeter and stand it on a few drops of water on the bench. Pour a little ether into the calorimeter and direct the rubber tube from a foot pump across the top. Open the windows so that a through current of air occurs (as ether gives an anaesthetic vapour) then press on the foot pump. The movement of air speeds up the rate of evaporation of the ether. If the calorimeter is touched from time to time it can be felt to be getting colder, and eventually will stick firmly to the bench as the water underneath it freezes. The latent heat required for evaporation has been taken from the air and water surrounding the calorimeter, causing cooling.

3 EXPANSION OF METALS, AND THE THERMOSTAT

(*a*) Using either the bar-and-gauge or the ball-and-ring apparatus, show that before heating the bar fits into the gauge or the ball goes through the ring. After heating the bar or ball strongly they will have expanded so that they no longer fit the gauge or pass through the ring.

(*b*) Take a bimetal strip and hold it firmly in a pair of tongs, or support it on a tripod. Heat it with a bunsen flame and note that it bends. Leave it to cool, when it will straighten again. Which metal has expanded the most? (Most bimetal strips are composed of brass and invar metals.)

(*c*) Look at a demonstration circuit which shows how a thermostat works. The circuit contains a bimetal strip with a 12 volt lamp placed close to it which will give off sufficient heat to cause the strip to bend and break the contact. The circuit is connected to a 12 volt supply of electricity.

4 ELECTRICAL CONDUCTORS AND INSULATORS

Make up a simple circuit consisting of a torch bulb in a holder connected to a 2 volt accumulator by insulated wires, but leaving a gap at one point. Place a number of objects made of different materials one at a time in the gap, so that each one in turn completes the circuit. If the material is a conductor the bulb will light, if it is an insulator the bulb will not light. Check that the parts of the circuit are properly connected before testing the materials by putting the bare ends of the two unconnected wires together at the gap, when the bulb should light. Materials you could test are: metals (silver, gold, brass, copper, magnesium, aluminium), plastic, glass, charcoal, graphite, rubber, chalk, wet earth, paper, porcelain, hair, wood, cotton, silk, wool.

5 ATTACHING A FLEX TO A 13 AMP PLUG

Remove the lid of the plug by undoing the screws on the underside between the pins. Hold the flex over the plug so that it extends 1 cm beyond the earth terminal then mark the outer covering of the flex at a point just inside the flex grip in the plug. Strip off the outer covering of the flex between this mark and the free end of the flex, taking great care not to cut into the coloured insulation round the three wires. Cut off the live (brown) and neutral (blue) wires 1 cm beyond the Live and Neutral terminals to which they will be attached. Remove the top 1 cm of coloured insulation from each of the three wires and twist the bared wires of each conductor to a point (do not allow any strands of wire to stick out). Take out the cartridge fuse to expose the Live terminal. Depending on the type of plug, either wrap the bare ends of each wire round the terminal and screw down, or push the wire through the central hole in the terminal then tighten the screw.

Connect the *green and yellow* wire to the *Earth* terminal
brown wire to the *Live* terminal
blue wire to the *Neutral* terminal.

Make sure that each wire is firmly attached, and try to leave a little slack on the earth wire. Screw down the cord grip to hold the flex firmly, replace the fuse, and then screw on the lid of the plug. (*See Fig.* 5.9)

Multiple choice questions

1 After-shave lotion has a cooling effect on the skin because it
a lubricates *b* stimulates *c* evaporates *d* condenses

2 The colour of the insulation round the live wire in a flex conforming to the international colour code is
a red *b* brown *c* green and yellow *d* blue

3 If a hairdryer is not all-insulated it must be earthed to
a bring the current from the mains
b make it more economical to use
c avoid fitting a fuse in the plug
d prevent an electric shock

4 Copper wires are used in the flex of a hairdryer because copper
a is a low resistance conductor
b gets hot as the electricity passes
c is a good insulator
d does not provide free electrons

5 The heat which is absorbed or given out when a substance changes its state is known as
a transfer heat *b* steam heat *c* latent heat
d dry heat

6 A bimetal strip is part of the structure of a
a thermostat *b* fan *c* square-pin plug
d heating element

7 The switch and fuse in an electric circuit are placed in the
a neutral conductor *b* earth wire *c* live conductor
d thermostat

8 The rate of production of heat by an electric current passing through a hairdryer heating element is measured in units called
a volts *b* watts *c* amps *d* ohms

9 A high resistance wire used in an electric heating element is made of
a nickel and chromium *b* steel and nickel
c tin and lead *d* copper, tin, and lead

10 One unit of electricity would be used by an appliance operating for 1·33 hours provided its wattage was
a 150 *b* 250 *c* 400 *d* 750

6 Dressing Out

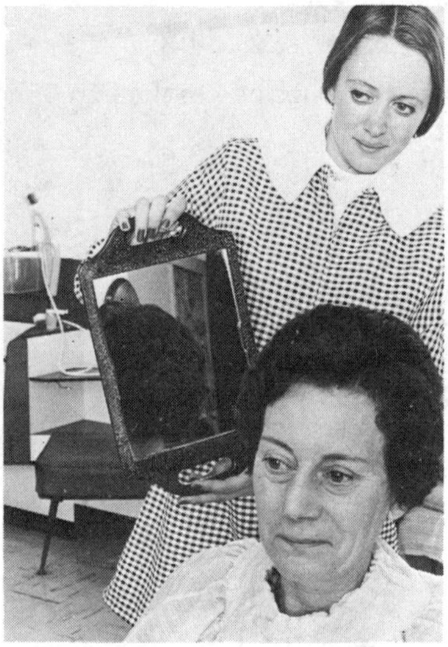

After the hair has been completely dried and the rollers removed, the first stage in dressing out the hair is to brush it through. When brushing or combing hair a certain amount of frictional or static electricity is formed.

Frictional or static electricity

When two good *insulators* are rubbed together they are found to develop opposite electrical charges because electrons are transfered from the surface atoms of one insulator to those of the other. The surface losing electrons then becomes *positively* charged, while that gaining electrons becomes *negatively* charged. These are *frictional* or *static* electric charges. If an *ebonite* rod is rubbed with a piece of *fur*, electrons are transferred from the fur to the rod which becomes negatively charged, leaving the fur positively charged. A *plastic* or *vulcanite* (hard rubber) comb, or a brush with *polythene* bristles will similarly gain a negative charge when drawn through human *hair*, which becomes positively charged. The frictional charges are only produced on good insulators, since with a *conductor* any electric charge would immediately be carried away to *earth*. *Hygroscopic* substances which are insulators, e.g. hair, will absorb water vapour from the air thus becoming better conductors, and losing any frictional charge to earth through the body. However, when hair is very *dry* on emerging from the hairdryer, an appreciable amount of frictional electricity will develop on brushing or combing it. Plastic and vulcanite, which are insulators and have water-repellent properties, hold a frictional electric charge for a considerable time. The opposite charges on the hair and brush (or comb) will cause them to be attracted towards one another. After brushing (or combing) hair vigorously the hairs will rise towards the brush (or comb) if it is held above the scalp.

In all atoms there are equal numbers of positive and negative electric charges, so that each atom is *electrically neutral*. This is true for both insulators and conductors. If a comb with a negative frictional charge is brought close to a conductor, the positive and negative electric charges in the conductor *separate*. The positive charges are attracted to the surface facing the comb, while the negative charges are lost to earth. This leaves the conductor with an *induced positive* charge. This can be shown by using small specks of tissue paper, which are conductors since they are slightly moist, and are in contact with the earth through the bench. The negative charge on the comb and the positive induced charges on the conducting specks of paper cause a force of attraction sufficient to make the paper stick to the comb. *Dust* particles become positively charged in a similar way, and are attracted to the negatively charged comb.

6.1 The effect of frictional electricity

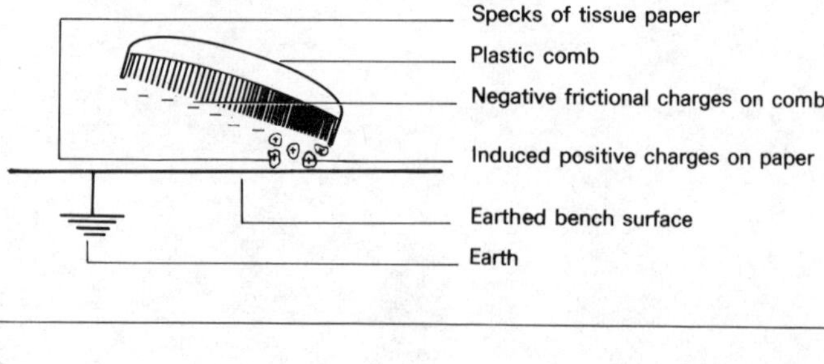

Hair is less likely to develop frictional electricity when dressing out if a 2% *cetrimide* solution is used as the final rinse before setting. Where the amount of frictional electricity makes hair difficult to dress out, *hair lacquer* can be sprayed onto the hair to counteract this effect. *Backcombing* and *backbrushing* which lift up the cuticle layers so that the surface of the hair is roughened, also help to keep the hair in place. Excessive backcombing or backbrushing however, have been found to damage hair.

Hair lacquers

These preparations, which are sprayed on to the hair after dressing out, are quick-drying because they contain a *volatile* solvent. As the solvent evaporates the *film-former* which was dissolved in it is left as a plastic coating round the hair.

6.2 Lacquer coating round hair

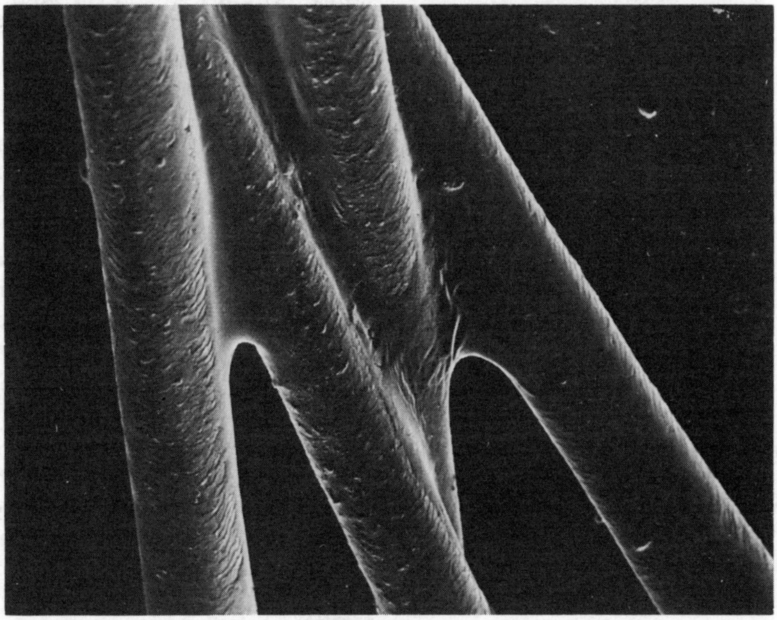

This coating stiffens the hair so that it remains in position, gives gloss as it reflects light, and waterproofs hair so that its hygroscopic property is reduced. The hair does not then absorb atmospheric moisture and lose its set. The plastic coating must be flexible to avoid an artificial appearance, and should not flake off on combing. The film-former should not be hygroscopic or the film will become sticky in a humid atmosphere (see Chapter 14).

The *solvents* used in hair lacquers are ethanol, industrial methylated spirit, or isopropanol. All these liquids dissolve the resins used as film-formers.

Ethanol is a thin colourless liquid with a slight smell, boiling at 78°C. It is soluble in water, so water/alcohol mixtures can be made. It is inflammable, and poisonous if drunk at concentrations exceeding 40%, so its production and sale are closely controlled by Law. It is heavily taxed which makes it expensive.

Industrial Methylated Spirit (I.M.S.) consists of 95% ethanol and 5% methanol. The methanol makes the liquid highly poisonous and so unfit to drink. It is a colourless liquid with the same properties as ethanol.

Isopropanol is a colourless liquid with a rather unpleasant smell which is difficult to mask. It has a boiling point of 82°C, and is soluble in water. It is not subject to the same legal controls as ethanol, and is a good cheap solvent for resins.

The *film-formers* are either natural or synthetic *resins*. Resins are plastic solids and are *organic* compounds. *Natural* resins contain essential oils which give them their characteristic smells. *Shellac* is a natural resin prepared from a secretion of an insect found in India called *Laccifer lacca*. Shellac produces a clear strong film, but it is slightly yellow and rather brittle. As it is not soluble in water it is difficult to wash out of the hair. It absorbs atmospheric moisture becoming sticky. *Polyvinyl pyrrolidone* (P.V.P. resin) is a synthetic resin soluble in ethanol containing a little water, and readily washes out of the hair. It is hygroscopic, becoming sticky in a humid atmosphere. This resin is also used in plastic setting lotions. *Polyvinyl acetate* (Gelva resin) is a synthetic resin which is combined with P.V.P. resin to form the *co-polymer* P.V.P./V.A., which is less hygroscopic than P.V.P. alone. *Isopropyl myristate* is usually added to the co-polymer as a *plasticizer* to modify the hardness of the film making it less brittle. Polyvinyl acetate is also used in plastic setting lotions. *Formaldehyde resin* is a good cheap film-former, soluble in both alcohol and water. The film is rather brittle so a plasticizer should be included in the lacquer, usually a *phthalate* or *lanolin*.

USING HAIR LACQUER

Hair lacquer should be sprayed directly onto the hair, care being taken to avoid spraying it on to the skin of the client's ears, neck, or eyelids, where it can cause *dermatitis*. Droplets of lacquer which remain suspended in the air because they have not reached the hair may be breathed in by the hairdresser and *damage* the lining of the *lungs*.

Light

Light is required for dressing out as the final effect is all-important for the confidence of the customer and whether or not they will come again. Light is a form of *energy*, which is absorbed by the *eyes* to allow *vision*. Clear vision depends on sufficient *light intensity*. In dim light very little detail is visible. Light travels in straight lines with the fastest known *speed* of 300,000,000 metres/second. A client's head, like other objects, is visible to the eye because light rays are *reflected* from it. When all the light rays falling on an object are either reflected or absorbed it is said to be *opaque*. Hair, metals, and black paper are opaque substances. If light passes through a substance it is *transparent*. Air, glass, clear plastic, and clean water are transparent substances. When light passes from one transparent substance into another, the light rays are bent or *refracted*. Different substances bend the light by different amounts. Light passing from a less dense substance or medium like air into a denser medium like glass is refracted towards the *normal*, which is a line at right-angles to the surface of the glass where the light ray hits it. The angle between the light ray and the normal in air (angle of *incidence*) is larger than the angle between the light ray and the normal in glass (angle of *refraction*).

In *translucent* substances such as frosted glass, non-clear plastic, and greaseproof paper some of the light passes through the substance the rest being reflected.

6.3 Refraction of light

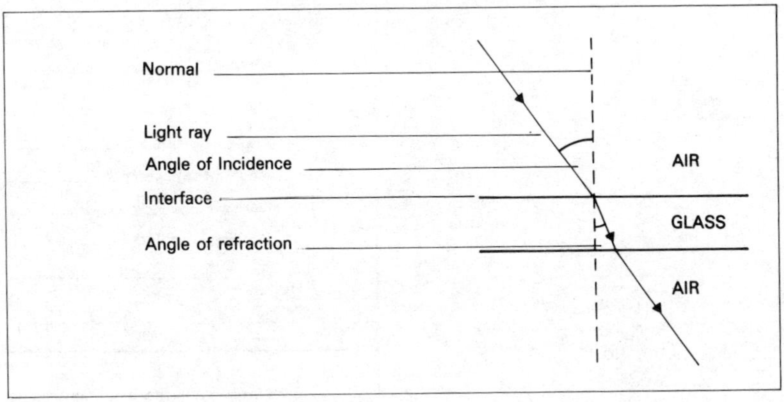

Reflection of light

Rays of light coming from an object will bounce back from a polished shiny surface making an *image* of the reflected rays in the observer's eyes. The shiny reflecting surface is a *mirror*. The image of the object appears to be as far behind the mirror as the object is in front of it. If a line is drawn at right-angles to the mirror the line is a *normal*. An incident ray hitting a mirror at the origin of the normal will bounce off at the same angle to the normal as the incident ray. These two angles are called the angle of *incidence* and the angle of *reflection*, and they are *equal* in size.

If you are brushing your client's hair in front of a mirror, holding the brush in your right hand, you see an *image* of yourself in the mirror where the image appears to be holding the brush in the left hand. This effect is known as *lateral inversion*.

Mirrors

The usual type of mirror used in the salon for dressing out is a *plane* mirror, which has a flat surface. It is made from a polished sheet of glass coated on the back with a layer of *silver* (expensive) or tin and mercury *amalgam* (cheaper), which reflects the light. If the back of the client's head is to be made visible to her, then two plane mirrors must be used. One mirror, which is *fixed*, is that in the dressing out table; the second one is a hand mirror held so that it is *inclined* (i.e. at an angle) to the fixed mirror. The hand mirror must be carefully placed, as the angles of incidence and reflection must be equal at both mirrors.

A larger than life-sized image for seeing detail is obtained by using a *concave* or inwardly curved mirror. This type of mirror is used when shaving or applying make-up, and it is necessary to be close to the mirror to obtain the *magnified* image. A *convex*, or outwardly curved, mirror will give a much *smaller* image over a wider area, and so is used for example as the driving mirror in a car.

6.4 Reflection in a mirror

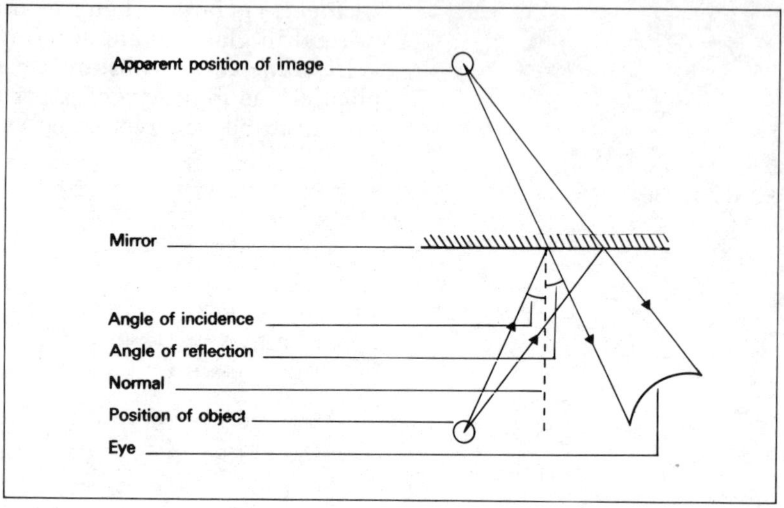

6.5 Using inclined mirrors

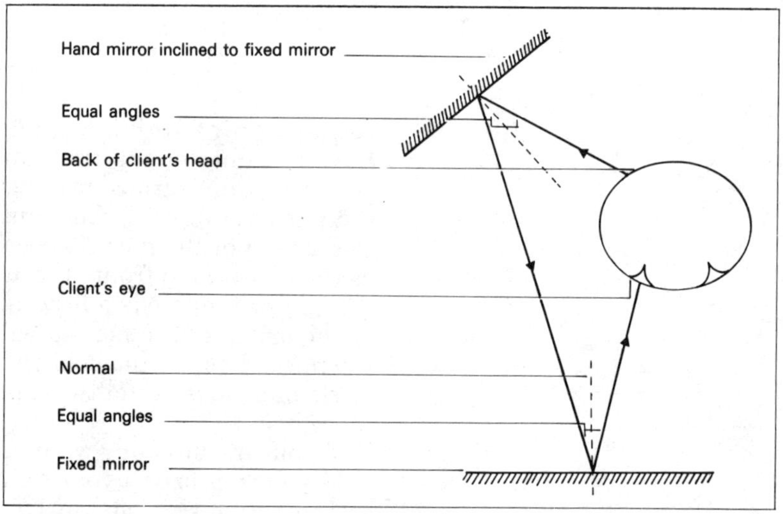

Diffusion of Light

Where the surface reflecting light is *rough* instead of smooth, light rays are scattered as they bounce off. This *scattering* of reflected rays produces *diffusion*. The light is evenly distributed, producing the softer effect of diffused light. The slightly roughened surface of a hair produced by the bands of cuticle will cause some diffusion of light, giving a soft shine to the hair. The *rougher* the hair surface the greater the proportion of light which is diffused, and the smaller the proportion which is reflected, so the *duller* its appearance.

Lighting in the salon

In many salons daylight does not provide enough illumination for seeing the client's hair clearly and comfortably. Light of low intensity causes *eye-strain* and unsatisfactory work. Plenty of light without *glare* or *deep shadows* is needed. Bright sunlight out of doors has an intensity fifty times as great as the light intensity inside the salon by a sunny window. The amount of light in the salon is affected by the *colour* of the walls and ceiling,

6.6 Diffusion of light from a rough surface

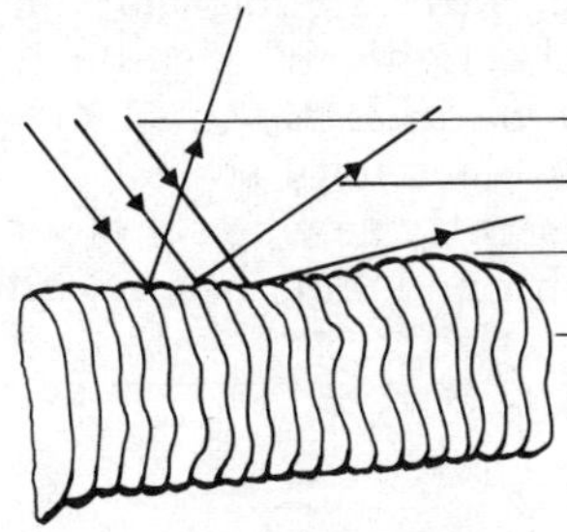

by the amount of *reflecting surface* (mirrors and shiny walls), and by the *shadows* produced by walls, doors, and equipment. Pale colours on walls and ceilings, large reflecting surfaces, and the absence of shadows, make the salon appear lighter. Dark colours, dull surfaces, and deep shadows have the opposite effect.

Some form of *artificial lighting* to increase the intensity of illumination is almost always required in the salon, even during daylight hours. A bright light source close to your line of sight either from a lamp, or reflected from a shiny surface, makes vision more difficult because it causes *glare*. It is also tiring for the eyes to look from a brightly lit object into deep shadow and back again, as the eye may take some little time to adapt to changes in light intensity. In dim light the *pupil* enlarges to let the maximum amount of light into the eye. Sudden bright light entering the eye through an enlarged pupil is damaging. It takes a few seconds for the pupil to contract and reduce the amount of light entering the eye. Contrasts between brightly lit, and shadowed, areas in the salon are to be avoided.

ARTIFICIAL LIGHTING

Artificial lighting is carried out by using *electrical energy* in appliances which convert it into *light* energy, plus a small amount of *heat*. These appliances are connected into a *lighting circuit*.

THE LIGHTING CIRCUIT

There is a separate lighting circuit from the mains supply, not connected to the power circuit of the salon. This lighting circuit is protected by a 5 *amp fuse* or *circuit-breaker* and so is unsuitable for power appliances. There are two ways in which a number of light fittings can be connected into a circuit. When for example light bulbs are connected *in series*, the electric current passing through the circuit goes through each bulb in turn. Any break in the circuit such as a faulty bulb or a bulb which is not making contact with the bulb holder, will stop the flow of current so that all the lights will go out, and there will be no indication where the fault lies. Each bulb glows less brightly than it would if only a single bulb was present in the circuit, since adding another bulb in series increases the resistance. If salon lights were wired in series each time a bulb burnt out all the salon lights would go out. Every time an additional light was switched on the bulbs already alight would dim. Obviously this method of wiring is unsuitable for salon lighting, although it is used for the strings of '*fairy lights*' that may be used decoratively at Christmas. The lights in a salon lighting circuit are therefore connected *in parallel*. By this method each lamp is connected to the source of electricity so that it forms a complete circuit, and glows as brightly as when it alone is switched on. Removing or switching off one lamp does not affect the others.

6.7a Bulbs connected in series

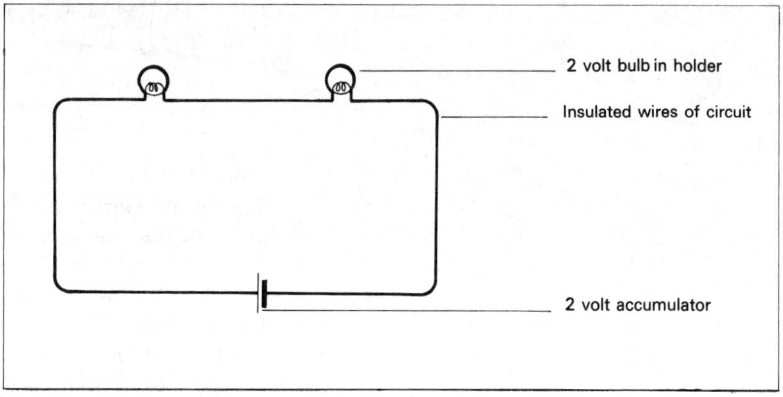

6.7b Bulbs connected in parallel

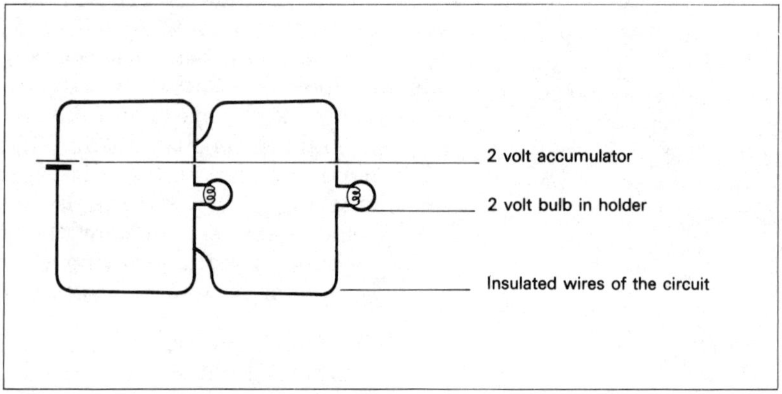

There are two types of light-producing appliances that may be used in the salon lighting circuit. These are the *tungsten filament lamp* and the *fluorescent tube*.

Tungsten filament lamps

The lamp consists of a glass *bulb* fitted with a brass cap bearing *contacts* for connecting it into the lighting circuit. The *filament wire* is supported in the centre of the bulb, and is made of *tungsten* because this metal has a high electrical resistance and a high melting point. The bulb is filled with an *inert gas* (argon or nitrogen) to prevent the tungsten wire burning away when it becomes white hot. The filament may be coiled once (*single coil*), or the already coiled filament may be coiled again (*coiled coil*). The coiled coil bulb gives 20% more light for a given wattage. Tungsten filament lamps should be of the same voltage as the salon supply, as they will then have an average life of 1000 hours. *Double-life* lamps with an average life of 2000 hours are available but produce less light for a given wattage. The life of a lamp is longer if it hangs *downwards*. Frequent switching on and off

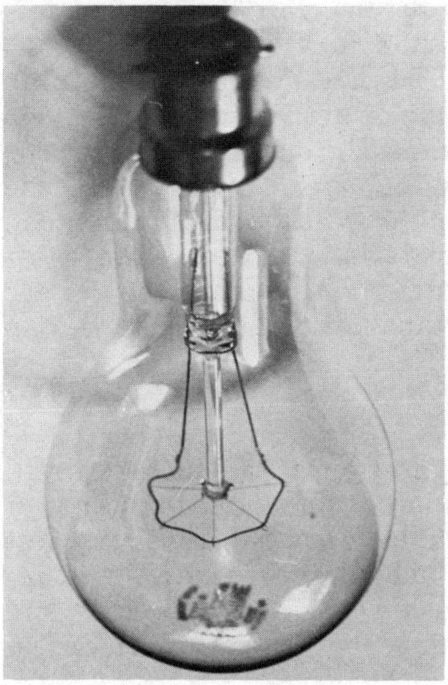

6.8 Clear bulb (coiled coil type)

shortens the life of a lamp. The light output of a lamp decreases as it gets older because the inside of the bulb *blackens* due to deposits from the glowing filament. *Dirt* on the outside of a bulb also decreases its light output. The glass bulb may be *clear*, giving a bright light which causes glare and sharp shadows. *Pearl* bulbs are translucent and so no clear image of the filament is visible. Glare is reduced as it produces *diffused* lighting. A salon floor area of 9 square metres requires a total wattage of 500 from tungsten filament lamps to give a really adequate light intensity. Lamps are available in a number of different sizes, 40, 60, 100, and 150 being the wattages normally used.

Fluorescent tubes

The fluorescent tube is filled with low pressure *mercury vapour*, and the electrical discharge which occurs through this vapour when the current is switched on produces *ultra-violet* radiation. The inside of the tube is coated with *phosphors* which *fluoresce* giving off visible *light* when the invisible ultra-violet radiation hits them. In the fitting, the tube has a *starting device*, and *control gear* to limit the flow of current after the tube is switched on, and then to keep it steady. Fluorescent tubes give three times as much light for the same amount of electric current used as do filament lamps. A 40 watt tube is equivalent to a 150 watt bulb in light output. Fluorescent tubes of different wattages are available; the longer the tube the higher the wattage. A fluorescent tube costs about five times as much as a filament lamp, but lasts about six times as long. The cheaper running costs (because of the lower wattage), and the longer life of a fluorescent tube make up for the fact that it is more expensive to buy and install. Switching on and off frequently will shorten the life of a fluorescent tube. A faulty tube should not be left switched on, as the insulation on the control gear may be damaged and a fire occur. Fluorescent tubes do not cause glare, and throw less shadow than filament lamps. Thus a salon with fluorescent tubes will be more evenly and more economically lit.

LAMPSHADES

Lampshades are usually used with tungsten filament lamps. An *opaque* lampshade will direct all the light downwards, strongly lighting a limited area, with shadows outside it. This type of shade is used with *spot-lights* to highlight any decorative features,

6.9 Opaque and translucent lampshades

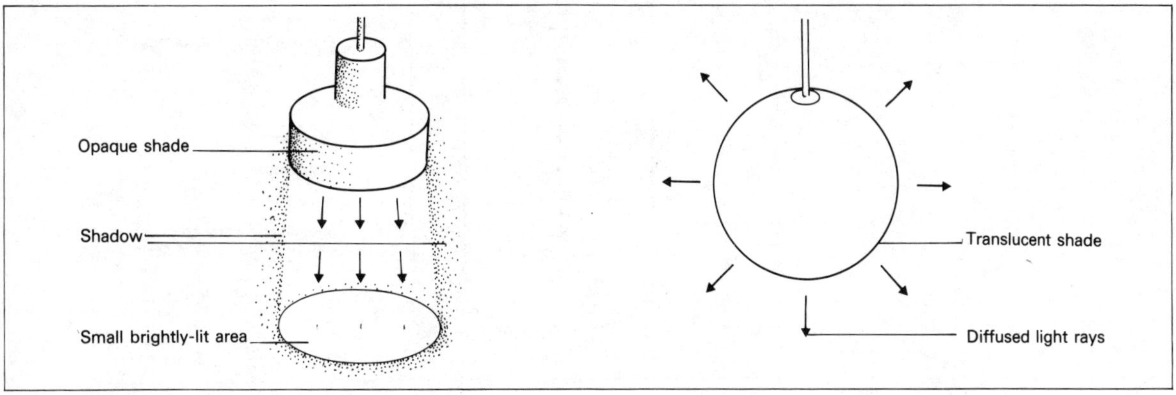

but is unsuitable for working under. A *translucent* lampshade will produce *diffused* lighting, reducing glare and giving less shadow, and is therefore more suitable for the salon.

Translucent lampshades should be *pale* in colour. Pale pink shades will give a *warmer* light; blue or green shades will give a *cold* hard light less suitable in a salon. The material of which the shade is composed should be easy to keep clean. A *dirty* shade reduces the amount of light getting through. Filament lamps can produce enough heat to ignite material which is close to or touching them. The higher the wattage of the lamp, the greater the heat produced, so it is important not to *exceed* the recommended wattage for any shade.

Emergency lighting

There should be a source of light in the salon which can still be used if the *mains* electricity supply is *interrupted* by a power cut or fault. A large *torch* powered by a dry battery is the best means of providing lighting in such an emergency. In a dry battery electricity is obtained directly from the chemicals contained in it, chemical energy being converted into electrical energy.

DRY BATTERY (DRY CELL)

A dry battery is one type of *primary cell*, making electricity by chemical processes during which there is an internal transference of electrons from one of its *terminals* to the other. One terminal has a surplus of electrons giving it a *negative* charge. At the other terminal there is a deficit of electrons, which leaves it with a *positive* charge. When the two terminals of the dry cell are connected by wires linking them to the light bulb, electrons flow through the wires (circuit) to even out their distribution. The flow of electrons through the high resistance wire in the bulb produces *light*. As electrons continue to be transferred inside the cell, the flow of current is maintained until the chemicals are used up. The electrons always flow in the same direction, so producing a *direct current*.

6.10 Flow of electrons in a torch circuit

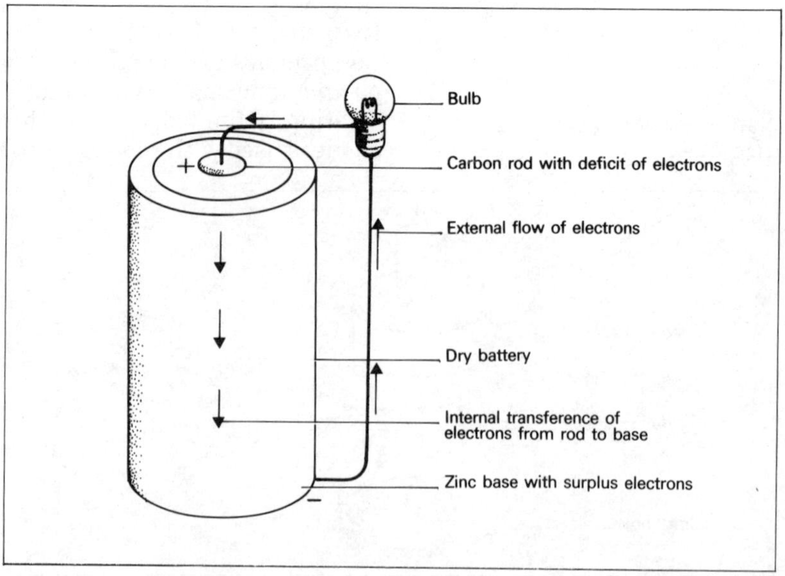

The *terminals* are provided by a *brass screw* in the central *carbon rod* which is *positive*, and the *base* of the *zinc casing* to the dry cell which is *negative*. The electrons travel from the positive to the negative terminals through the *electrolyte* (see Chapter 10), which is a paste of *ammonium chloride*. Surrounding the carbon rod is a black *depolarizing* material which prevents the collection of hydrogen bubbles round the rod. Gas bubbles round the carbon electrode would stop the flow of current. The ammonium chloride paste is sealed into the zinc case by layers of sawdust, sand, and pitch, which prevent leakage from the cell and support the carbon rod. A *tar paper washer* separates the carbon rod and the zinc case at the base of the cell to prevent the two electrodes from touching.

6.11 Vertical section through a dry cell

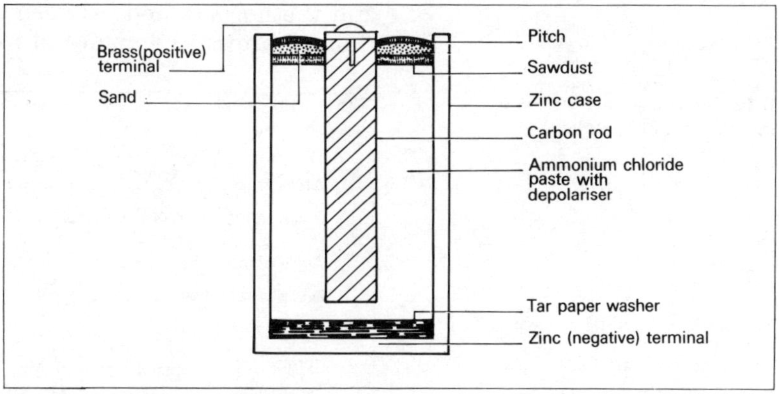

Practical work

1 FRICTIONAL (STATIC) ELECTRICITY

(*a*) Brush or comb the hair vigorously, then hold the brush or comb above the scalp. The hairs will be attracted upwards by the production of opposite charges on the brush or comb and the hair.

(*b*) Tear up a piece of tissue paper into the smallest possible pieces. Comb the hair vigorously then hold the comb just above the pile of tissue paper pieces. The frictional electricity produces a negative charge on the comb which induces a positive charge on the paper pieces, so that they are attracted to the comb.

2 HAIR LACQUER SOLVENTS

Take two test-tubes one containing a flake of shellac, and the other a very small amount of P.V.P. resin. Add 5 cm of water to each test-tube, shake well, and observe carefully whether either type of resin dissolves in the water. Repeat the experiment, adding a different liquid to each of the two resins. Each time two clean dry test-tubes must be used for testing the solubility of the resins. Liquids which may be tested are: ethanol, industrial methylated spirit, isopropanol, carbon tetrachloride, and a 50/50 mixture of water and ethanol. Notice the smell of each liquid you test, and note if you recognize it as being present in any particular hair lacquer you use in the salon. Which of these liquids are likely to be used as solvents for hair lacquer?

3 TO MEASURE THE ANGLES OF INCIDENCE AND REFLECTION

Place a large sheet of plain white paper on the bench. Support a plane mirror vertically towards the back of the paper. Draw a line in front of the mirror to mark its position. Place two large pins a few cm apart in a line which when extended would meet the mirror at an angle. The pins must be vertical, so stick them firmly into the bench through the white paper. Look into the mirror and move your head until the images of the two pins are in line. Then place a pin in front of the mirror so that the two images are covered by this pin. Keeping your head in the same position place another pin so that it covers the pin previously placed and the two images. Remove the four pins and use a ruler to join up the pin holes to produce an incident ray and a reflected ray. The two lines should meet at a point on the line drawn in front of the mirror. From this point, using a protractor to measure a right-angle, draw in the normal between the incident and reflected rays. Measure the angles between the incident ray and the normal, and between the reflected ray and the normal, thus obtaining the angles of incidence and reflection.

6.12 Measuring the angles of incidence and reflection

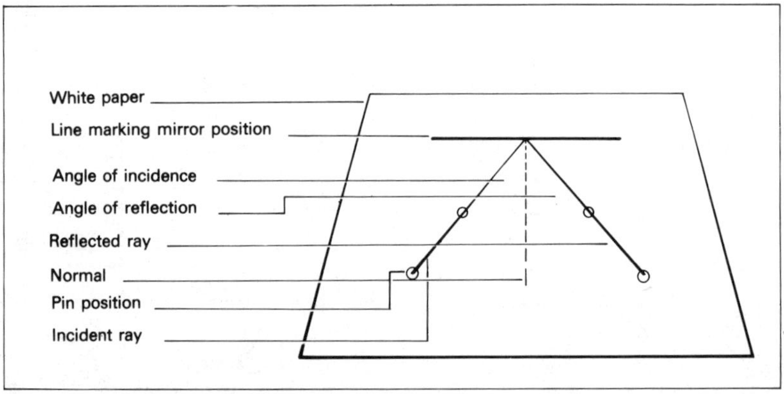

4 TO SHOW REFRACTION OF LIGHT

Place a sheet of plain white paper on the bench and put a glass block in the centre. Draw round the glass block to mark its position on the paper. Behind the block place two pins vertically, so that a line joining them and continued to the block would meet it at an angle which is not a right-angle. From the front look at the pins through the block, and place a pin in front of the block so that it covers the two pins as you see them through the glass. Keeping your head in the same position place another pin so that it hides the other three pins. Join the pin holes on each side of the block and extend each line until it reaches a line marking the position of the block. Remove the block and join the lines across the oblong marked on the paper. Note the change in direction of the line as it enters and leaves the glass block.

5 CONNECTING LIGHT BULBS IN SERIES AND IN PARALLEL

(*a*) *In series* Take two bulb holders containing torch bulbs and join them together by means of insulated wires so that they form a line. Connect each end of the line with one of the terminals of a 2 volt accumulator. Both bulbs should light, glowing faintly. Failure of the bulbs to light indicates a faulty connection somewhere in the circuit. Unscrew either of the glowing bulbs, and note that both bulbs go out. Remove one bulb in its holder from the circuit, and connect the remaining one to the free terminal of the accumulator to complete the circuit. Note that this single bulb now glows more brightly than before.

(*b*) *In parallel* Starting from the circuit with a single light bulb connected as in (*a*), connect a second bulb between the two terminals of the bulb holder already in the circuit. Note that this second bulb glows as brightly as the first bulb. Unscrew either of the two bulbs and note that the other bulb remains alight.

6 PREPARATION OF HAIR LACQUER

P.V.P./V.A. 60/40 (resin)	4 g
Isopropyl myristate (plasticizer)	1 g
Ethanol (solvent)	80 g
Perfume	0·5 ml (cm^3)

Weigh a small beaker on a rough balance, add a further 80 g to the weights, and pour the ethanol into the beaker until a balance is obtained. Add a further 1 g weight and pour in the isopropyl myristate until it again balances. Weigh out the resin separately then dissolve it in the liquids in the beaker. Finally stir in the perfume. Pour the lacquer into a screw-top bottle, so that it is stored in an air-tight container. It can be transferred to a spraying bottle immediately before use.

Multiple choice questions

1 As a ray of light hits the surface of a glass block and enters into the denser medium it is
a refracted *b* reflected *c* inverted *d* diffracted

2 Hair will stick to a plastic comb which is being vigorously drawn through the hair due to its
a high frequency *b* electric current
c frictional electricity *d* high conductivity

3 Excessive backcombing of hair leads to a roughening of its surface which causes light rays hitting it to be
a radiated *b* diffused *c* diluted *d* diffracted

4 The hand mirror surface used in the salon to allow a client to view the back of her head is
a convex *b* polaroid *c* concave *d* plane

5 The inclusion of a plasticizer in an aerosol hair lacquer is designed to
a improve the solubility of the resin
b vaporise the liquid *c* make the film more flexible
d dilute the solvent

6 When looking into a concave mirror held close to your face your image will be
a exactly life-size *b* a little less than life-size
c considerably magnified *d* greatly reduced in size

7 The solvent commonly used in hair lacquer because it is cheap and effective is
a isopropanol *b* polyvinyl pyrrolidone
c carbon tetrachloride *d* amyl acetate

8 Hair lacquer should be used sparingly and sprayed directly onto the hair because it could damage the
a cuticle of the hair *b* lining of the lungs
c elasticity of the skin *d* cortex of the hair

9 A salon lighting system should produce illumination which is free from glare and shadows as economically as possible. The best type of appliance for this purpose is a
a clear filament lamp *b* pearl filament lamp
c fluorescent tube *d* spot light

10 The ceiling lamps forming part of a salon lighting circuit are
a in series *b* incident *c* inclined *d* in parallel

7 Bleaching Hair

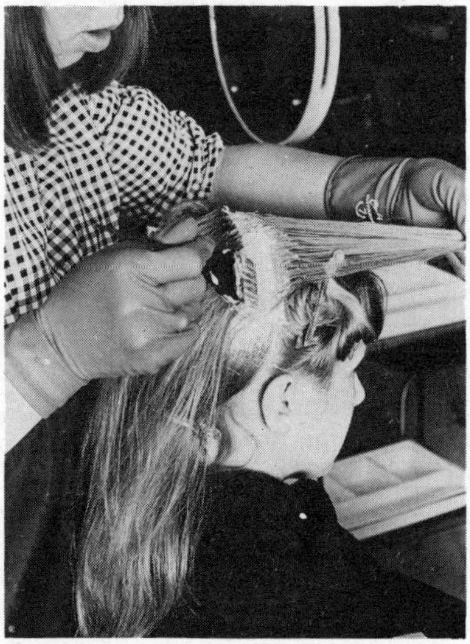

When hair is bleached, a chemical change occurs in the pigment present in the cortex of the hair. This chemical change is brought about by the action of oxygen gas which is supplied by the bleach.

Oxygen is a colourless gas without taste or smell, which forms 21% of the air. It is needed by plants and animals for the process of *respiration*, and if it is absent, death occurs. As oxygen dissolves slightly in water, soluble oxygen is available for the respiration of water plants and animals.

As well as the uncombined oxygen molecules in the air, the earth's surface contains oxygen combined with other elements, in compounds. *Compounds* consisting of any single element joined with oxygen by a chemical change are called *oxides*. Hydrogen combined with oxygen forms hydrogen oxide, which is *water*. The chemical change in which substances combine with oxygen is *oxidation*. Oxidation may take a number of forms.

Burning (or *combustion*) is one type of oxidation where the chemical change usually occurs very rapidly, producing both light and heat as a *flame*. When an element burns there is a *weight increase*, as it has joined with oxygen to form an oxide: e.g. Magnesium + oxygen = magnesium oxide (ash).
Burning *magnesium* produces the bright white flame needed in taking a flash photograph.

Substances will burn very much more fiercely in oxygen than in air, only one-fifth of which is oxygen. The browning of old newspapers is also burning, but occurs very slowly over many years. Eventually the paper becomes black (scorched) and falls to pieces (ash). Other forms of oxidation which also occur fairly slowly are *rusting* and *bleaching*. During rusting, iron combines with oxygen in the air, the rust produced being *iron oxide*. The presence of *water* is needed for this chemical change to occur.

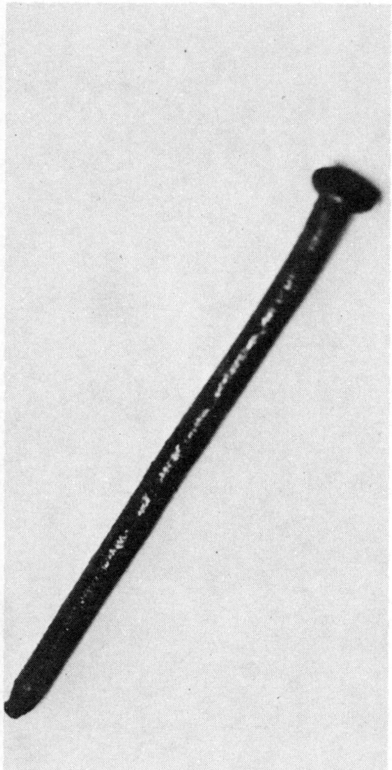

7.1 Burning (left)

7.2 Rusting (right)

Bleaching is the oxidation of coloured substances, to give new *colourless* substances.

Oxygen can be obtained from the air, as it is possible to separate it from the gaseous mixture. The air is first liquified by compressing it and cooling it in a special type of refrigerator. This causes the gases to change their state, becoming liquids. If the liquid air is then warmed up, the liquid nitrogen evaporates first as it has a lower boiling point than liquid oxygen. Oxygen will evaporate as the temperature is raised to its boiling point. Oxygen gas is forced under pressure into steel cylinders, and sold for commercial use as a *breathing aid*, and to produce the very hot *oxyacetylene flame* used for welding steel.

Oxygen can also be obtained from *water*, which splits up into hydrogen and oxygen when an electric current passes through it (see Chapter 3).

Neither of these two methods are suitable for obtaining a supply of oxygen for *salon* use. In the salon, oxygen is obtained from an inorganic compound called *hydrogen peroxide*. Peroxides are oxides which have more than the usual amount of oxygen combined with the other element. They readily *break down* to release this additional oxygen, leaving behind the *lower* oxide.

Hydrogen peroxide will break down slowly to produce *atoms of oxygen* and *water*, which is the lower oxide of hydrogen. This chemical *decomposition* is very slow, particularly at low temperatures. It can be speeded up by heating, or by adding a *catalyst*, which is a substance required only in very small amounts and which remains unaltered at the end of the chemical change. A black powder called *manganese dioxide* is a very effective catalyst, and so are most *alkalis*. The catalyst normally used with hydrogen peroxide solutions in the salon, is the alkali *ammonium hydroxide*, or the salt *ammonium carbonate*. Hydrogen peroxide, because it supplies oxygen, is an oxidizing agent.

Hydrogen peroxide, as a pure substance, is a colourless syrupy liquid. Weak solutions of it can be prepared by the action of acids on other peroxides, e.g. *phosphoric acid* on *barium peroxide*. The hydrogen from the acid combines with the oxygen from the peroxide, while the barium combines with the rest of the acid molecule (acid radicle) to form an insoluble salt *barium phosphate*, which can be removed by filtering.

$$\text{Phosphoric acid} + \text{barium peroxide} \rightarrow \text{hydrogen peroxide} + \downarrow \text{barium phosphate.}$$

The solutions must be kept cold, or the newly formed hydrogen peroxide breaks down immediately into water and oxygen gas.

Hydrogen peroxide is an acidic substance. It would damage hair and skin if applied in its pure state. In hairdressing it must be used in *dilute solution*, dissolved in distilled water.

Because hydrogen peroxide slowly decomposes at normal temperatures, solutions should be *stored* away from heat and light in a cool dark place, using dark glass or opaque plastic bottles as containers. The stopper should be replaced in the bottle as quickly as possible after using the solution, as dust getting into the bottle will speed up decomposition of the hydrogen peroxide. Because hydrogen peroxide solutions for salon use are difficult to store for long periods without deterioration, manufacturers add *stabilizers* to them. These are chemicals which have the opposite effect to a catalyst, and so slow down decomposition. Very small amounts of *acid* (phosphoric or salicylic) are added as stabilizers.

Strengths of solutions

The hydrogen peroxide solutions used are available in a number of strengths. The strength of these solutions may be measured in two ways: percentage strength and volume strength. *Percentage* strength is the *weight* in grammes of pure *hydrogen peroxide* present in 100 g of the solution, e.g. a 3% solution contains 3 g of hydrogen peroxide and 97 g of water in 100 g of the solution. *Volume* strength is determined by the *volume* of *oxygen* gas produced when the hydrogen peroxide present in the solution decomposes. It is the volume of oxygen gas in ml (cm^3) given off on heating 1 ml (cm^3) of the solution, e.g. 10 volume strength means that 10 ml (cm^3) of oxygen gas will be liberated on heating 1 ml (cm^3) of the solution. As 1 ml (cm^3) of a 3% solution of hydrogen peroxide will liberate 10 ml (cm^3) of oxygen gas, this 3% solution is also of 10 volume strength. For the relation between percentage strength and volume strength see Table 1.

Table 1. Comparing Volume strength and % strength of hydrogen peroxide solutions

Volume strength		% strength
10 volume strength	≡	3% strength
20 volume strength	≡	6% strength
30 volume strength	≡	9% strength
40 volume strength	≡	12% strength
100 volume strength	≡	30% strength

40 *volume* strength is the *maximum* strength of any hydrogen peroxide solution that can be used on the hair without causing

7.3 Peroxometer

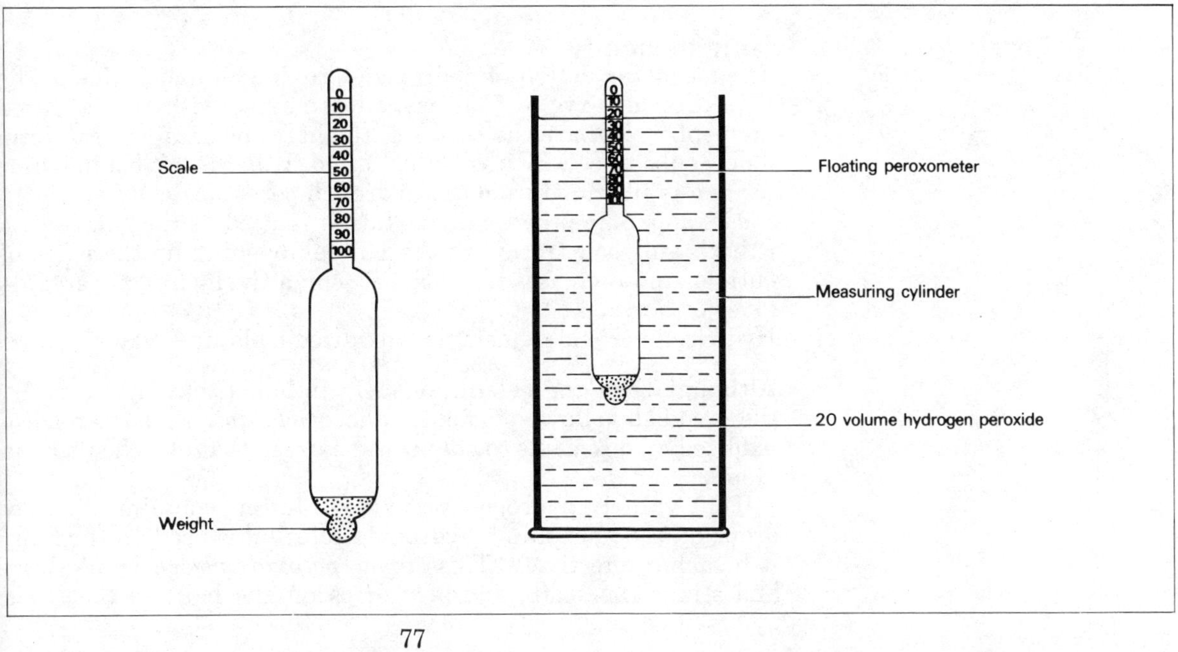

damage. 100 *volume* solutions must *never* be used on the hair. The volume strength of any hydrogen peroxide solution can be measured by using a *peroxometer*. This is a special type of *hydrometer* having a scale which is marked out in volume strength instead of relative density. The density of hydrogen peroxide solutions of different strengths is not the same, so the peroxometer will float at different depths in the various solutions.

Diluting solutions. If a hydrogen peroxide solution of a required strength is not available it can be made from a stronger solution by *dilution*, which involves adding the correct volume of *distilled water*, by using the following formula:
Actual volume strength—Required volume strength = Parts of water to be added.
See Table 2 for examples using this formula.

Table 2. Dilution of hydrogen peroxide solutions

Volume strength of stock solution	–	Required volume strength	=	Parts of water needed for dilution	Parts of hydrogen peroxide solution	Parts of distilled water	Ratio of parts of hydrogen peroxide solution to parts of water
100	–	60	=	40	60	40	60 : 40 = 3 : 2
100	–	20	=	80	20	80	20 : 80 = 1 : 4
40	–	30	=	10	30	10	30 : 10 = 3 : 1
40	–	20	=	20	20	20	20 : 20 = 1 : 1
40	–	10	=	30	10	30	10 : 30 = 1 : 3
30	–	20	=	10	20	10	20 : 10 = 2 : 1

Hair bleaches

The *bleaching* action of hydrogen peroxide on hair is due to the liberation of *oxygen*. The oxygen combines with the coloured pigment *melanin* in the cortex of the hair and *oxidizes* it to form a new substance which is not coloured. *Water* is left behind after oxygen is liberated from the hydrogen peroxide.

0·88 ammonium hydroxide solution is used as the *catalyst*, as it both aids penetration of the hair by opening up the rings of cuticle, and increases the speed at which the hydrogen peroxide gives off oxygen.

Hydrogen peroxide + melanin → oxidized melanin + water
(melanin: coloured; oxidized melanin: colourless)

Although the *dark* melanin pigment in hair is bleached rapidly, the reddish-yellow pigment, *phaeomelanin*, is less readily oxidized, and remains to colour the hair, so that bleached hair is blonde.

If 40 volume hydrogen peroxide solution containing a few drops of 0·88 ammonium hydroxide solution is used on the hair, it bleaches effectively. This *simple peroxide bleach* is alkaline, and stings the scalp, and also drips off the hair, so that it is uncomfortable and inconvenient to apply. The drip can be prevented by mixing the two substances with the salt *magnesium carbonate*, which is a white powder. This mixture forms a *bleaching paste* (white henna). This type of paste may still be sufficiently alkaline to cause the scalp to sting, so to reduce the pH to below 9·5, *ammonium carbonate* or sodium acetate can be used instead of ammonium hydroxide. This produces a stable pH of 8·5. The steady production of oxygen from the bleaching paste can be improved by adding '*boosters*' in the form of *peroxy salts* (potassium and ammonium persulphate). Liquid and paste bleaches must always be rinsed out of hair, or the cuticle will be roughened, and the hair may become brittle, or swell and disintegrate.

Heat from the steamer will speed up the chemical change in which melanin is oxidized.

Hair brighteners

Brighteners are very *weak* bleaches, which put blonde highlights into darker hair, or lighten naturally blonde hair. They consist of 10 volume hydrogen peroxide solution with a wetting agent and conditioner added. Quaternary ammonium compounds such as *cetrimide* are usually added as they serve both purposes. Brighteners are allowed to dry on the hair.

Yellowing of bleached hair may occur due to the action of ultra-violet rays in sunlight, or by the use of *alkaline* soap shampoos.

Practical work

1 OXYGEN

(*a*) *Preparation* In a boiling tube held by a stand and clamp, place 5 cm of 20 volume hydrogen peroxide solution. Assemble the rest of the apparatus as in the diagram, filling the gas jar with water before placing it on the beehive shelf in the trough of water. Add a pinch of manganese dioxide to the peroxide in the boiling tube, and very quickly put in the stopper. Bubbles of oxygen gas produced in the boiling tube are collected in the gas jar, displacing the water. When the gas jar is full of oxygen gas, slide a glass plate between it and the beehive shelf, and remove the covered gas jar. Collect a second gas jar of oxygen.

(*b*) *Burning in oxygen* Take a deflagrating spoon containing a little magnesium and ignite it at a bunsen flame. Immediately place it in one of the jars of oxygen gas, and notice the increased

7.4 Preparation of oxygen

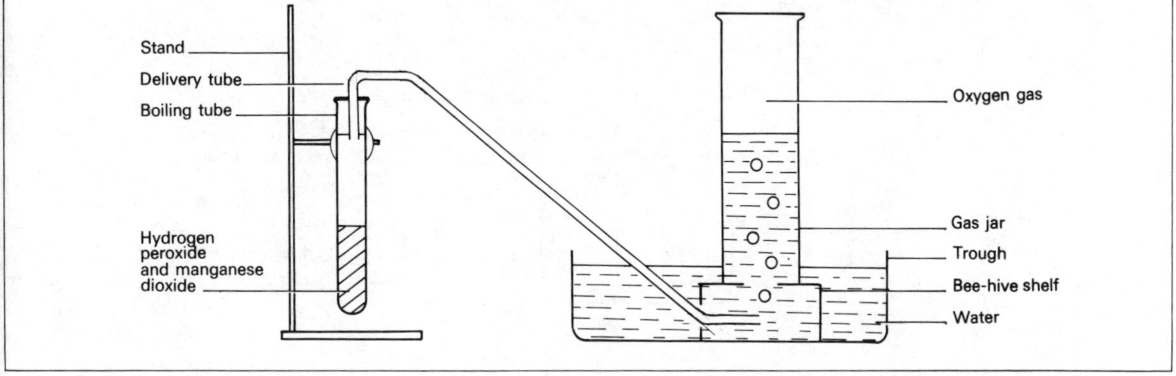

brilliance of the flame (CARE—the very bright light can damage the eyes). Repeat the experiment, using burning sulphur, or glowing charcoal, in place of the magnesium.

2 INCREASE IN WEIGHT ON BURNING

Take a crucible and lid, and weigh them both together on a chemical balance. Then separately weigh out 0·5 g magnesium ribbon, and place it in the crucible. Support the crucible on a pipe-clay triangle on a tripod. Hold the crucible lid in a pair of tongs, but do not place it on the crucible. Heat the crucible with a bunsen flame until the magnesium ignites and then place the lid on the crucible to keep all the smoke particles inside. The lid must be slightly raised from time to time to keep the magnesium burning. When the magnesium is completely burnt, allow the crucible to go cold, then reweigh the crucible and its contents, together with the lid. Add 0·5 g to the weight of the empty crucible and lid. This total should be less than the final weight of the crucible, lid, and ash.

3 RUSTING

(*a*) Take about a teaspoonful of iron filings and wrap them in a piece of muslin to form a bag. Attach the bag of filings by cotton to one end of a glass rod, and cover with a gas jar inverted in a trough containing water. Mark the water level in the gas jar, and leave for a week. Note the change in level of the water inside the gas jar, and the rusting of the iron filings. Rusting is a process in which one component of the air is removed.

(*b*) Take two test-tubes, and place a few small iron nails in each one. In one tube place a little water so that the nails have contact with both water and air. Completely fill the second tube with water that has been boiling for at least half an hour, to remove all the dissolved air. Into the tube place a tight rubber bung from which projects a short piece of glass tubing ending in 5 cm of rubber tubing. Close the rubber tubing with a clip. In this tube, the nails are in contact with water, but air has been completely excluded. Observe both groups of nails after one week for signs of rusting. One component of the air is required for rusting to occur.

4 HYDROGEN PEROXIDE

(*a*) *Preparation* Take 5 ml (cm^3) of syrupy phosphoric acid (corrosive so handle carefully) in a large test-tube, and add 5 ml (cm^3) of distilled water. Cool the contents by running water

7.5 Rusting experiment

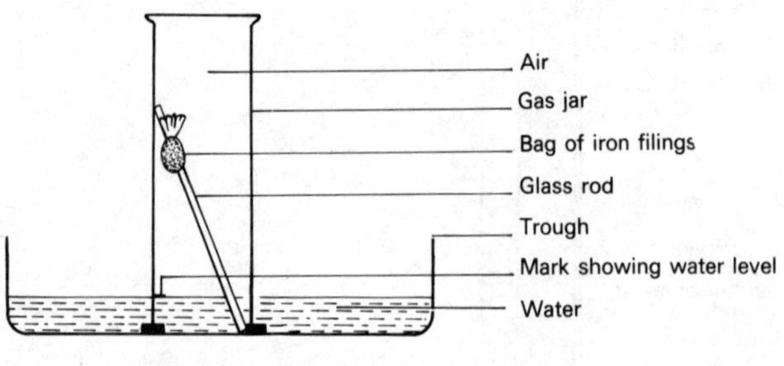

from the cold tap over the outside of the test-tube for two minutes. Add three saltspoonsful of barium peroxide a little at a time, cooling the test-tube with cold water as before several times while adding the barium peroxide. Heat is produced during the chemical change, and will decompose the peroxide unless the cooling is very thorough. Filter the solution to remove the insoluble barium phosphate, and collect the solution of hydrogen peroxide which comes through as the filtrate. Add a little manganese dioxide to show that it liberates oxygen.

(*b*) *Volume strength.* Into a 100 ml measuring cylinder place 5 ml (cm^3) of 10 volume hydrogen peroxide solution, and add 1 ml (cm^3) of a liquid detergent, e.g. Teepol, as a foam-former. Add a pinch of manganese dioxide on to the peroxide, and shake the cylinder rapidly from side to side to aid the production of oxygen foam. The volume of the foam produced is approximately the same as the volume of oxygen gas that would be produced.

1 ml (cm^3) of 10 volume peroxide$\rightarrow$10 ml (cm^3) of oxygen (foam)
5 ml (cm^3) of 10 volume peroxide$\rightarrow$50 ml (cm^3) of oxygen (foam)

Repeat the experiment using 20 volume hydrogen peroxide solution, and note the volume of foam produced.

(*c*) *Using the peroxometer*, check the strengths of a number of different hydrogen peroxide solutions.

5 BLEACHING ACTION OF HYDROGEN PEROXIDE ON HAIR

Obtain some clippings of naturally dark hair and tie with cotton to form five small bundles. Wash the hair bundles in soapless detergent solution, rinse thoroughly, and blot dry with a paper towel. Take five boiling tubes and place a hair bundle in each. Label the tubes 1 to 5. Take a large beaker and half fill it with water. Warm to 37°C, and maintain the water at this temperature. Add the following substances to the five tubes:

Tube 1 2 cm of 20 volume hydrogen peroxide solution (not stabilized),

Tube 2 2 cm of 20 volume peroxide + 5 drops of 0·88 ammonium hydroxide,

Tube 3 2 cm of 20 volume peroxide + 5 drops of 0·88 ammonium hydroxide + 1 drop of soapless detergent,

Tube 4 2 cm of 20 volume peroxide + 5 drops of dilute phosphoric (or sulphuric) acid,

Tube 5 2 cm of distilled water + 5 drops of 0·88 ammonium hydroxide.

Place all five test-tubes in the warm water, and maintain it at 37°C for half an hour (to imitate scalp temperature). Observe each test-tube for the production of bubbles of oxygen. After half an hour remove the bundles of hair from each test-tube in turn, and rinse each bundle thoroughly before placing it on a similarly numbered piece of paper towel to dry. Compare the bleaching effect of the various solutions on the hair bundles. Explain which substances act as stabilizers for hydrogen peroxide. Tube 5 without any peroxide acts as a control experiment, to show that ammonium hydroxide alone has no bleaching effect.

Multiple choice questions

1 If 3 ml (cm^3) of pure hydrogen peroxide is dissolved in water to give 25 ml (cm^3) the percentage strength of that solution is
a 3% *b* 4% *c* 12% *d* 25%

2 When hydrogen peroxide is applied to the hair in a bleach, the change in colour of the hair is due to
a oxidation *b* neutralization *c* reduction
d precipitation

3 When a hydrogen peroxide solution is described as being '20 volume' this means
a 20 ml (cm^3) of the solution is used
b 1 ml (cm^3) is added to 20 ml (cm^3) of water
c it is a 20% solution
d 1 ml (cm^3) solution will provide 20 ml (cm^3) oxygen

4 To obtain 20 ml (cm^3) of 30 volume hydrogen peroxide solution from a 40 volume solution we must use
a 10 ml (cm^3) peroxide + 10 ml (cm^3) water
b 15 ml (cm^3) peroxide + 5 ml (cm^3) water
c 5 ml (cm^3) peroxide + 15 ml (cm^3) water
d 20 ml (cm^3) peroxide + 20 ml (cm^3) water

5 Manganese dioxide is added to hydrogen peroxide solution when oxygen is prepared because it acts as
a an oxidizer *b* a catalyst *c* an element
d a stabilizer

6 The % strength of a 30 volume hydrogen peroxide solution is
a 0·3% *b* 3% *c* 9% *d* 30%

7 Rust forms when the following substances are all present
a oxygen, water, and iron *b* oxygen, water, and tin
c iron, water, and tin *d* tin, iron, and oxygen

8 Combustion, bleaching, and rusting are all examples of
a decomposition *b* oxidation *c* physical change
d catalysis

9 The material providing the bulk in a bleaching paste is
a sodium bisulphite *b* ammonium persulphate
c magnesium carbonate *d* ammonium carbonate

10 If scalp sting is not to occur, the maximum pH of any hairdressing lotion must be
a 6·5 *b* 7 *c* 8·5 *d* 9·5

8 Permanent Waving

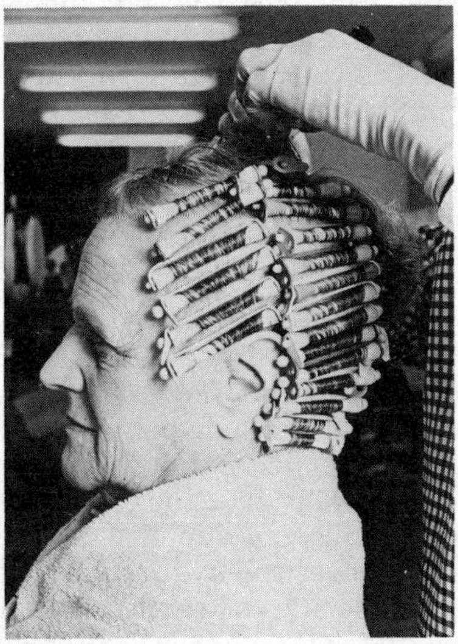

During the process of permanent waving irreversible changes in the keratin molecules of hair occur. These chemical changes can be brought about in two ways, cold waving and heat waving. The cold waving method is the one used today.

Cold permanent waving

The process of cold permanent waving affects the keratin in the cortex of the hair by its chemical action on the *disulphide* bonds. These bonds occur in the *cystine* amino-acid components of the *polypeptide* chains making up the keratin molecules (see Chapter 4).

FIRST STAGE

Some of the disulphide bonds are first broken by the action of a *reducing agent* which supplies *hydrogen* atoms to the keratin molecules. The two *sulphur* atoms which are joined to form the disulphide bond each become attached to a hydrogen atom instead of to one another. By this chemical change two *thiol* groups are formed from the broken disulphide bond, and the single cystine molecule becomes broken into two *cysteine* amino-acid molecules. This chemical change is *reduction.*

The cold wave perming lotion which is applied to the hair contains the reducing agent which breaks the disulphide bonds. It consists of a solution of *ammonium thioglycollate* which is a salt of *thioglycollic acid.* The strength of the perming lotion is important, as too concentrated a solution will permanently damage hair. For *Home perms* a 4·5% solution is supplied, while for *salon* use a 5·5% solution is used for *bleached* or *tinted* hair, and a 6·5% solution for *normal* hair. The longer the perming lotion remains on the hair the more disulphide bonds it will break. Thus the *time* the perming lotion is left on the hair is important. If too many disulphide bonds are broken the hair will break up, so perming lotion must not be left on the hair for too long. Too short a time will mean that not enough disulphide bonds are broken to increase the extensibility of the hair. The *pH* of the perming lotion is critical. If the solution is too *acid* its effect on the hair is too slow, but if the solution is too *alkaline* the perming lotion acts as a *depilatory.* A pH of 9 to 9·5 is considered to be most suitable. As perming lotion gives off *ammonia gas* it becomes less alkaline the longer it remains on the hair.

Cold wave perming lotion is made by adding 0·88 *ammonium hydroxide* solution to a solution of *thioglycollic acid,* when the chemical change called *neutralization* occurs, to form the salt *ammonium thioglycollate.* Excess ammonium hydroxide solution is then added until the pH reaches 9 to 9·5. Thioglycollic acid is a colourless liquid with a characteristic unpleasant smell. It is damaging to the eyes, and burns the skin in concentrated

8.1 Action of cold wave perming lotion

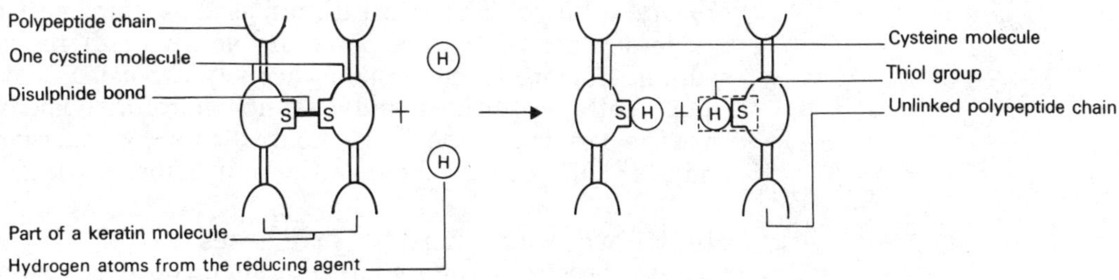

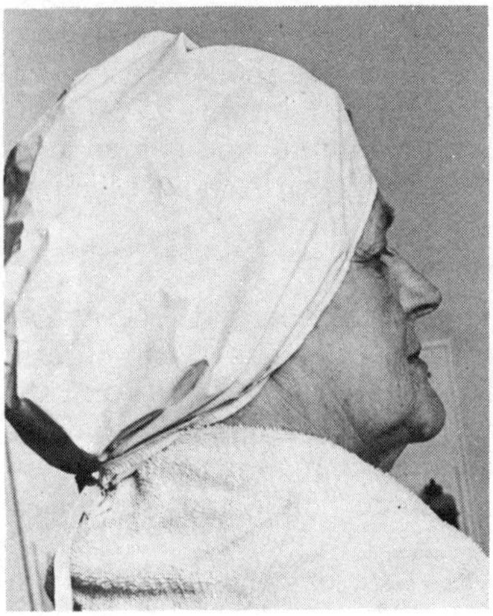

8.2 Perming cap in use

solution. Perming lotions usually contain a *conditioner* either cetrimide or P.V.P. resin (see Chapter 4).

After applying the perming lotion to the hair, the *shape* of the keratin molecules is changed physically to produce *waves* by winding the hair round *rollers*.

THE PERMING CAP

The scalp is covered by a perming cap once the winding is completed. This is an *insulating* layer (see Chapter 14) of paper and plastic to retain the scalp *heat*. The chemical change which occurs when the cold wave perming lotion is applied requires a temperature which is not too low, or the rate of the reaction will be too slow. The heat produced by the scalp is sufficient, provided it is not lost too quickly.

SECOND STAGE

After the perming lotion has been rinsed out of the hair the *second stage* in the cold permanent waving process is carried out. The hair is treated by an *oxidizing agent* so that *disulphide* links will *re-form* in new positions and so hold the hair permanently in its new shape. The oxidizing agent applied is known as the 'neutralizer' although the chemical change it brings about is *oxidation* and not neutralization. The oxygen supplied by the *oxidizing agent* in the 'neutralizer' removes the *hydrogen* atoms from the *thiol* groups in the *cysteine* molecules of keratin so that two adjacent *sulphur* atoms will be free to form a new disulphide bond. The hydrogen and oxygen atoms join to form *water*.

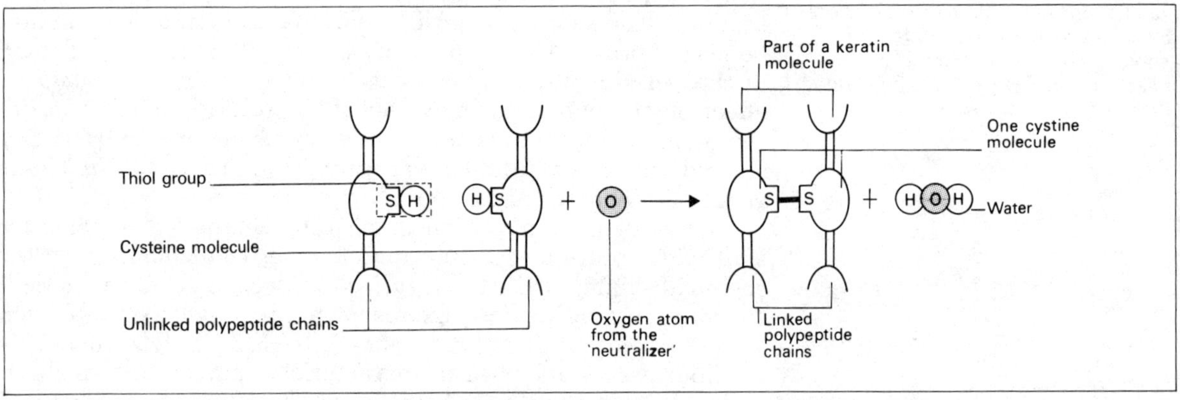

8.3 Action of the 'neutralizer'

'*Neutralizers*' are solutions containing the *oxidizing agent* and a *surfactant* to act as a *wetting agent*. The oxidizing agent used may be 20 volume *hydrogen peroxide* solution, or 5% *sodium bromate* solution. The 'neutralizers' used in Home perms contain the less reactive *sodium perborate* as an oxidizing agent, as sodium bromate forms a spontaneously *explosive* mixture with thioglycollate solutions, and must not therefore come in contact with the perming lotion. Some 'neutralizers' contain *conditioners*, and are then not rinsed out of the hair before setting.

Heat permanent waving processes

In these processes the hair is first shampooed to remove sebum which would slow down the penentration of the hair by the perming lotion. Each portion of hair is coated with *perming lotion*, and the hair *wound* on curlers to change the shape of the keratin molecules. The hair is then heated so that water in the hair is turned into *steam*. The heated perming lotion breaks down some of the *disulphide* bonds by the chemical change of *hydrolysis*, where the bonds are attacked by water. The new waved shape is fixed by the formation of new cross-linkages which are *sulphide* bonds, occurring in another keratin amino-acid called *lanthionine*. The breakdown of disulphide and the formation of new sulphide bonds are a *continuous* process.

The *heat* which changes water in the hair to steam during heat permanent waving is obtained by a number of different methods. In the *Falling Heat* (Wireless) method heaters which have been previously warmed by *conduction* from an electric heater are placed over each portion of hair wound on its curler. Conduction is a method of heat transfer through solids where heated molecules pass on heat to the molecules next to them. Heat is transferred from the heater to the hair by conduction. An insulating rubber pad below each heater prevents the scalp from being burned. In the *Exothermic* (Chemical) method the heat is produced by a chemical change instead of by electricity. Chemical pads containing *calcium oxide* (lime) are placed over the wound hair. The calcium oxide reacts with water in the hair to form *calcium hydroxide* (lime-water), the chemical change being exothermic as it produces a good deal of heat. *Care* must be taken when handling chemical pads, as there is enough moisture in the skin to cause the exothermic reaction and produce a burn. They must also be prevented from touching the client's skin, e.g. on the back of the neck, for the same reason.

HEAT WAVE PERMING LOTION contains a mixture of *alkali*, which aids penetration of the hair, and a sulphite, usually *sodium bisulphite*. The alkalis which are used are *ammonium hydroxide* and *sodium borate* (borax).

Table. Comparing cold and heat waving

	Cold waving	**Heat waving**
Process	In 2 stages	Continuous
Bonds broken	Disulphide	Disulphide
New bonds formed	Disulphide	Sulphide
Amino-acid involved	Cystine	Lanthionine
Chemical Changes	1st stage is reduction 2nd stage is oxidation	Hydrolysis

Straightening processes for curly hair

The reasons for curliness of natural hair are not certain. It does not appear to be due to the shape of the hair in cross-section (as not all round hairs are straight or all flattened hairs curly) as has been suggested. Curly hair may form because the end of the hair follicle is bent, so that the developing hair follows the curved shape of the follicle. The process for straightening curly hair uses the same reagents that are used in *cold permanent waving*, but as more *concentrated* solutions. The hair is treated with a 10% solution of *ammonium thioglycollate* incorporated into a thick cream, and having a pH of 10. This is combed through the hair to break the *disulphide* cross-links so that the hair straightens. The hair is then rinsed with water and *oxidised* with *hydrogen peroxide* solution to re-form disulphide bonds which will hold the hair in its new straight shape.

Where hair is very curly, as in African models, a stronger chemical straightener may be needed containing *sodium hydroxide* (caustic soda). This strongly alkaline chemical breaks the disulphide bonds between the polypeptide chains of the keratin so that the hair can be straightened. The sodium hydroxide forms around 5% of a cream hair straightener, the preparation having a very high pH of between 10 and 14. The following stringent safety precautions are necessary when this type of preparation is used. It must not be used on *European* hair, which could be considerably damaged in the process. The scalp must be covered by a protective layer of *petroleum jelly* before applying the caustic straightener. Great care must be taken to avoid getting the caustic straightener on unprotected skin, or in the eyes. The hairdresser must wear protective gloves. If the client complains that her scalp stings the straightener must be washed off immediately. The maximum *time* for the straightener to be left on even the coarsest hair is 8 minutes. The hair may dissolve if it is left on for a longer time.

After completely rinsing away the straightening cream with water, the hair is shampooed to remove the protective petroleum jelly and an oily *conditioner* applied to the hair before setting and drying.

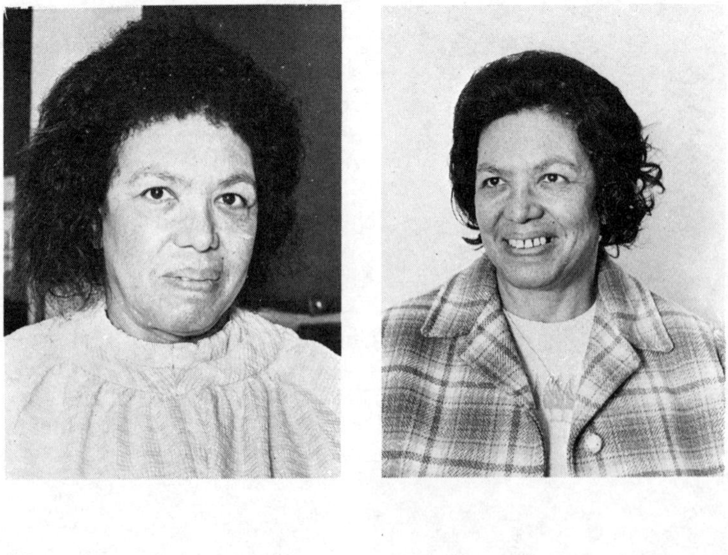

8.4 The same model with curly and straightened hair

The effect of the cuticle on hair waving processes

The *cuticle* keratin takes up water less readily than the cortex keratin. It will therefore act as a *chemical barrier* to water-soluble hairdressing preparations, including perming lotions and 'neutralizers'. This may explain the often experienced resistance of fine hair to permanent waving processes, since fine hair contains proportionately more cuticle keratin than coarse hair (40% : 20%, see Chapter I).

Practical work

1 NEUTRALIZATION OF THIOGLYCOLLIC ACID WITH AMMONIUM HYDROXIDE SOLUTION

Into a large evaporating dish pour 6% thioglycollic acid solution until the dish is half full. Place a test-tube in a test-tube rack and pour into it 1 cm of 0·88 ammonium hydroxide solution, taking care not to breathe in the choking vapour. By means of a dropper pipette transfer one drop of ammonium hydroxide solution to the thioglycollic acid solution, and stir with a glass rod. Dip a small piece of pH paper into the solution in the dish, and note the pH. Continue to add ammonium hydroxide solution drop by drop, stirring after each addition and testing the solution with pH paper, until a pH of 7 is obtained. Neutralization has now been carried out. Continue adding ammonium hydroxide solution until a pH of 9 is obtained, when your solution will be a cold wave perming lotion.

2 PERMANENTLY WAVING HAIR

Take a number of long hairs and wind them tightly round a glass rod so that the hairs do not lie over one another. Fix both ends of each hair to the rod by adhesive. Place the rod in a 6% solution of ammonium thioglycollate having a pH of 9, prepared as in Experiment 1. Leave the rod in this solution for 20 minutes then remove it. After rinsing thoroughly with water, place the rod in 10 volume hydrogen peroxide for 20 minutes. Rinse the rod then air dry it, and then remove the hairs which should be tightly curled, and remain curled after stretching or wetting.

3 HEAT PRODUCTION FROM CALCIUM OXIDE

Take a crucible and half fill it with calcium oxide. Place the crucible on a pipe-clay triangle supported on a tripod, and heat it very strongly with a bunsen flame for 10 minutes to thoroughly dry the calcium oxide. Cover the crucible with a lid, and leave it to cool. When it is quite cold place the crucible in the palm of one hand and press your fingers round the outside. Using a dropper pipette allow two drops of cold water to run down the inside of the crucible on to the calcium oxide. Notice that the crucible becomes very hot at this point due to the chemical change between the calcium oxide and the water.

4 TO DETERMINE THE pH OF COMMERCIAL COLD WAVING LOTIONS

Take a series of small beakers and into each one place 10 ml of a different commercial cold waving lotion (use both salon and home-perm types). Into each solution dip a piece of pH paper, note the colour and obtain the pH from the colour chart.

Multiple choice questions

1 When a cold wave lotion has a pH above 9·5 it is likely to act as
a an acid *b* an astringent *c* an oxidizer
d a depilatory

2 The substance used in exothermic pads which undergoes a chemical change in contact with water is calcium
a bicarbonate *b* oxide
c carbonate *d* hydroxide

3 The reducing agent present in cold wave perming lotion is
a ammonium thioglycollate *b* ammonium hydroxide
c thioglycollic acid *d* hydrogen peroxide

4 The chemical change which occurs in keratin on the addition of hydrogen peroxide during cold permanent waving is
a reduction *b* sulphonation *c* neutralization
d oxidation

5 The keratin cross-links broken by cold wave perming lotion are
a salt bonds *b* hydrogen bonds *c* disulphide bonds
d peptide bonds

6 A substance which provides hydrogen atoms during a chemical change is
a an oxidizing agent *b* a reducing agent *c* a wetting agent *d* an emulsifying agent

7 One cream used to straighten curly hair is effective because it contains
a ammonium thioglycollate *b* calcium hydroxide
c sodium perborate *d* quaternary ammonium compounds

8 Cold wave perming lotion is
a neutral *b* acidic *c* alkaline *d* exothermic

9 The action of the 'neutralizer' on keratin during cold permanent waving is to remove hydrogen atoms from the
a hydrogen bonds *b* thiol groups *c* disulphide bonds
d amino groups

10 The perming lotion used in some forms of heat permanent waving contains sodium
a bisulphite *b* bicarbonate
c sesquicarbonate *d* sulphate

9
Tinting Hair

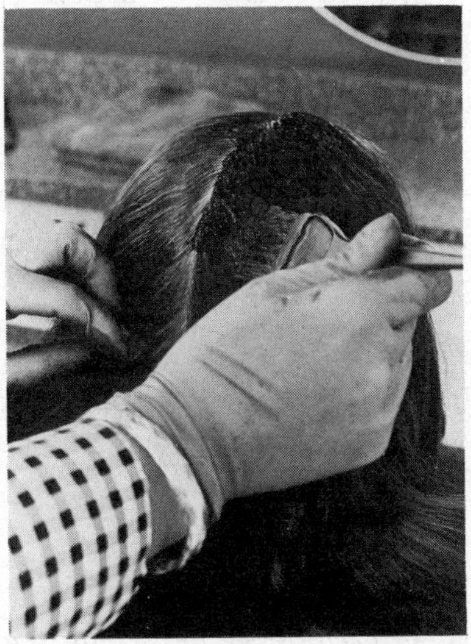

Hair dyes or tints may affect the hair in either of two ways. The dye may form a surface *coating* held by the scaly cuticle, or it may *penetrate* the cuticle and be deposited in the cortex of the hair. Where a dye forms a surface coating it gives the hair a dull appearance. A more natural appearance is obtained when the dye is deposited in the cortex of the hair, as the clear uncoated cuticle reflects light and gives a shine to the hair. Dyeing hair is a difficult process because keratin is a very dense material and difficult to penetrate. Many dyes are composed of large molecules which do not easily enter the hair through the tightly fitting cuticle layers. The colouring materials used to tint hair are obtained from three sources. They are *natural vegetable* dyes, *inorganic* dyes, and *synthetic organic* dyes.

Natural vegetable dyes

Until a century ago all the colouring materials in use were obtained from living things, the two dyes that were used on the hair being obtained from plants. *Henna* is a preparation containing the orange dye *Lawsone* obtained from the leaf of the Egyptian privet (Lawsonia). Henna takes a long time to penentrate the hair shaft at body temperature. *Camomile* is a golden yellow dye obtained from the flowers of the camomile plant which grows as a weed in this country. This dye only provides *surface* colour, its molecule being too large to get through the cuticle. Natural dyes are not poisonous and not likely to act as irritants.

Inorganic dyes

Certain *metallic salts* can be used to dye hair but the colour is slow to develop, and as these dyes are deposited on the outside of the hair, they give a dull effect. They also cause problems where hair is bleached or permed afterwards, so are little used today. The dye is produced as a result of a *chemical change* between the metallic salt and another reagent. The dye may be produced by *reduction* of a metal salt (e.g. cobalt, chromium, or copper sulphates) to produce a dark coloured deposit of metal which coats the hair. *Pyrogallol* is used as the reducing agent. A dye may also be produced by reaction of the metal salt (e.g. lead acetate) with sodium sulphide to form a metal *sulphide* dye (lead sulphide) which coats the hair. The finely divided metal and metal sulphides deposited are insoluble in water, so do not wash out of the hair. They are not skin irritants, but they do stain the skin as well as the hair.

Synthetic organic dyes

All the modern dyes used for tinting hair are *organic* compounds, being synthetic dyes obtained from *coal tar*. They are of three types; *oxidation*, *nitro*, and *acid* dyes.

1 OXIDATION OR PARA-DYES

This type of dye is obtained by *oxidizing* a colourless *dye-base*. The dye-base may be either *para-phenylenediamine* or *para-toluenediamine*. It is oxidised by *hydrogen peroxide*, and forms large coloured molecules inside the cortex of the hair. The increase in *size* of the molecules is due to several smaller molecules joining together during the process of *polymerisation*. Any dye left on the outside of the cuticle will wash away, the clear cuticle giving the hair gloss. The dye-base must be packed in tubes under *nitrogen* instead of air to prevent oxidation. Some oxygen usually penetrates through the tube cap so that the first quantity of dye-base out of the tube is already coloured by *air-oxidation*. 0·1% *sodium sulphite*, which is a *reducing* agent, may be added to the dye-base to prevent darkening in the tube. The colour of the dye usually fades slightly in *ultra-violet* rays, particularly in the case of para-toluene compounds. Para-dyes may irritate the skin causing *dermatitis*, particularly para-phenylenediamine, and for this reason its use in hair dyes is prohibited in France, Austria, and Germany where only para-toluene dye-bases may be used. A 4% incidence of allergy in 1000 tested persons has been shown, so that a *skin test* 48 hours before using a para-dye on a client for the first time is an essential

9.1 Camomile plant

precaution. The hairdresser must protect her hands by wearing *rubber gloves* when applying a para-dye.

2 NITRO-DYES

These dyes are similar to para-dyes in their chemical structure, as they too are diamines, but nitro-dyes are already coloured. They are not very soluble in water, so *benzyl alcohol* is used as a solvent to carry the dye into the cortex of the hair by penetrating the cuticle. Although nitro-dyes have a low solubility in water, they will eventually wash out of hair after shampooing a few times.

3 ACID DYES

Acid dyes are sponged onto the hair mixed with an *organic acid* (e.g. citric or tartaric acids) to give a pH between 4 and 2·5 which makes the dye stick to the hair. Acid dyes have large *coloured* molecules so do not normally penetrate into the cortex unless the hair has been damaged by over-bleaching or perming, which tend to make it more porous. The coloured dye molecules are held as a coating round the cuticle, and as they are water-soluble they readily wash off.

Hair colouring preparations

TEMPORARY COLOUR RINSES

These consist of an *acid dye* which is rinsed through the hair and then dried on during setting. The colour is removed entirely by the first shampoo, and may wash off in rain or steam.

COLOURED SETTING LOTION

This is a setting lotion containing a suitable *acid dye* which will attach itself at intervals along the *P.V.P.* molecule which acts as the *film-former* (see Chapter 4). On drying the film-former sets as a coloured plastic film on the hair. It washes out with the first shampoo.

COLOUR SHAMPOO

These shampoos do not produce any marked colour change in the hair but they brighten faded hair and add highlights. The natural dye *camomile* may be added to the detergent, but it is more usual in modern colour shampoo for a *nitro-dye* to be used. Alternatively colour shampoos may contain an *acid dye* together with the detergent and an *organic acid* to give a pH around 5. A more acid pH may cause irritation of the scalp.

HAIR COLOUR RESTORERS

Preparations are still on the market designed for home use to colour white hairs. They contain a *metallic salt* dye.

SEMI-PERMANENT DYES

These are either *nitro-dyes* used with a benzyl alcohol 'carrier', or diluted *para-dyes* which are either oxidised by oxygen in the air, or mixed with 10 volume hydrogen peroxide solution. The colour usually persists for up to six shampoos since the dye penetrates into the hair cortex, but it slowly washes out.

PERMANENT DYES

These dyes remain in the hair colouring it permanently. Although they may fade slightly, particularly in strong sunlight, they do not wash out. The natural vegetable dye *henna* is a permanent dye, and so are the *metallic salt* dyes, but their use has been largely discontinued except in cases where a person is *allergic* to the modern para-dyes. *Para-dyes* are the main permanent colourings used today both on naturally coloured, and on greying or white hair. The *dye-base* and *hydrogen peroxide* solution are mixed immediately before use and applied together since the chemical change of *oxidation* occurs slowly enough for the reagents to have penetrated the cuticle before the reaction has proceeded very far. The mixture is *alkaline* to cause swelling of the hair to aid penetration, and to catalyse the breakdown of hydrogen peroxide. An excess of the dye-base is used because the rate of oxidation slows down rapidly towards the end of the application time. 20 volume hydrogen peroxide solution is used unless lighter shades than the natural colour are required. Then 30 volume solution must be used.

The application time of 20 to 40 minutes can be reduced by applying *heat* which speeds up the rate of the chemical changes. Heat may be applied by means of the *accelerator* or the *steamer*.

The accelerator

The accelerator consists of a *hood* inside which a number of small *bulbs* are fitted to produce *infra-red* heating rays when electricity passes through them. The 12 volt bulbs are wired in series (see Chapter 6), with two bulbs to each circuit. This means that in each wiring circuit the current passes through the two bulbs one after the other. If one bulb becomes loose or broken the other bulb wired in the same circuit will not heat either, the circuit having been broken by the fault. The machine has a *three-heat switch* (see Chapter 5) controlling the intensity of radiation, and a *time switch* normally set to give a four-minute heating period. It is protected, in case a *short-circuit* occurs, by a 3 *amp fuse*. The bulbs must be kept clean to remain effective and should be wiped once a week with a damp sponge while the accelerator is unplugged. When used during oxidation tinting on the 'medium' switch position, the time required for the colour to develop is cut to 4 minutes.

9.2 Accelerator

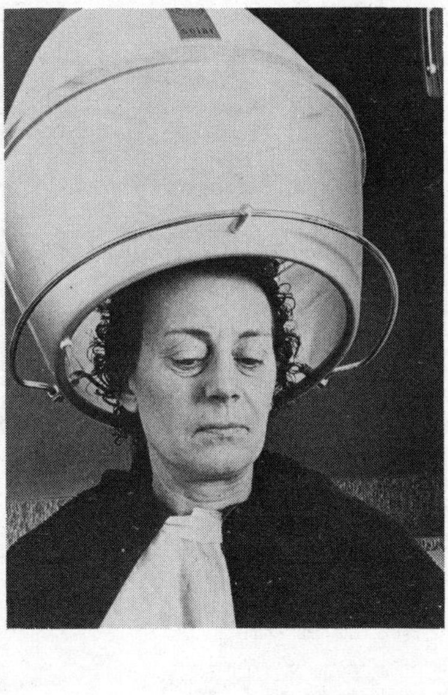

The steamer

The steamer consists of a *kettle* connected to a *hood. Distilled* water is placed in the *reservoir* and runs down into the kettle. Distilled water should always be used to prevent the deposition of *scale* which will form in the kettle if *hard* tap water is used. The water is heated by the electrical *heating element* in the kettle and produces steam which passes into the hood through small holes in a tubular *manifold.* A *thermostat* and *three-heat switch* control the heating element. The steamer produces *moist heat* which speeds up the chemical changes during tinting, having the same effect as the *dry heat* from the accelerator.

Reducers

These are chemicals which will remove oxidation dyes from the hair and skin. They comprise two solutions which are applied to the hair one being *sodium bisulphite* and the other *sodium formaldehyde sulphoxalate*. They remove colour by *reduction* and are themselves removed from the hair by an *oxidizing rinse*, using a dilute solution of *hydrogen peroxide*.

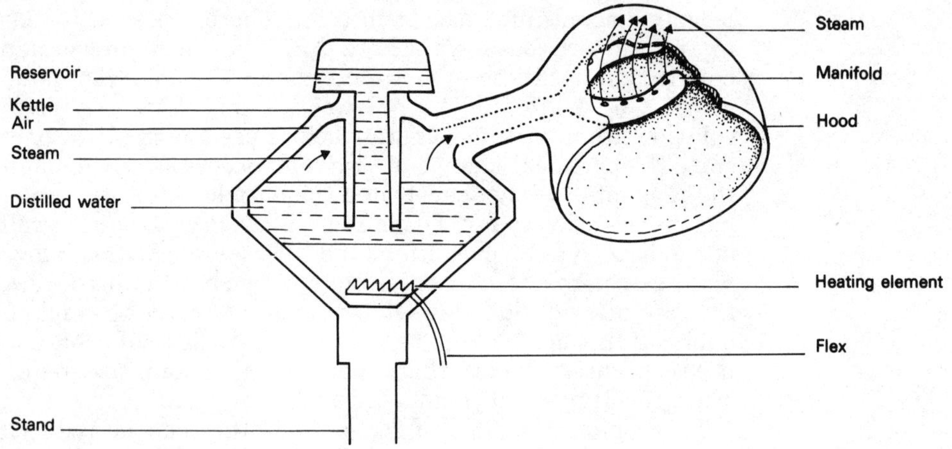

9.3 The steamer

Light and colour

The impression of colour obtained from dyes is due to the nature of *white light* and the way that *pigment* molecules *absorb* and *reflect* light. White light can be split up into a number of components by passing it through a *prism*. This process is *dispersion*, and is caused because the prism bends the various components of white light by different amounts. We see seven components of white light on dispersion appearing as different colours. Each colour consists of light *rays* which travel in a wave-like manner. The distance between the crest of a wave and the one following it is the *wave-length*. Light rays of different colours have different wave-lengths. These seven component colours of white light are a *spectrum*. *Red* light is at one end of the spectrum, being bent the least by the prism and having the *longest* wave-length. This is followed by orange, yellow, green, blue, indigo, and violet. *Violet* light is bent most by the prism and has the *shortest* wave-length.

9.4 Dispersion of light

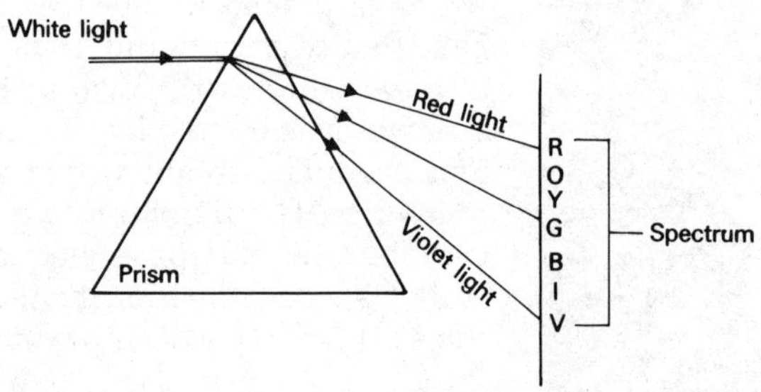

If white light can be split up into its coloured components then it should be possible to combine coloured lights to produce white light. This is known as *colour mixing*. It is also possible to combine selected coloured lights to give a variety of colour effects. The *colour triangle* is a device to show the effects of colour mixing for light rays (*N.B.* it does not apply to pigments such as dyes and paints).

9.5 Wave-length differences

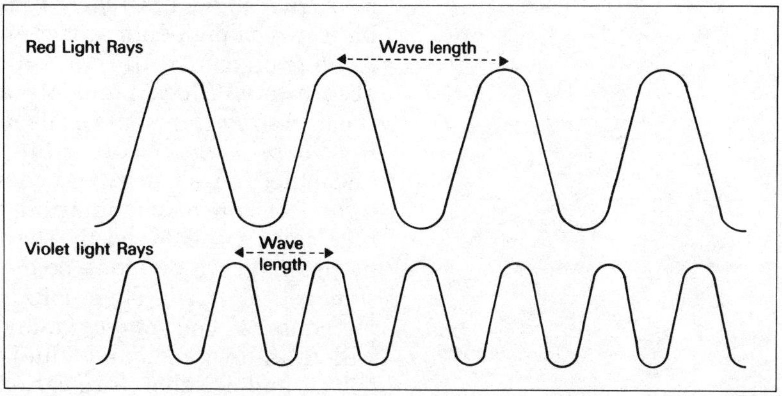

9.6 Colour triangle

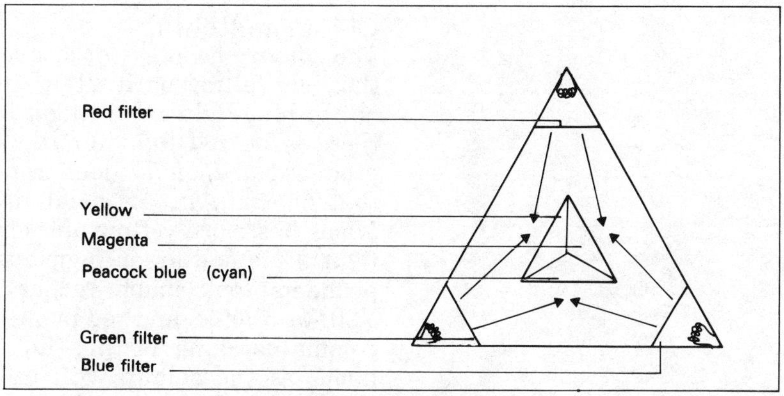

It is found that if *red*, *green*, and *blue* light are combined at the centre of the colour triangle *white* light is seen. Red, green, and blue are the *primary* colours of light. Adding red and green light produces *yellow* on the side of the inner triangle on which these two colours fall. Similarly, red and blue give *magenta*, and green and blue give *peacock blue* or *cyan*. Yellow, magenta, and peacock blue (cyan) are the *secondary* colours of light. Secondary colours can be combined with the primary colour opposite to them in the colour triangle to form white light, e.g. yellow (2 parts) + blue (1 part) = white. The pairs of primary and secondary colours which together form white light are *complementary* colours. This is colour mixing by *addition*.

Colours can be removed from white light by passing it through *filters*. A *red* filter allows only the *red* component of white light to pass through but stops all other colours. A *yellow* filter lets through both *red* and *green* light but stops blue light. A *magenta* filter lets through *red* and *blue* light but stops green. On passing *white* light through a yellow and then a magenta *filter* only *red* light would emerge. This is colour mixing by *subtraction*.

Pigments

The colour of hair is due to the *pigment* molecules it contains. *Dyes* and *paints* contain pigment molecules. They produce colour by absorbing light rays of certain wave-lengths which fall on them, and reflecting others. Pigments differ from filters as the latter allow certain rays to pass through them instead of reflecting them, but both pigments and filters absorb some of the rays. *Red* pigments *reflect* red light and absorb green and blue light. *Green* pigments reflect green light and absorb red and blue. A *white* pigment will reflect all the colours of light and does not absorb any. *Black* pigments absorb all the light falling upon them. *Yellow* pigments reflect green and red light but absorb the *complementary* colour blue. A *magenta* pigment reflects red and blue and absorbs the complementary green light. If *white* light falls on a combination of yellow and magenta pigments blue light is absorbed by the yellow, and green light absorbed by the magenta pigment, so *only red* light is reflected, i.e. yellow + magenta = red. Thus colour mixing by *subtraction* occurs in pigments. *Yellow, magenta,* and *cyan pigments* (often incorrectly called yellow, red, and blue) can be used to make any other colour and are therefore called the *primary colours* of pigments.

Colour matching

The colour of a *pigment* or dye will be affected by the colour of the *light* falling on it. Hair *tinted red* looks red in white light, but in blue light it will look black as it absorbs blue light and there is no red light for it to reflect. The white light that is produced *artificially* does not have a spectrum identical with that of *sunlight.* Artificial light produced *by electric filament lamps* has more yellow and less blue and green light than sunlight. Blue and green pigments therefore look dull, and purple pigments look much redder in this type of artificial light. Yellow, orange, and red pigments look much brighter. Accurate colour matching is thus not possible under electric filament lamps as the colours will differ from those seen in daylight. Artificial light produced by *fluorescent strip* lights of the 'daylight' type has a composition more closely resembling sunlight, and so is much better for colour matching.

Practical work

1 USING A METALLIC DYE

Take a 4% solution of a metallic salt such as copper sulphate or cobalt sulphate and brush the solution on to a hank of light coloured hair or white wool. Dip the coated hair into a freshly prepared alkaline pyrogallol solution for 10 minutes. This acts as a reducing agent leaving a brown deposit of metal on the hair or wool, which does not rinse off with water.

2 USING AN ACID DYE

Take a hank of light coloured hair tied together with cotton, and a piece of white wool, and place them in a small beaker. Take 10 ml (cm^3) of dilute acetic acid (4N) add a small amount of acid dye from the tip of a spatula and pour the mixture into the beaker. Suitable dyes would be I.C.I. Lissamine Green or Coomassie Black. Leave the wool and hair in the dye for ten minutes then remove them, and rinse in water. The wool and hair will both be coloured by the dye.

3 TO PRODUCE A SPECTRUM

(*a*) A projector consisting of a lamp with a lens in front is used as a source of white light. If a prism is placed in front of this lamp a spectrum will be produced on a sheet of white paper placed on the bench in front.

(*b*) If a diffraction grating (15,000 lines/inch) is placed in front of a projector lamp light source a spectrum will be produced on a screen or sheet of white paper placed in front of it.

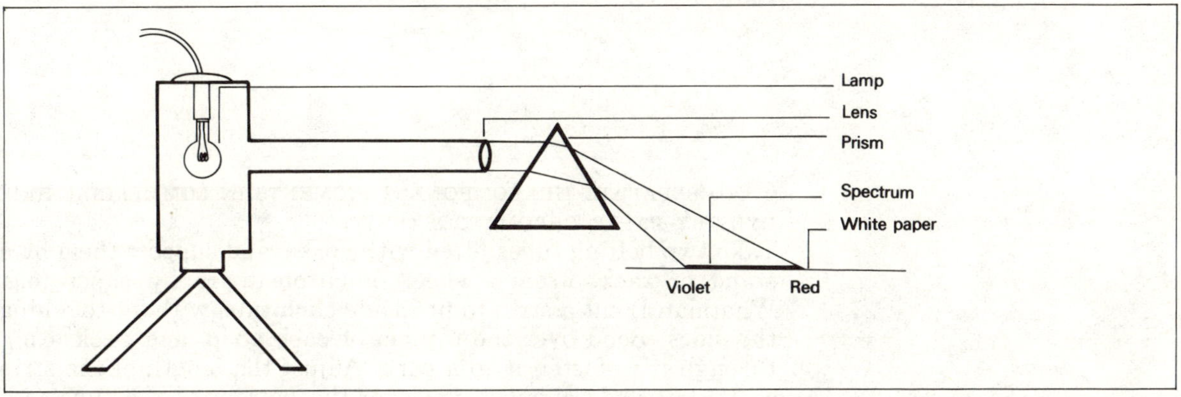

9.7 Using a prism to produce a spectrum

4 COLOUR MIXING

(*a*) Using coloured filters placed on an overhead projector complete the following table:

Filters placed on projector	Observed colour
Cyan + magenta	
Magenta +	Red
Yellow +	Green
Cyan + yellow + magenta	
Green + magenta	
Yellow + blue	

(*b*) Place three filters, cyan, magenta, and yellow, on an overhead projector so that they overlap as in the diagram. Write down the colours observed in the areas marked 1, 2, 3, and 4.

5 THE APPEARANCE OF DYES IN COLOURED LIGHT

Observe a number of coloured cards or squares of coloured fabric under different colours of light produced on a screen by placing

9.8 Overlapping filters

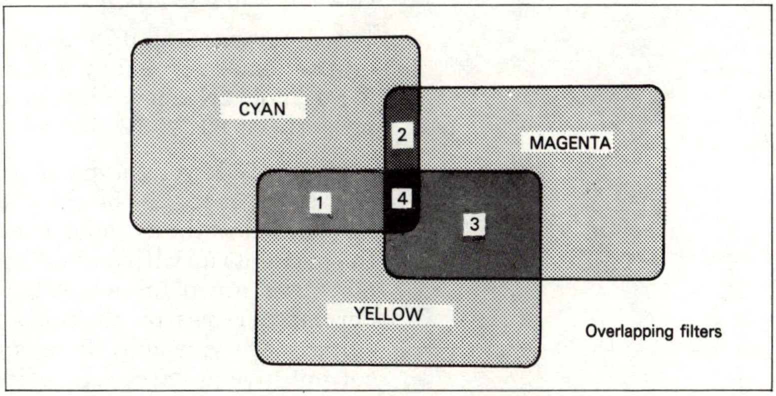

a series of coloured filters on an overhead projector, e.g. red, blue, yellow, and green filters. Record your results as a table as shown below:

Colour in white light	Colour of illumination	Observed colour

6 TO SEPARATE THE COMPONENT PIGMENTS IN COMMERCIAL HAIR DYES BY PAPER CHROMATOGRAPHY

Take two boiling tubes fitted with corks, and support them by a stand or rack. From a sheet of chromatography paper (e.g. Whatman I) cut a strip to fit inside each tube without touching the sides. Bend over the top cm of each strip, and stick a pin through it to fasten it to a cork. Adjust the length of the strip so that it ends about 1 cm from the bottom of the tube (see diagram).

9.9 Separation of pigments by paper chromatography

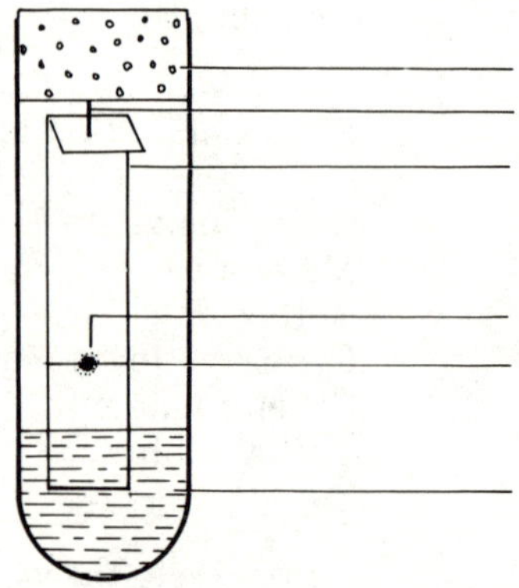

Remove the paper strips (still attached to the corks) and rule a pencil line 2 cm from the bottom end of each. By means of a short capillary tube place a spot of a commercial hair dye (preferably a dark colour), or a coloured ink, in the centre of the pencil line on each paper strip. Pour a different solvent into the two tubes to a depth of 2 cm. Suggested solvents:

1 Sodium citrate; 0·88 ammonium hydroxide; water; in the proportions 2 : 5 : 100 by weight.
2 Butanol; 2N ammonium hydroxide solution; ethanol; in the proportions 60 : 20 : 20 by volume.

Carefully lower the paper strips back into the tubes. *Do not* let the paper touch the sides of the tubes, and the solvent level must be below the dye spot. The solvent rises up the paper drawing the pigments up with it at different rates, so that separate patches of colour are obtained. After half an hour remove the paper chromatograms from the tubes and dry them. How many different colours are you able to see on the chromatograms? Does one solvent give a better separation than the other?

Multiple choice questions

1 Para-toluenediamine forms large coloured molecules in the presence of one of the following agents

a wetting *b* oxidizing *c* hydrolysing *d* reducing

2 A skin test for allergy must be given 48 hours before the first application of one of the following dyes

a nitro *b* metallic *c* oxidation *d* vegetable

3 The organic substance lawsone would be found in a

a temporary colour rinse *b* henna application
c tinted setting lotion *d* camomile shampoo

4 Heat is transfered to hair from a salon accelerator by

a ultra-violet radiation *b* thermal conduction
c convection currents *d* infra-red radiation

5 A combination of primary and secondary coloured lights of suitable illumination to give white light would be

a yellow and blue *b* red and yellow
c cyan and green *d* magenta and yellow

6 The process by which light is split up into a spectrum of colours is

a diffusion *b* filtration *c* inversion *d* dispersion

7 Hair which has been permanently dyed with henna will absorb the following colours of the spectrum

a all except red and orange *b* only red *c* only blue
d all except blue

8 Light produced by electric filament lamps differs from sunlight in having an increased proportion of light of the following colour

a red *b* blue *c* yellow *d* violet

9 To tint hair to a lighter than natural colour the volume strength of the hydrogen peroxide solution used with the dye-base is

a 10 *b* 20 *c* 30 *d* 40

10 Colour shampoo may contain any of the following dyes except

a camomile *b* para-dye *c* acid dye *d* nitro-dye

10 Hair Growth and Hair Loss

Hair follicles begin to form in the skin of the unborn baby by small regions of the epidermis growing down into the dermis, where specialized patches of *dermal cells* occur which will produce the hair papilla. The first hairs that grow from the base of these follicles in the unborn baby are called *lanugo* hairs, and are shed in the eighth month of pregnancy. The follicles then produce *vellus* or *terminal* hairs, depending on the region of the skin where they occur. At *puberty* the effect of the *sex hormones* is to cause some follicles which were producing vellus hair to form terminal hair, e.g. under the arms, in the pubic region, and in the beard region in males.

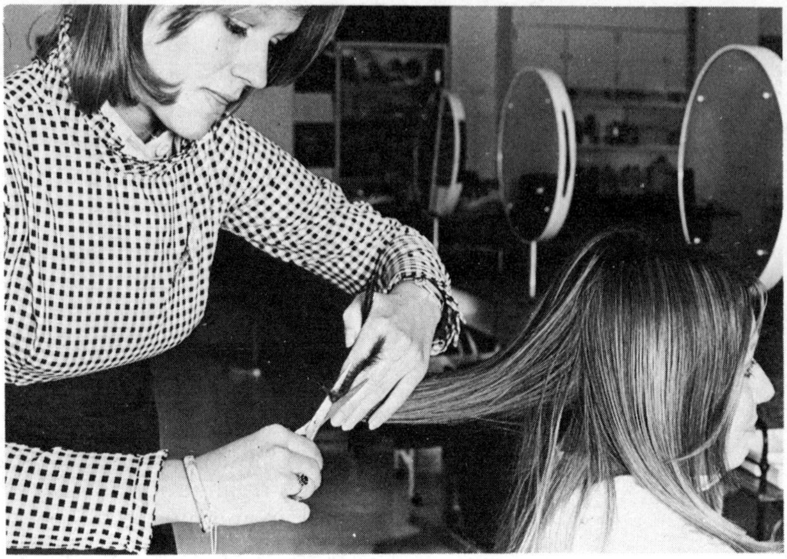

Growth at the hair root

The growing region of the hair is the *bulb* which occurs at the bottom of the hair follicle. In the lower part of the bulb known as the hair *matrix* the cells are dividing very rapidly and the new cells are pushed upwards as they form. The cells of the matrix are all alike, unpigmented, and the fastest growing cells of the body. As the cells are pushed up to form part of the *upper bulb* they begin to change in shape, *differentiating* into cuticle, cortex, and medulla. They also become horny and die. In the bulb, pigment is injected into the cortex by the *melanocytes*. In older people melanocytes stop producing pigment in some of the hair follicles. It is the mixture of unpigmented and coloured hairs which causes *grey* hair (canities). The *inner root sheath* is also formed by the matrix and grows up alongside the cuticle of the hair with which it interlocks. The large amount of food and oxygen required by the actively growing matrix are supplied by the blood in the knot of blood capillaries forming the *dermal papilla*.

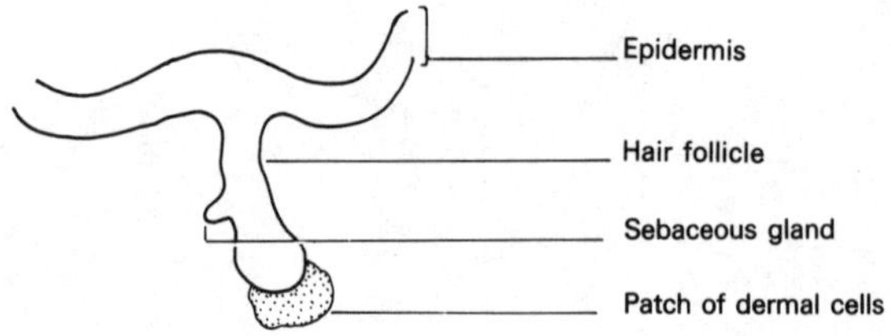

10.1 Development of hair follicle

Hair growth cycle

In each follicle a period of hair *growth* is followed by a *resting* period. The growing phase is known as *anagen*, and the resting

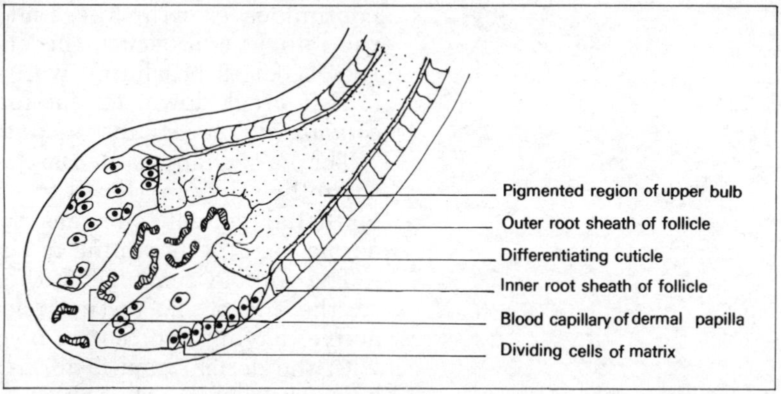

10.2 Hair root

phase as *telogen*. The breaking down period before telogen is called *catagen*. At any one time some of the body's hair follicles are growing and some are resting. On the scalp, resting follicles occur at random and form around 13% of the total. The hair follicles in different parts of the body have growing and resting phases of different lengths. A *scalp* hair *grows* for a period between $1\frac{1}{4}$ and 7 years, with 3 years being an average growing period. *Catagen* lasts 2 weeks, and the follicle then has a *resting* period of 3 to 4 months. *Eyebrow* and *eyelash* hairs grow for 1 month and have a resting period of $3\frac{1}{2}$ months. *Body* (vellus) hairs grow for 3 months and have a resting period of $2\frac{1}{2}$ months. At the end of the resting phase a *new* hair will normally begin to grow from the follicle and the original hair will be *shed*. Thus

10.3 Hair growth cycle 1
Hair growth cycle 2

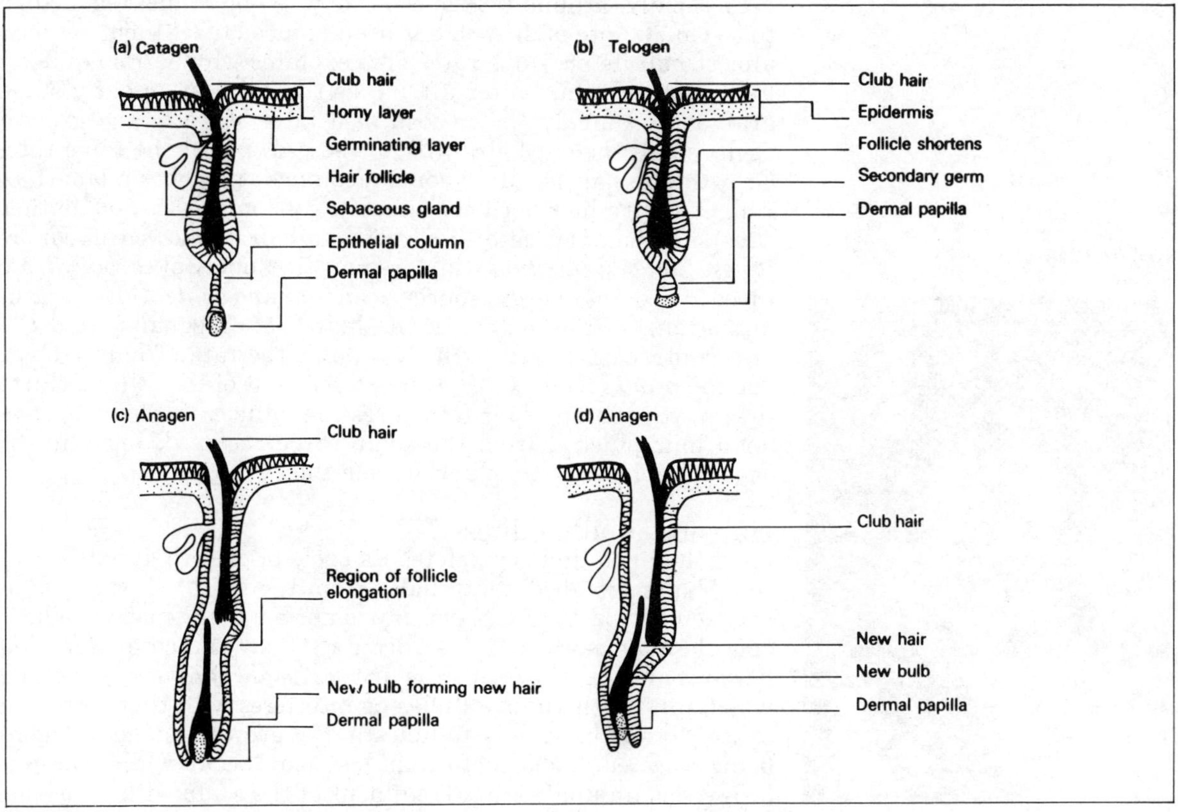

continuous growth, loss, and replacement of hair occurs. As the follicle approaches the end of its growing phase the hair root becomes brush-like while the bulb and lower part of the follicle break down, except for a strand of cells, the *epithelial column*, which remains in contact with the dermal papilla.

The hair is now called a *club hair* because of its shape, and the follicle has shortened to about half its original length. The epithelial column shortens to form the *secondary germ*, the dermal papilla remaining in contact with it.

The follicle remains in this condition throughout telogen. At the end of the resting phase the secondary germ becomes active, having two *centres* of growth. Its lower end in contact with the dermal papilla forms the new *bulb*, producing a new hair. The upper part of the secondary germ forms the new cells which lengthen the follicle below the club hair. The lengthening of the follicle keeps pace with the growth of the new hair, so that the hair tip remains positioned just below the end of the club hair. Only when the follicle is fully grown does the tip of the new hair push past the base of the club hair.

The new hair grows up to the surface, and the old hair is removed by brushing or combing, or drops out of the follicle.

Rate of hair growth

The rate of hair growth is *fastest* between the ages of 15 and 30 years, and is slightly faster in women than in men. On the scalp the average rate of hair growth is 0·35 mm per day, although a hair does not grow at the same rate throughout its growth cycle. When the hair tip reaches the level of the skin surface it grows very rapidly, around 0·38 mm per day. When it has reached 25 to 35 cm, its rate of growth has been reduced to 0·21 mm per day, almost half its previous rate. This explains why hair so quickly looks uneven again after a trim, as the hairs in an early stage grow more quickly than those in a later stage of the growth cycle, so all the cut hairs will not be growing at the same rate. Growth of a hair is rarely continued once it reaches a length of 1 m. *Cutting* a hair does not affect its rate of growth, and neither does shaving. The rate of growth of hair is slowed down by *illness* and *malnutrition* which reduce the supply of *carbohydrate* (needed as an energy source), and *amino-acids* (for keratin formation), to the matrix of the hair root. Pregnancy and the oral contraceptive pill both slow down the rate of hair growth due to *hormonal* effects. *Plucking* a hair out of the follicle starts the growth of a new hair from a resting follicle. It takes 147 days for a hair plucked from the scalp to be replaced, but only 61 days to replace a hair plucked from the eyebrow.

10.4 Traction alopecia

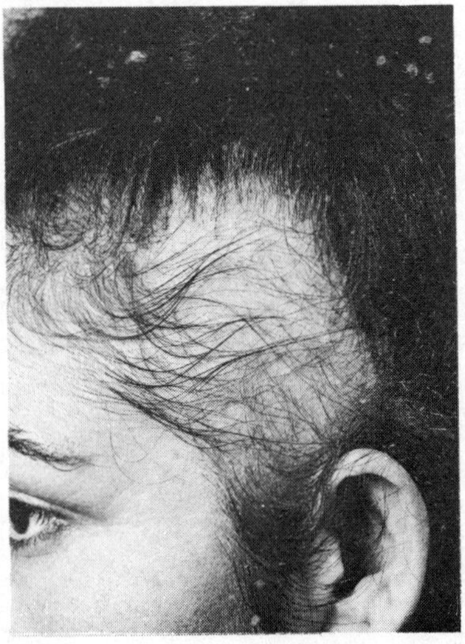

Hair loss and baldness

As each hair follicle completes its cycle of growth at a different time, hairs are shed continually from the scalp. A *hair loss* of between 50 and 100 hairs per day is normal for the scalp. Where considerably more hair loss occurs it may indicate *ill-health*, nervous or skin *disease*, or the onset of *male baldness*. Anything which injures the hair follicles or interferes with their function causes loss of hair, only follicles in the growing stage (anagen) being affected. Thus scalp hair loss may occur while the eyebrows remain unaffected. Treatment of the scalp with *X-rays* or administering *lithium salts* will usually cause all the scalp hairs to fall out. Such treatment is known as *epilation*. A number of different types of *Alopecia*, or baldness of the scalp, are recognised. Certain types of alopecia are associated with hairdressing. Excessive pulling or *traction* of the hair will loosen it at the base of the follicle, or cause it to break off at scalp level. Over-vigorous use of nylon hairbrushes, particularly on fine hair, may cause hair loss on the top of the head. Dragging back the hair tightly in a *pony-tail* or *bun* may cause the edges of the hair-line in the frontal and temporal regions to recede due to hair loss. Tight curlers or brush-rollers, particularly if used daily, may cause irregular bald patches with fringes of broken hairs over the ears and mid-line scalp. All these types of alopecia disappear when the traction is removed.

10.5 Alopecia areata

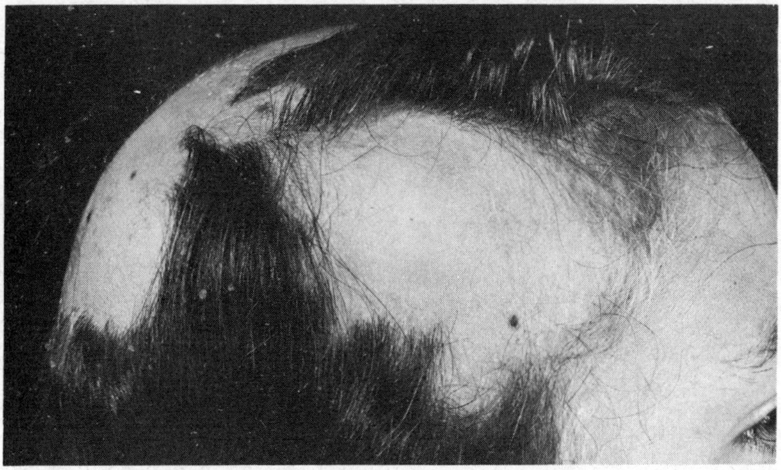

Soapless shampoos may cause *diffuse hair loss* with oiliness of the scalp. Thinning hair is becoming more common in young women, which may be due to the present use of soapless shampoo. *Permanent waving* lotions and *bleaches* may cause hair to break with too frequent use, as they make hair brittle and reduce its elasticity. *Nervous disorders* are thought to be the cause of baldness in some cases. *Alopecia areata*, or *patchy* hair loss, producing round bald patches on the scalp with smooth glossy skin, is of this type. Alopecia areata normally clears up spontaneously. If the entire scalp is affected the condition is known as *Alopecia totalis*.

10.6 Male baldness

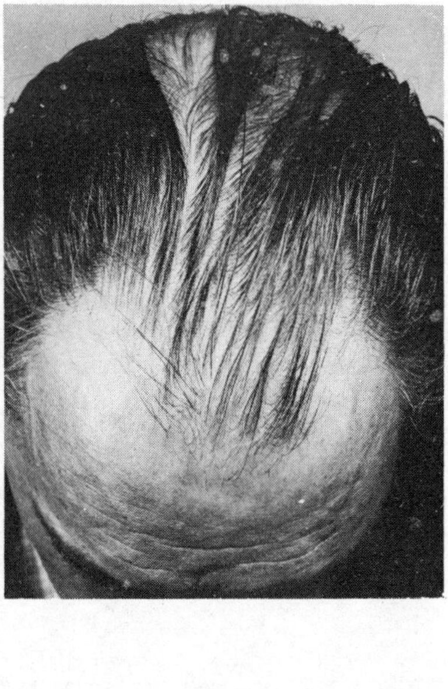

Trichotillomania is a form of incomplete alopecia where irregular bald patches occur with a few short hairs in them. This is caused by a nervous disorder where patients pull out their hair.

For examples of baldness due to *skin diseases* see Chapter 16.

MALE BALDNESS is a condition in which loss of hair from the scalp develops gradually and symmetrically, starting at the temples and crown. 95% of baldness in men is of this *patterned* type and is not associated with ill-health or disease. Heredity, male sex hormones, and increasing age all affect the onset of male baldness. The tendency for hair loss to occur in a particular pattern is *inherited*. Hair loss does not occur in women who have inherited the same pattern because *male sex hormones* are required to stop hair growth in the follicles. They can, however, pass the pattern on to their sons. Baldness increases with *age*, the blood supply to the hair bulb becoming much reduced. Some of the follicles turn over to the production of very fine colourless *lanugo* hairs, others stop producing hairs altogether. At this time the blood supply to the *sebaceous* gland attached to the hair follicles increases enormously, and the sebaceous glands enlarge and become more active. This produces the characteristic shine of the bald scalp. There is no acceptable way of preventing or arresting the development of male patterned baldness by treating the scalp.

Depilatories

The *removal* of hair is a long-established cosmetic practice, although the hair which is removed varies in different cultures and fashions. The places from which hair is commonly removed in women are the upper lip, the armpits, and the legs. *Superfluous hair* (*Hirsuties* or *Hypertrichosis*) on the upper lip may be due to an *inherited* racial trait, or due to *hormone inbalance* as in older women after the menopause. *Electrolysis* is the only effective means available of removing unwanted hair permanently. *Temporary* removal of hair can be brought about by *shaving*, *plucking*, or the use of chemical, wax, or abrasive *depilatories*.

ELECTROLYSIS

The body tissues contain a salty fluid which will conduct an electric current and is therefore an *electrolyte*. When dissolved in water, salts form negative and positive electrically charged groups called *ions*, and it is the presence of these ions which allows the solution to conduct electricity. The electricity passes into and out of the electrolyte by *electrodes* which are connected by wires to the source of the electric current. The two electrodes are the *anode* bringing current into, and the *cathode* taking current out of, the electrolyte.

10.7 Electrolysis

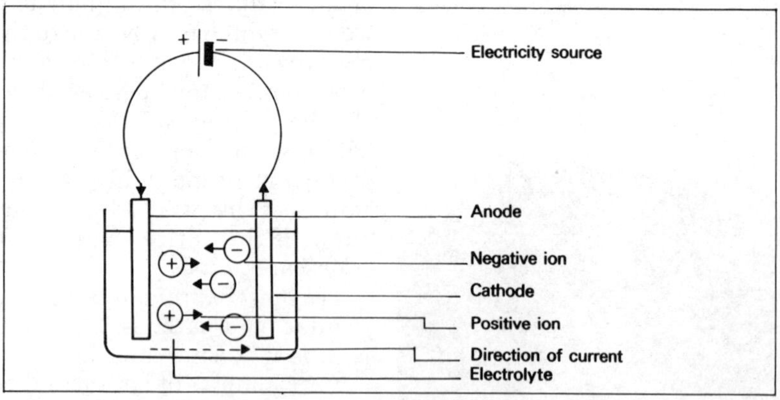

There are two methods of 'electrolysis' used for removing facial hair in women. These are *galvanic* electrolysis and *diathermy*. In galvanic electrolysis a small *direct* electric current is applied to the skin through an *anode* consisting of a piece of *sponge* soaked in salt solution. The current travels through the skin where the tissue fluid acts as the electrolyte, to the *cathode* which is the electrolysis *needle*. This is a steel or platinum needle, often bent at an angle, which has been inserted down to the base of the hair follicle. From the needle the current passes back to the source. The *electric current* destroys the hair root and loosens the hair so that it can be lifted out of the follicle after 5 to 20 seconds.

Diathermy uses a *high frequency alternating* current (see Chapter 11) which produces *heat* at the tip of the insulated *needle* to destroy the hair root in a fraction of a second. The needle is connected to the diathermy machine so that the current to and from the hair follicle passes in the needle, and the *resistance* of the needle causes *heat* to be produced in it. Diathermy is more often used because more hairs can be treated in a given time. The skin may become red or sore after 'electrolysis' but these effects should not last more than a few hours. Infection, scarring, and pitting of the skin can occur unless 'electrolysis' is skilfully applied.

10.8 Hair removal by galvanic electrolysis

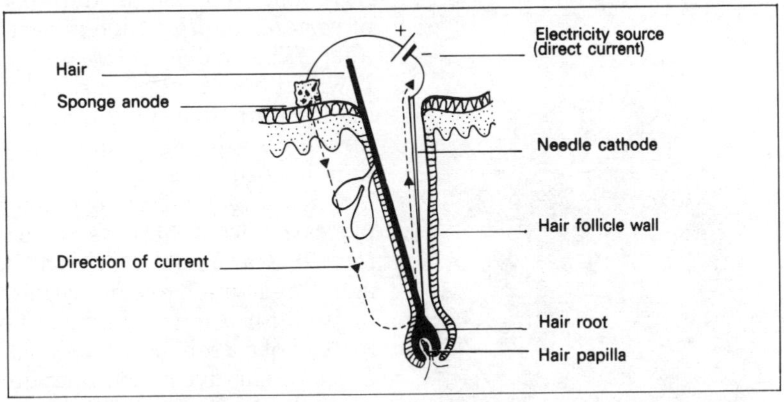

CHEMICAL DEPILATORIES

Chemicals act as depilatories when they break down the *keratin* molecules of the hair. The hair then breaks into small pieces and can be wiped away. The older chemical depilatories contained *barium* or *sodium sulphide*, and had an unpleasant 'bad eggs' smell. Modern depilatories contain *calcium thioglycollate* made alkaline by calcium hydroxide to give a pH between 10 and 12·5. These depilatories have a smell like that of cold wave perming lotion which also contains a thioglycollate. The pH of cold wave lotion must be below 9·5 or it will act as a depilatory. Because the cornified layer of the skin, like hair, is composed of *keratin*, chemical depilatories will also affect the skin and must not be left on for longer than the specified time given by the manufacturer. Before using a chemical depilatory for the first time it is advisable to test it on a small area of the skin. Chemical depilatories should be used only on *healthy* undamaged skin and no other chemicals, e.g. *antiperspirants*, applied to the skin within 24 hours. Chemical depilatories are used to remove hair from the armpits and legs.

10.9 Use of wax depilatory

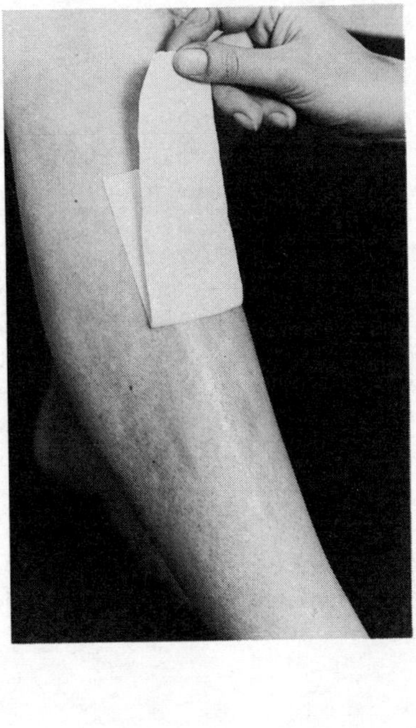

DEPILATORY WAXES usually contain a mixture of *paraffin waxes* and *beeswax* blended to produce a solid with a low melting point. It changes its state from solid to liquid just above skin temperature. The wax is *melted* and spread on to the skin which cools it slightly so that it *solidifies* as a strip. The wax strip is pulled quickly away from the skin in the opposite direction to that in which the hair grows, so that all the hairs embedded in the wax will be removed. Depilatory waxes are mainly used to remove facial hair.

ABRASIVE DEPILATORIES are rubbed lightly over the skin and cut off the hairs at skin level, so producing the same effect as shaving. *Pumice* stone or *emery* gloves are used on the legs as abrasive depilatories.

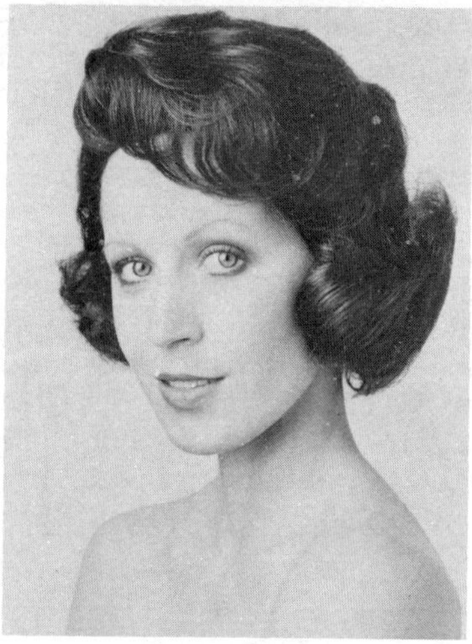

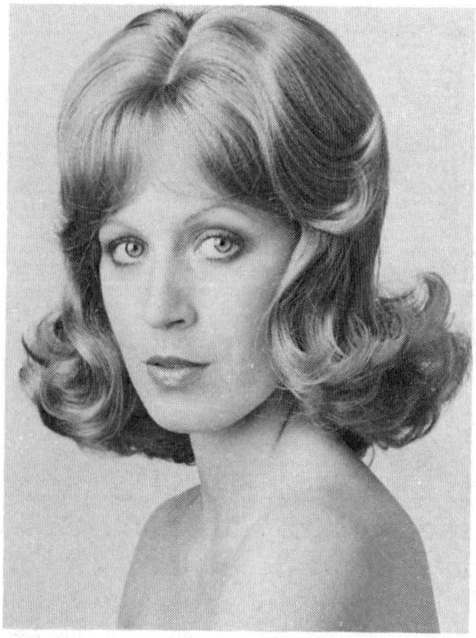

10.10 Women's wigs—modacrylic and human hair

Wigs and hairpieces

The *fibres* used for making wigs are either *human hair* or *modacrylic*, a man-made *synthetic* fibre similar to acrylic fibres such as Courtelle. Synthetic fibres are produced from long chain molecules, or *polymers*, built up from simple organic chemicals derived from oil or coal tar. *Hairpieces* are usually made of *human hair*, as they must blend in with the wearer's hair and so have a similar colour and texture. Human hair consists of fibres of *variable width* which gives the characteristic 'natural' appearance. It has a deep *lustre* and its colour does not fade. On burning it will flare slightly, particularly if much lacquer has been used on the hair. It is *hygroscopic*, absorbing water vapour from the air which reduces the amount of *static* electricity produced on the hair by brushing. It is easy to *set* and is readily re-styled. A *dry-cleaning fluid* is recommended for cleaning wigs and hairpieces made of hair as water rots the base. *Modacrylic* fibres (Dynel, Kanekalon, Teklan) have a much more *uniform width*, and fibres which are finer than the average for human hair must be used for a natural effect. The fibres also have a *surface gloss* instead of a deep lustre which detracts from a natural appearance. Some of the dyes used change colour becoming slightly redder, as well as fading, in strong light. Modacrylic fibres *melt* but do not flare. They are not hygroscopic and will *retain static* electricity which makes them less manageable than human hairs. They have to be *set* by using *heat* (82°C), and are difficult to re-style. Wigs made from modacrylics are uncomfortable in *warm* conditions because they trap a layer of insulating air in the wearers own hair below. Modacrylic wigs are best washed in *lukewarm water* and *shampoo* and dried naturally.

Practical work

1 ELECTROLYSIS

Connect a copper electrode by a wire to the positive (red) terminal of a Nife battery. Connect a D.C. ammeter measuring a current up to 1 amp to another copper electrode by a wire, and join the other terminal of the ammeter to the negative (black) terminal of the battery. Half fill a large beaker with 3% sodium chloride solution, place the electrodes in the salt solution, and take a reading of the current flowing through the ammeter. Replace the salt solution in the beaker by the following liquids in turn: methylated spirit, sucrose (sugar) solution, distilled water, and very dilute sulphuric acid. Which of these liquids are electrolytes?

2 DEPILATORY ACTION OF THIOGLYCOLLATES

Make an 8% solution of thioglycollic acid by adding 8 ml (cm^3) of thioglycollic acid to 92 ml (cm^3) of distilled water in a 100 ml (cm^3) measuring cylinder. Divide this solution between two

10.11 Electrolysis experiment

beakers. Using a dropper pipette add 0·88 ammonium hydroxide solution (CARE. Do not inhale the choking fumes) one drop at a time to each beaker in turn. Stir the solution with a glass rod and test its pH with pH paper after adding each drop of alkali. Adjust the pH in one beaker to 9, and in the other beaker to 14. Add some hair clippings to each beaker and leave them in the solution. After 30 minutes remove some of the hairs from each beaker, rinse them in water, and test by pulling gently to see if the hair breaks up. After a further 30 minutes remove a little more hair from each beaker, rinse, and test again. The hair can be left for further periods of time if necessary. Compare the depilatory effect of the two solutions.

3 HAIR LOSS

Count the number of hairs you remove from your scalp each day for one week, when brushing or combing your hair. Work out the daily average loss by dividing the week's total of hairs removed by seven. Compare your average with that of other students.

Multiple choice questions

1 From which of the following regions of the skin does hair growth occur?

a germinating layer *b* dermal hair papilla
c outer root sheath *d* inner root sheath

2 When a hair is in the resting condition it is known as

a a lanugo hair *b* the anagen stage *c* a club hair
d a secondary germ

3 The condition called Alopecia areata has the following symptoms

a round bald areas on the scalp
b hair recedes at the temples
c hair becomes thinner on the crown
d hair grows on the upper lip in women

4 The frequent cutting of hair to maintain a short style

a slows down hair growth
b increases the thickness of the hair fibres
c increases the rate of hair growth
d has no effect on the rate of hair growth

5 Skin will conduct an electric current, the salty tissue fluid acting as an

a electrode *b* ion *c* electrolyte *d* anode

6 The active ingredient of most modern depilatory creams is Calcium

a oxide *b* thioglycollate *c* sulphate *d* carbonate

7 The man-made fibre most commonly used for making wigs is

a keratin *b* nylon *c* modacrylic *d* courtelle

8 The hygroscopic property of natural hair has the effect of

a making it dry rapidly
b increasing the amount of sebum
c making it likely to flare on burning
d reducing the amount of static electricity

9 The property which makes some waxes suitable for use as depilatories is

a a crystalline structure *b* a low melting point
c they resist a change of state
d they change hair chemically

10 Cells of the hair shaft differentiate into cuticle, cortex, or medulla cells in the

a matrix *b* inner root sheath *c* epithelial column
d upper bulb

11 Scalp Treatments

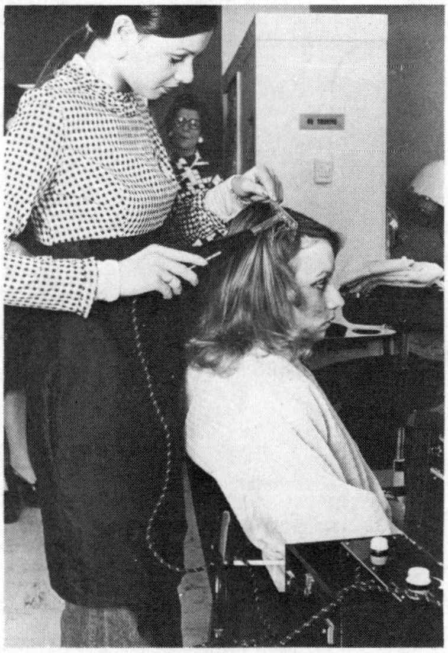

The intended effect of the various types of scalp treatment given in addition to the normal salon service of shampooing, setting, tinting, etc., is to improve the *circulation* of blood to the scalp. An improved blood supply brings more food and oxygen to the scalp which makes the sebaceous glands more active and encourages hair growth.

11.1 Vibro-machine in use

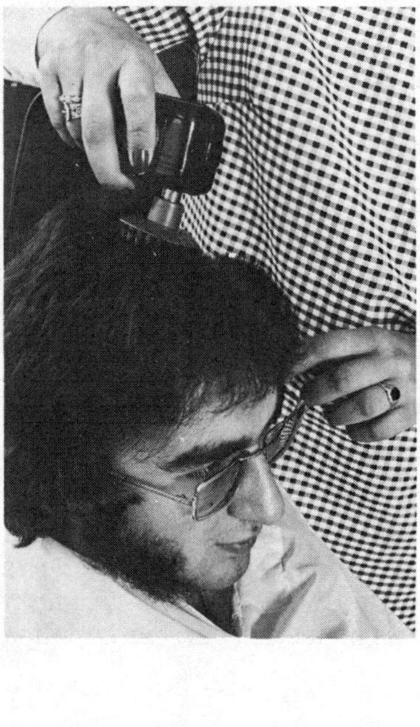

Heat treatments
Heat will increase the blood supply to the scalp by causing the blood *capillaries* in the dermis to *dilate*. The source of heat may be either the steamer, accelerator (see Chapter 9), hot towel, or hot oil. For a *hot oil* treatment a vegetable oil, e.g. *olive oil*, is warmed to 55°C and then brushed on to the hair. In addition to the heating effect, the oil will *condition* very dry hair. For a *hot towel* treatment the towel is soaked in water at 60°C, wrung out thoroughly, and wrapped tightly round the client's head. The accelerator transfers heat to the scalp by *radiation*; the steamer, hot oil, and hot towel do so by *conduction* (see Chapter 14).

Massage
This treatment increases the blood supply because *friction* (rubbing) produces *heat*. Massage may be *manual*, using the fingers to produce the friction. Small circular movements of the finger tips move the scalp over the underlying bones of the cranium to which it is loosely attached. The *weight* of the body is used in pressing with the fingers. *Pressure* is the *weight* divided by the *area* of surface it is resting on. The smaller the surface area that a given weight has contact with, the greater the pressure. In manual massage the pressure on the scalp will be greater if only the *tips* of the fingers are in contact with the scalp.

Massage can also be carried out with a *vibrator* massage machine (vibro-machine). In this machine an *electric motor* (see Chapter 14) vibrates a *shaft* to which rubber *applicators* are attached. The vibration produces friction between the applicator and the scalp, and the blood supply is increased.

High frequency treatment
The high frequency apparatus consists of a *machine* to which glass or metal *electrodes* are connected by leads, through an *insulated handle*. The electrodes transfer the electric current to the scalp. The *mains* electricity supply must be changed by the machine to produce the small, high voltage, *high frequency* current used in the treatment.

THE MAINS ELECTRICITY SUPPLY
The flow of electrons making up an electric current (see Chapter 5) may be steady and in one direction only. This is known as a *direct* current (D.C.). On the other hand the direction of flow of electrons in a circuit may reverse many times a second, when the current is said to be *alternating* (A.C.). A complete *cycle* is said to have occurred when the current flows one way, then changes and flows in the opposite direction in the circuit. Thus the current has changed direction at the beginning of each cycle, and changes again half-way through it, so changing direction *twice* in every cycle. The *number of cycles* in each *second* is the *frequency* of the current.

Large scale electrical *generators*, or *dynamos*, at the power stations which produce the mains electricity supply, usually give an alternating current. The *mains* current has a *frequency* of 50 cycles/second, now called 50 hertz (Hz). This means that there is a change of direction 100 times every second. In a dynamo the current is produced by rotating a *coil* of wire between the two poles of a *magnet*. The movement of the wire across the lines of force in the magnetic field (see Chapter 17) produces an *induced* electric current in the wire.

11.2 Dynamo generating an alternating electric current

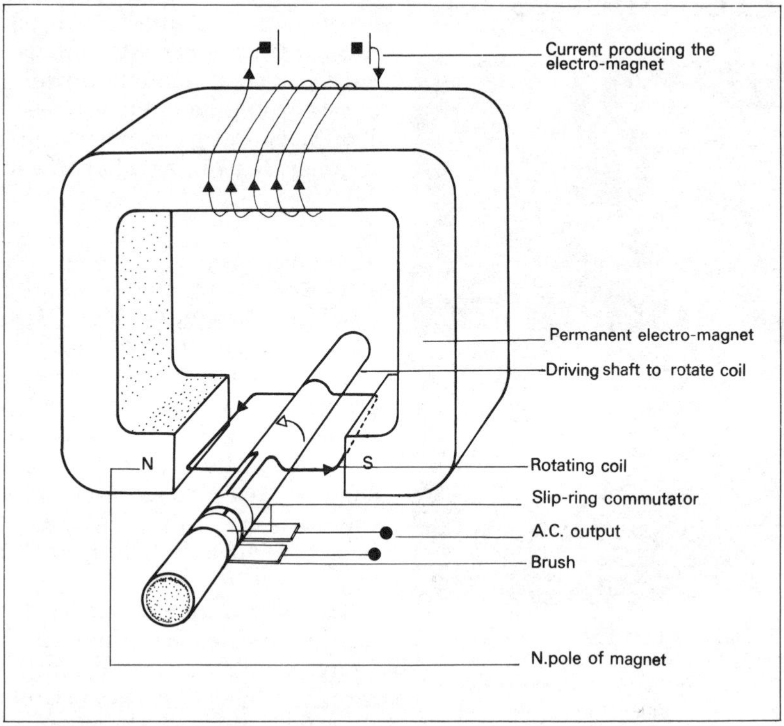

In most cases it is immaterial whether A.C. or D.C. current is used. Electric heating and lighting are unaffected by the direction of flow of the current. Galvanic electrolysis for hair removal, and re-charging *secondary cells* (accumulators) with a *battery charger*, are two processes which require a direct current. If only alternating current is available and a direct current is required, it must be changed by a *rectifier*. This allows electrons to pass through it in one direction only, so that A.C. becomes D.C. The electricity produced in power stations has a *high voltage*, being at a pressure of 11,000 volts. This current passes into the power lines of the *National Grid*, and is transmitted through them at a pressure of 132,000 volts, because at this *higher voltage* less electricity is converted into heat and wasted. To increase the voltage between the power station and the National Grid a *step-up transformer* is required.

11.3 National Grid lines and pylons

When the electricity arrives at the outskirts of a town, its voltage must be *reduced* to 240 volts by a *step-down transformer*. This 240 volt supply then comes into the salon. The changes in the mains electricity which occur in the high frequency machine are produced by the *induction coil* incorporated into it.

THE INDUCTION COIL

The induction coil has a *core* composed of a bundle of *soft iron* wires. Wound on top of the core are two coils of wire which are completely insulated from one another. The inner or *primary* coil is of thick wire and carries a large electric current supplied by a battery in the primary circuit. The *secondary* coil outside it has a very large number of turns of a much thinner wire. When the primary circuit is complete the current flowing through it *magnetizes* the soft iron wires of the core which therefore becomes an *electromagnet.* The primary circuit contains a *contact breaker.* This consists of a strip of *springy metal* which presses against a metal *pin.* The primary current goes through this springy metal strip and then through the pin. When the core becomes magnetized it attracts a soft iron *block* on the contact breaker and pulls the springy metal strip away from the pin, thus *breaking* the primary circuit. When this happens the core loses its magnetism so the soft iron block is no longer attracted. The springy metal strip then bends back and presses against the pin, *completing* the primary circuit again. There is a *condenser* in the primary circuit which prevents sparks being produced between the metal strip and the pin of the contact breaker.

Each time the circuit is *broken* the current *falls rapidly* in the primary coil. This change in the primary current produces an *induced* electrical pulse of *high voltage* in the *secondary* coil. When the current starts to flow in the primary circuit it takes a little while to build up, so that a *slow change* occurs and the electric *pressure* induced in the secondary coil is *small.* When the primary circuit is *broken* the current *stops* immediately so the electric *pressure* induced in the secondary coil is *large.* This pulse of high voltage (pressure) electricity in the secondary coil sparks across the *spark gap.* These pulses occur very frequently because contact is made and broken very rapidly by the contact breaker. The current is therefore said to have a *high frequency.* It changes direction as the contact is made and broken and therefore is an *alternating* current.

11.4 Induction coil

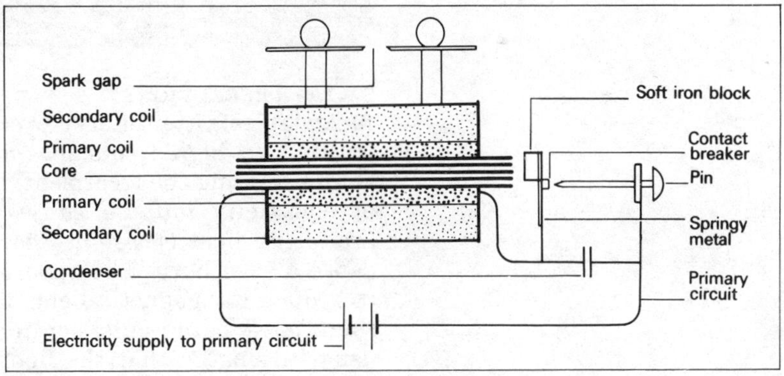

HIGH FREQUENCY MACHINE

In the high frequency machine the *mains* supply is connected to the primary coil of the induction coil, and provides the current in the *primary* circuit. The *frequency* of the mains alternating current is increased from 50 Hz to around 20,000 Hz by the machine, and the *voltage* is increased to over 2000 volts. The current however is very small, remaining too small to penetrate far enough into the body to cause an electric shock.

THE ELECTRODES

The high frequency current produced by the machine is transfered to the *electrodes* inside which the sparking occurs. This generates electrical *eddy currents* which are converted into *heat* in the skin in contact with an electrode. The higher the frequency of the current the greater the loss from eddy currents, and the greater the heat produced. Eddy currents remain at the *surface* of the skin; they do not penetrate. The *glass electrodes* which are hollow may be shaped like a *rake* or a flattened *bulb*, and are drawn over the scalp. Alternatively, the *metal electrode* is held in one of the client's hands and the insulated handle in her other hand, while the operator massages the client's scalp with her fingers.

11.5 High frequency electrodes—glass (rake and bulb) and metal types

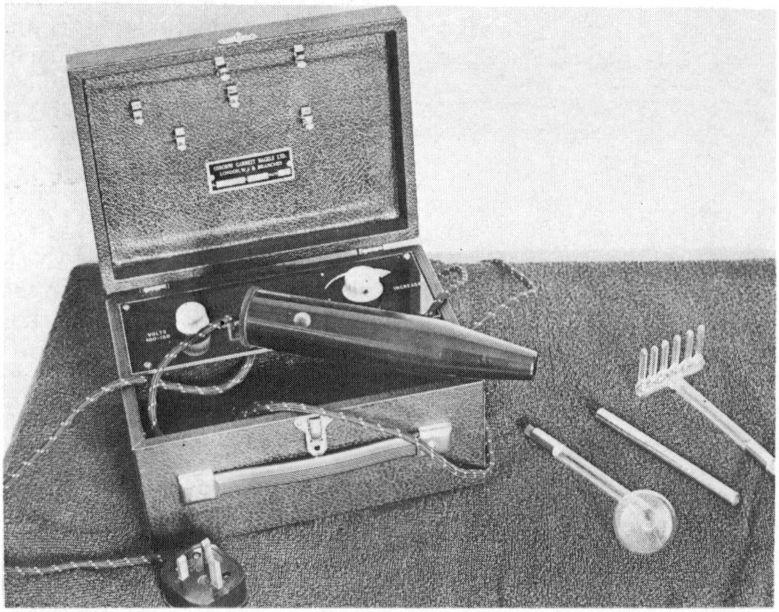

SAFETY PRECAUTIONS

Metal objects (jewellery) worn by the client and likely to be within the high frequency *magnetic field* should be removed before starting the treatment. Because metal is a good *conductor* of electricity *induced eddy currents* will circulate within it producing heat (*resistance heating*), which may be sufficient to cause a skin burn. The apparatus should be effectively *screened* to reduce its magnetic field. The clients hair must be dry, and there must be no cuts, scratches or bruises on the scalp. It is usual to ensure that the floor is dry in the part of the salon where treatment is being given. The electrodes should be *sterilized* after use by wiping them over with ethanol, or placing them in a sterilizing cabinet.

OZONE

The electric *spark* produced by the induction coil in the high frequency apparatus produces *ozone*, a gas with a characteristic smell, which is noticeable when giving a high frequency treatment. Ozone molecules are composed of *oxygen atoms* joined in groups of three, whereas in gaseous oxygen molecules the atoms are in pairs. Ozone is an *antiseptic*, as it readily gives off the third oxygen atom which will destroy micro-organisms (see Chapter 15). At high concentrations, ozone becomes poisonous.

Multiple choice questions

1 A transformer would be used to change
a A.C. into D.C. *b* the electrical pressure
c the frequency of the current
d the wattage of the current

2 The frequency of the electric current supplied to the salon by the Electricity Board is
a 20 Hz *b* 50 Hz *c* 250 Hz *d* 20,000 Hz

3 The high frequency machine is able to increase both the voltage and the frequency of the mains supply because it contains
a an induction coil *b* a rectifier *c* a vibrator
d a dynamo

4 The outer coil of wire in an induction coil in which a high frequency current is induced is described as
a magnetic *b* primary *c* secondary *d* step-down

5 An electric current in which the direction of flow of electrons is continually reversing is
a an eddy current *b* a transformed current
c an alternating current *d* a direct current

6 The gas with antiseptic properties produced when a high frequency treatment is given is
a oxygen *b* chlorine *c* argon *d* ozone

7 The increased flow of blood to the scalp during manual massaging is caused by
a frictional heat *b* mechanical vibration
c static electricity *d* latent heat

8 A client's jewellery should be removed before starting a high frequency treatment as it may become
a magnetized *b* electrified *c* heated *d* insulated

9 The large scale production of electricity in a power station is by a
a transformer *b* rectifier *c* motor *d* generator

10 The voltage at which an electric current is distributed on the National Grid is
a 240,000 *b* 132,000 *c* 11,000 *d* 240

12 Manicure and Pedicure

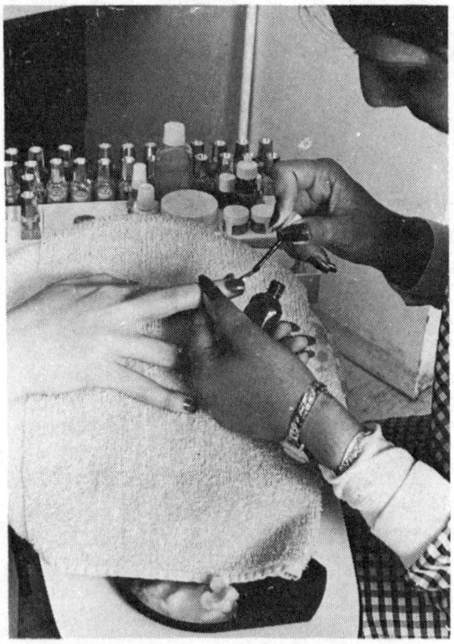

Nails occur on the end section of each finger and toe, and are protective structures developed from the *epidermis* of the skin. A hairdresser's hands are very conspicuous, so they should be well cared for, and look as attractive as possible. Many salons provide a manicure service for their clients.

Structure of nails

Each nail is a horny curved plate made of *keratin*. The nail plate consists of the *root*, or buried part, the *body*, forming most of the visible part, and the free *edge*. The nail root is inserted into the epidermis which splits horizontally the upper part forming the *nail fold* and *cuticle*, and being the remains of the horny layer. The part of the epidermis lying below the nail fold and nail root is the *matrix*, which extends forward below the half-moon or *lunula*. The matrix is part of the *germinating* layer of the epidermis, and is the region from which the nail grows. The nail plate is a thickening of the *clear* layer of the epidermis.

In the *nail bed* below the body of the nail, the dermis is *ridged*, instead of having the usual projecting papillae. The colour of the *blood* in the dermal capillaries shows through the transparent nail plate, which looks pink.

Growth of nails

On average, nails *grow* 0·1 mm each day, although finger nails grow faster than toe nails, and nail growth is faster in summer than in winter. Some *illnesses* have an effect on nail growth, and may cause horizontal *ridges* in the nail. Nails grow by the division of cells of the *matrix* at the base of the nail and it is probable that the nail bed also plays a part in nail growth.

Effect of diet on the nails

Nails become rough, brittle, and deformed if the diet is deficient in *iron*. Increased *calcium* in the diet (from drinking extra milk) improves the shine on nails, and hardens them. Brittle nails can also be treated by taking up to 7 g of *gelatin* a day (by eating table-jelly cubes).

Care of the nails

The finger nails should be *filed* from each side towards the centre, to produce an oval shaped nail plate. An *emery board* is best for this purpose, making the free edge less likely to break or split. The nails should not extend far beyond the end of the finger, because of the danger of scratching the client.

The *toe nails* should be cut *straight* across, and kept as *short* as possible. Long toe nails may cut the skin on adjacent toes, or become ingrowing.

12.1 Surface view of nail
Section through end of finger (right)

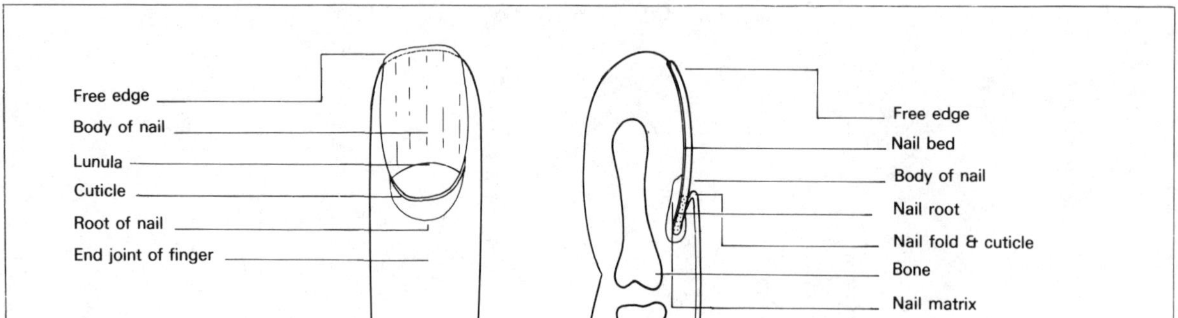

Before attempting to push back the *cuticle*, the hands or feet should be soaked in warm water, to prevent cracking of the cuticle. Cotton wool soaked in *cuticle remover* and wrapped round an orange stick, may be used to push the cuticle back from the lunula. If the cuticles dry and crack, they readily become infected. *Cuticle cream* or hand cream rubbed into the cuticles after washing the hands will help to counteract dryness.

A *nail brush* and warm soapy water should be used to remove all traces of dirt from below the free edge of the nail. Nails are damaged by strong *detergents* which remove fatty material, leaving the nail brittle. Over-use of nail lacquers and removers have a similar harmful effect.

Nail cosmetics

These include cuticle remover and cuticle cream, nail varnish, and nail varnish remover.

CUTICLE REMOVERS

These are very weak solutions (2%) of the alkalis *sodium hydroxide* or *potassium hydroxide*, which are caustic, and dissolve away the cuticle. Alkalis also remove *sebum* from the skin, so that the area round the base of the nail may dry and crack. A skin softener like *glycerol* may be added to the cuticle remover to counteract this drying effect.

12.2 Applying cuticle remover

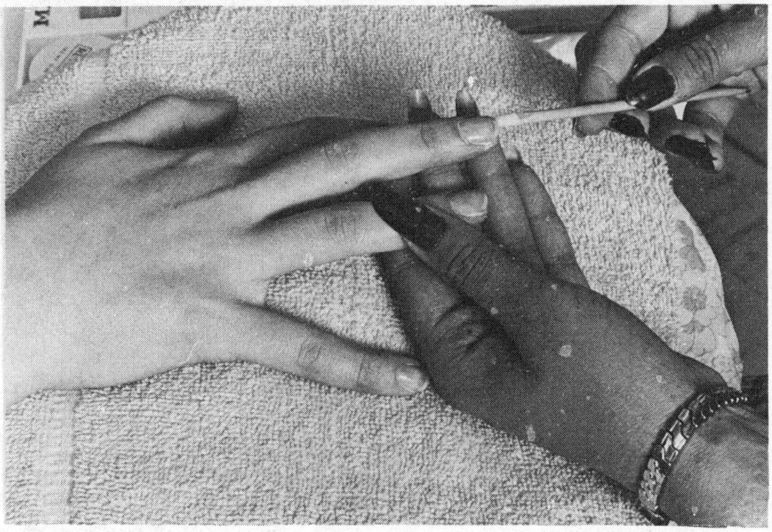

CUTICLE CREAMS

These are protective creams consisting of emulsions of *mineral oils* and water. *Beeswax* is usually included as an emulsifying agent.

NAIL VARNISH

After evaporation of the *solvent*, the lacquer which is left behind as a film on the nail is *nitrocellulose*, which holds the colour. As a nitrocellulose film does not stick to the nail very well, and chips readily, it is mixed with *formaldehyde resin*. This is a synthetic resin, which toughens the film, and helps it to stick. Other substances called *plasticizers* are added to give the lacquer film elasticity and prevent flaking. *Phthalates* are frequently used as plasticizers in nail varnish. All these materials

are dissolved in a mixture of *volatile solvents*, which evaporate at different rates, e.g. *acetone* evaporates very rapidly, *amyl acetate* more slowly. If the solvent evaporates very rapidly and the lacquer dries too quickly, the nail varnish does not flow well, and brush marks show on the nail. Very rapid evaporation of the solvent will *cool* the nail by removing *latent heat* from it. Atmospheric water vapour may then *condense* on the drying cold lacquer film and cause *cloudiness*. Too high a proportion of less volatile solvents will mean that the lacquer takes an inconveniently long time to dry. *Pearl* nail lacquers contain natural pearl essence obtained from fish scales (herring). Nail lacquers are *inflammable*, and must be kept away from heat and flames.
Base coat is a lacquer which is applied to the nail first, and allowed to dry before brushing on the coloured nail lacquer. Base coat contains an increased amount of resin, and is used to 'key' the lacquer on to the nail.

NAIL VARNISH REMOVER

Acetone is used as it dissolves nail varnish readily. As acetone is also a *fat solvent* it removes sebum from the skin round the nail, drying the cuticle. A little *glycerol* or *oil* is usually included in nail varnish remover to counteract the drying effect.

Care of the hands

The hairdressers hands are likely to suffer from the effects of being continually in and out of *water*, and having prolonged contact with *detergents* and other chemical solutions. This leads to *chapping*, which is a drying and roughening of the skin, deep cracks often developing in the *horny* layer. The skin is only supple and pliable when water forms 10% of its total weight. When immersed in water for some time, the horny layer of the epidermis will absorb a lot of additional water and *swell*. The stresses produced by the increasing volume break up the horny layer, displacing groups of cells. When the hands are removed from water and dried, the horny layer tries to return to its original size and shape, but some of the displaced cells remain sticking up at the surface, which is therefore rough. Evaporation of water is particularly rapid if *cold winds* are present, so chapping is worse in winter than in summer.

Detergents and alkalis also remove the natural *oily* secretion from the skin and this increases water loss from the horny layer. Normally the film of sebum retards evaporation of water from the skin surface. Where skin is dry, roughened, and cracked, germs can enter, and *infection* occur.

The best *protection* for the hands when hairdressing is to wear *rubber gloves*. When this is not acceptable, *barrier creams* designed for 'wet work' should be smoothed into the hands before starting work, and will need to be reapplied every three or four hours. *Hand cream* should be rubbed into the hands and left on overnight, to counteract the harmful effects of water and detergents. Hand cream is an *emollient*, or skin softener, consisting of an oil-in-water *emulsion*. The water it contains is absorbed by the horny layer, while the oil helps to prevent water loss by evaporation. It will also help to hold down the groups of projecting cells where the skin is roughened. A 2 : 1 mixture of *water* and *glycerol* can be applied to the hands at night, instead of hand cream. Glycerol is a *humectant*, being *hygroscopic*, so that it absorbs and holds water. Glycerol must never be used on the skin unmixed with water, or it will withdraw water from the epidermis and add to the drying effect.

Germs may collect on the skin of the hands, or under the nails, when cleaning the salon, or using the lavatory. The hands should always be washed, and the nails scrubbed, after either of these activities, or germs will spread on to tools, gowns, towels, or the client's skin or hair, from the hairdresser's infected hands.

Some of the hairdressing lotions used can inflame the skin, causing *dermatitis* (see Chapter 16). Oxidation *tints* and cold-wave *perming lotions* in particular may do so. A hairdresser should always protect her hands by wearing rubber gloves when applying these preparations.

Care of the feet

Hairdressing involves standing for many hours of the day and causes a good deal of strain on the feet. This is increased if the *muscles* of the feet are weak, and if the hairdresser adopts a *bad posture*. Aching feet result in irritability and loss of skill. The *shoes* worn by a hairdresser at work must be well-fitting and comfortable, with room for the toes to move independently. Ill-fitting shoes cause *corns* which are painful epidermal thickenings caused by pressure of the shoe on the skin. The *arch* of the foot should be supported, so that a low, but not completely *flat heel* is preferable. *Stockings* or tights should be the correct size, and should be washed daily. Sweat produced by the feet will be

12.3 Foot-toning exercises

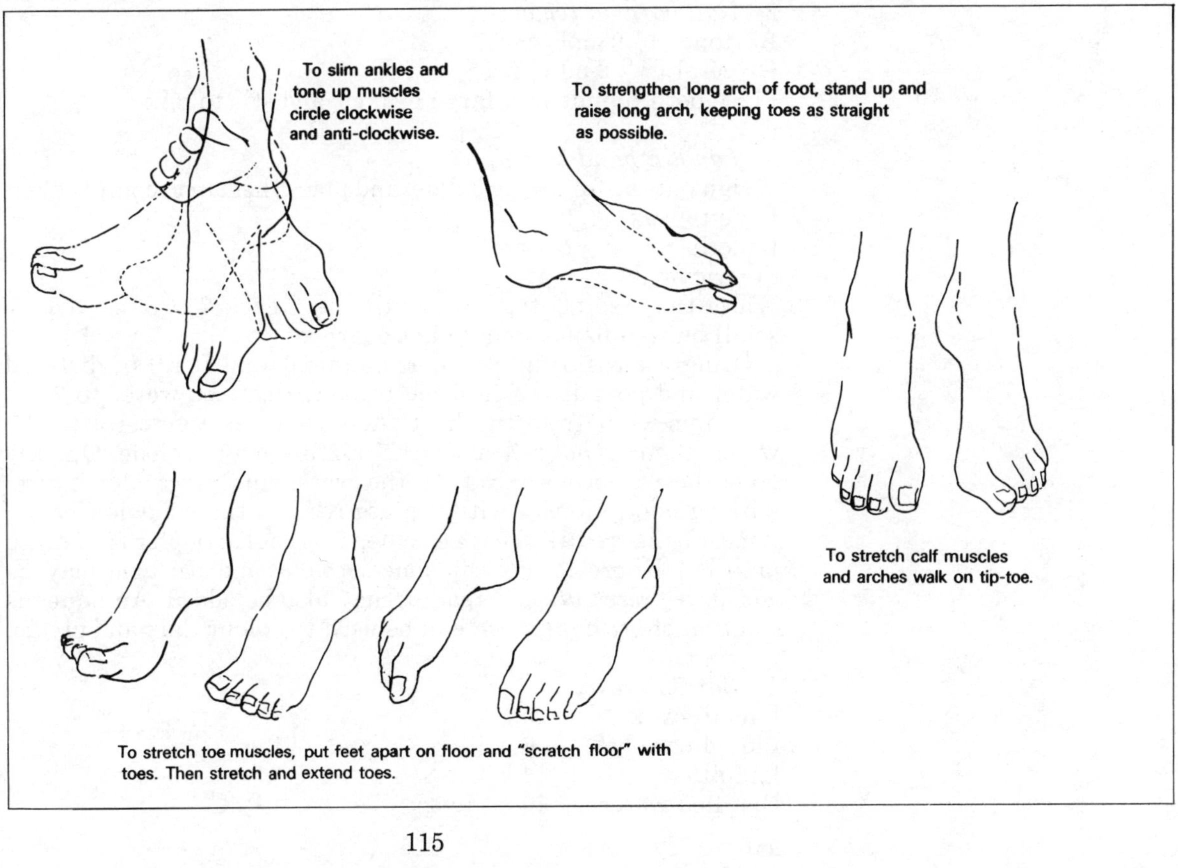

absorbed by the stocking, and if left on for any length of time will be broken down by bacteria and cause an unpleasant smell. Washing restores *elasticity* to the stocking fibres, so that holes and ladders are less likely to occur when stockings are pulled on and off.

The feet should be washed daily, and thoroughly dried, particularly between the toes, as warmth and moisture encourage attack by germs. *Talcum powder* (which is a mixture of calcium carbonate, talc, and magnesium stearate), smoothed on to the foot, and between the toes, will absorb some of the sweat. Any painful thickening of the outer horny layer of the skin can be removed by rubbing with soap and a *pumice* block while washing the feet.

Exercises which strengthen the muscles of the feet are shown on the previous page.

Practical work

PREPARATION OF COSMETICS FOR USE ON THE HANDS

1 *Cuticle remover*

Potassium hydroxide pellets	2 g
Distilled water	80 ml (cm^3)
Glycerol	20 ml (cm^3)

Dissolve the potassium hydroxide pellets in the distilled water in a large beaker. Potassium hydroxide is very caustic, so do not handle the pellets. Weigh them out on a filter paper, and use this paper to transfer them to a beaker containing the distilled water. Add the glycerol when the pellets have dissolved.

2 *Nail varnish remover*

Acetone	98 ml (cm^3)
Glycerol	2 ml (cm^3)

Place both liquids in a large beaker, and stir to mix.

3 *Lanolin hand cream*

Weigh out the following solids, and place them in a small beaker.

Lanette wax	9 g
Lanolin	6 g
Stearic acid	5 g

Warm these solids together until they reach 75°C. Use a very small bunsen flame, and do not overheat.

Using a measuring cylinder, obtain 100 ml (cm^3) of distilled water and pour it into a large beaker. Heat the water to 75°C, then remove it from the heat. Add 4 ml (cm^3) glycerol to the water, then do *not* reheat or the mixture may explode. Quickly pour the warmed waxes into the water and glycerol mixture stirring continuously with a glass rod. As the emulsion cools, it must be stirred all the time. When it is cool enough to pour into jars, but before it has thickened, *colour* and *perfume* may be added. A *preservative* (Nipagin) may also be added. An aqueous solution of *brilliant green* can be used to colour the hand cream.

4 *Barrier cream*

Lanette wax	20 g
Liquid paraffin	6 g
Lanolin	4 g
Distilled water	70 ml (cm^3)

Place the first three ingredients in a small beaker, and warm them to 75°C over a small flame. Do not overheat these oils and waxes. Heat the distilled water to 75°C in a large beaker, then pour the wax mixture steadily into the water, stirring all the time with a glass rod. Continue to stir, and add perfume, then pour into pots before the mixture thickens.

Multiple choice questions

1 The skin of the hands is more readily infected after frequent immersion in hot water and detergents because it
a loses water from the dermis *b* becomes dry and cracked
c secretes extra sebum *d* loses its epidermis

2 Nails are composed of a substance called
a matrix *b* gelatin *c* lunula *d* keratin

3 Acetone is used as a nail varnish remover because it is
a a fat solvent *b* a lacquer solvent *c* a volatile liquid
d an emollient liquid

4 A preparation containing nitrocellulose, pigments, resin, and suitable solvents would be
a cuticle remover *b* hand cream *c* corn remover
d nail varnish

5 Nails may become brittle following
a pressure on the nail bed *b* infrequent cutting
c over-use of lacquer and remover.
d excess calcium in the diet

6 Glycerol must not be used on the skin unmixed with water because it is
a emollient *b* hygroscopic *c* corrosive *d* caustic

7 Plasticizers are included in nail lacquer because they
a evaporate the solvent *b* prevent flaking of the lacquer
c dissolve nitrocellulose *d* give a pearly appearance

8 The nail plate is a modified
a epidermis *b* dermis *c* germinating layer
d cuticle

9 Rubber gloves should be worn when tinting because the tint
a removes sebum from the skin *b* may cause dermatitis
c stops transfer of germs to the client
d prevents chapping of the skin

10 A base coat may be applied under nail varnish to
a increase viscosity of lacquer
b prevent allergy due to the dye
c prevent brushmarks showing
d 'key' the lacquer to the nail

13 General Physiology and Health

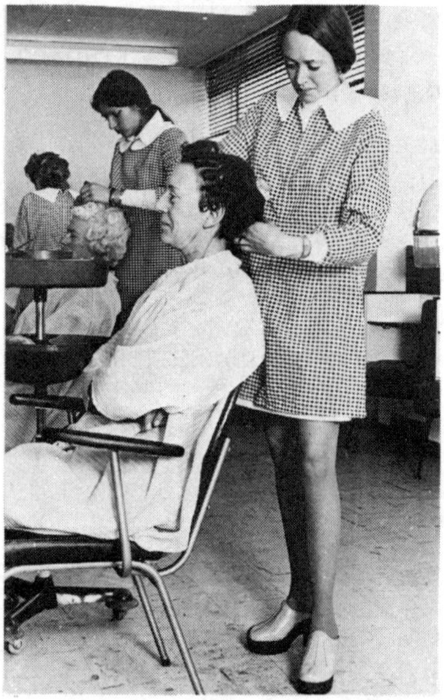

The *human body* has a characteristic structure or *anatomy*, and carries out a number of living processes. The study of the ways in which these processes occur is known as *physiology*. The efficient functioning of the body in carrying out the living processes is what we call *good health*.

Like all other living things, the human body is built up from very small units of living material called *cells*. These cells are of a number of different types. Where a group of similar cells occur together they form a *tissue*, e.g. a group of muscle cells will form muscle tissue. Each tissue has its particular use in the body. The tissues are arranged to form larger structures called *organs*, which have one, or a related group of functions, e.g. the *heart* is the organ with the function of pumping blood round the body.

The living processes of the body are concerned with the use and supply of *chemicals* and *energy*, and with the removal of *waste*. These processes are collectively called *metabolism*, and include nutrition, respiration, excretion, movement, growth, reproduction, and repair. The living processes must continue in spite of changes inside and outside the body, otherwise death occurs. This is known as *steady-state control* and is an important factor in keeping healthy. The nervous system is concerned in steady-state control through its action on metabolism. *Reproduction*, by producing new generations of human beings, perpetuates human life in the world.

Movement and posture

Movements of the body are brought about by the combined action of the *skeletal* and *muscular* systems.

THE SKELETAL SYSTEM

This is composed of a large number of separate bones, and has three main functions. It acts as a *framework* to support the body; it *protects* the softer organs, e.g. the skull protects the brain; it is used for the *attachment* of muscles. The bones act as *levers*, hinged at the *joints*, which can be pulled into different positions by muscles attached to the bones on either side of the joint. The muscles end in very strong inelastic *tendons*, by which they are attached to the bones. The bones are held together at the joints by very strong bands of tissue called *ligaments* which permit the correct movement of the bones.

The skeletal system consists of *axial* and *appendicular* parts. The *axial* part is made up of the *skull* and the spine or *vertebral column*, composed of thirty-three small bones called *vertebrae* lying one on top of the other. In the chest, or thoracic region, twelve pairs of *ribs* curve round the sides from the vertebrae. The upper ten pairs connect in front with the *sternum* or breastbone to form a cage-like protection for the heart and lungs. The last two pairs are the floating ribs.

The *appendicular* skeleton consists of the shoulder girdle, the arms, the hip girdle and legs. The shoulder girdle has the *clavicle*, or collar bone in front, and the *scapula* or shoulder blade at the back. The hip girdle, or *pelvis*, is a complete ring of bone connecting with the vertebral column at the back.

Both the arms and legs are built on the same plan of a single upper long bone below which lie two thinner long bones, side-by-side, connected to the hands and feet by a number of small bones at the wrist and ankle. The names of the individual bones are shown on the diagram of the skeleton (13.1).

13.1 Human skeleton side view (only left arm and leg included)

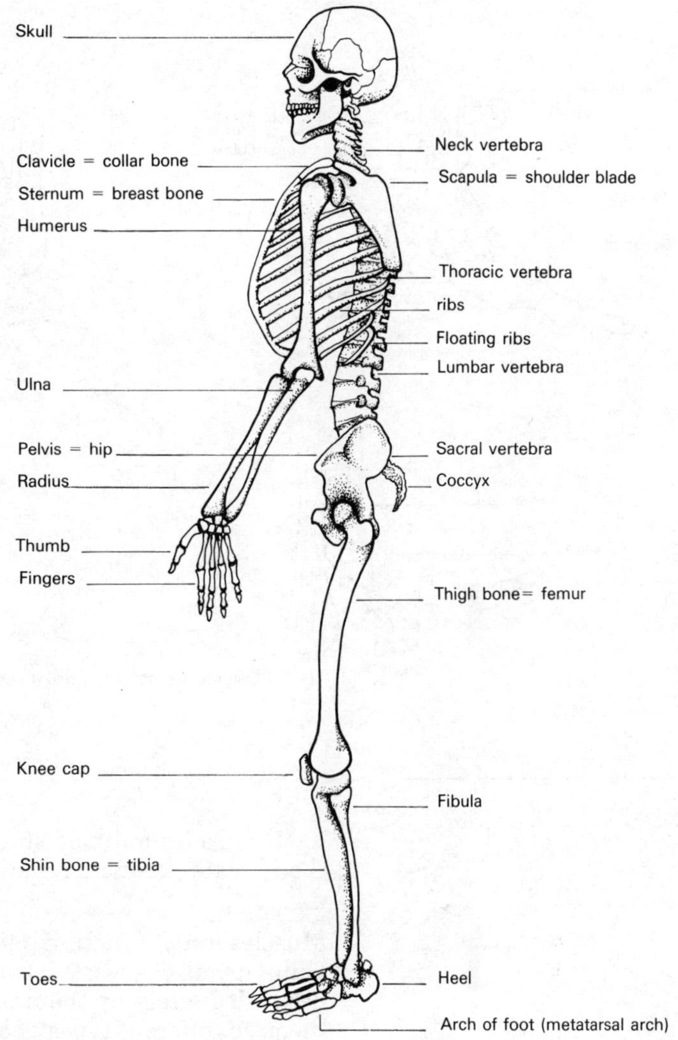

THE MUSCULAR SYSTEM

Muscles can only work by *pulling*, never by pushing. When a muscle is *working*, it uses up energy to make the fibres that compose the muscle shorten, or *contract*, becoming fatter. When a muscle is not working it is *relaxed*, but cannot stretch itself again. Most of the muscles that cover the bones are arranged in pairs which work together, so that one is contracting while the other is relaxing. Such *antagonistic pairs* of muscles move the limbs, e.g. calf and shin muscles form a pair which lower and raise the foot.

The muscle which is contracting moves the bones, which then stretch the relaxed muscle. Skeletal muscles of this type can be contracted at will, being *voluntary* muscles. A *nerve* brings the stimulus which starts the muscle contracting.

A different type of muscle occurs in many of the internal organs, e.g. in the walls of the stomach, and in the heart. Such muscles contract and relax spontaneously and are said to be *involuntary*.

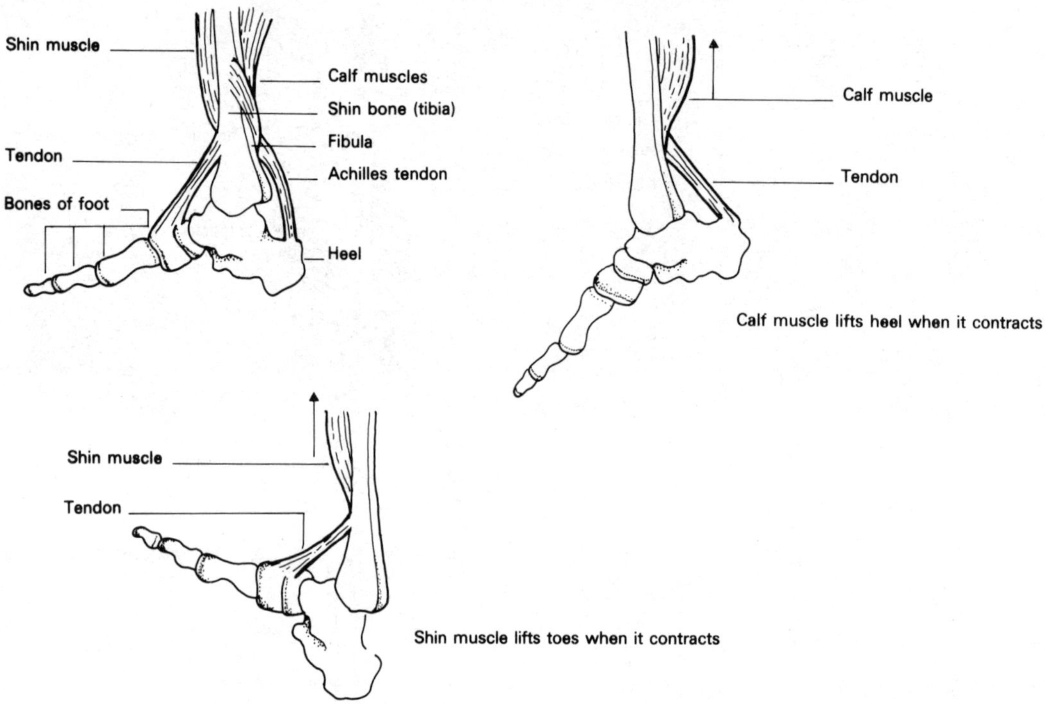

13.2 Muscles moving the foot

All muscles must be supplied with food and oxygen, and have their waste-products removed, by the *blood* supply.

EXERCISE

Muscles only function efficiently if they are used regularly. Unused muscle wastes away, or *atrophies*. Many muscles are used adequately by the hairdresser while at work, but not all of them, so different types of activity (walking, dancing, games and sports) are necessary to keep every muscle functioning well. *Exercise* also stimulates the circulation of the blood which brings a supply of food and oxygen to all parts of the body. During exercise, breathing occurs more rapidly, so the body obtains more oxygen. Exercise also improves digestion and appetite and the elimination of waste-products from the body.

POSTURE

Muscles maintain *posture* as well as bringing about movements in the body. Very little muscle action is needed to stand upright since the joints involved are almost vertically above one another, provided the bones of the skeleton occur in their correct positions.

Correct standing posture occurs when the weight of the body is carried equally on both legs, the natural slight curves of the spine are maintained, the hips and shoulders are level, and the head is held up, so that it is balanced on top of the spine. Common *faults* of standing posture are round shoulders, standing with most of the weight on one leg so that hip and shoulder girdles are tilted, and hollow back. Hollow back often results

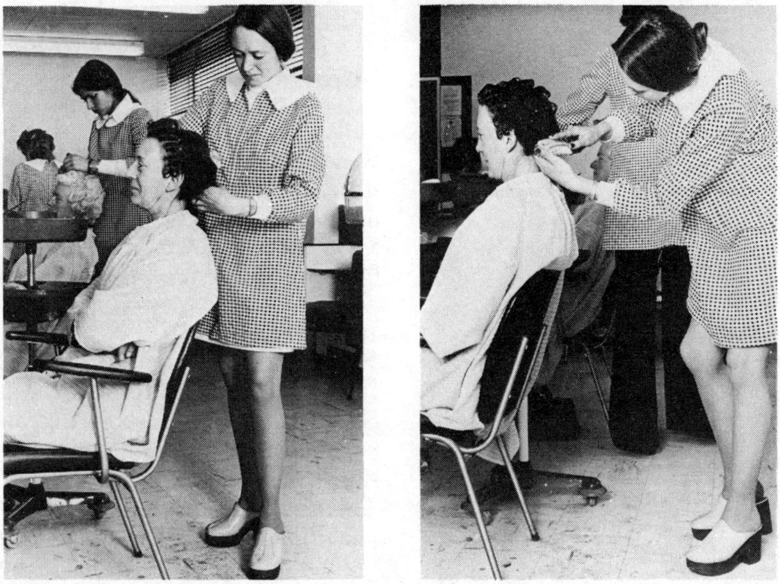

13.3 Good and bad standing posture

from wearing shoes with very high heels, or is a posture adopted by very tall girls in an attempt to look shorter.

Correct sitting posture requires the hips and most of the thighs to be supported by the chair. The bones should form a right-angle at the hip and knee. Common faults in sitting posture occur when the back and thighs are not supported, and only the base of the spine is in contact with the chair. Sitting with one leg tucked under the body puts considerable pressure on some of the blood vessels, so that the blood cannot circulate freely.

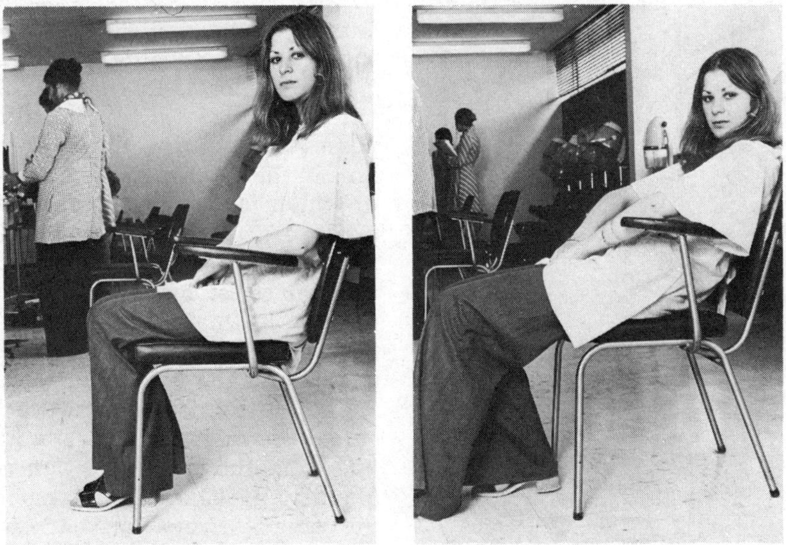

13.4 Good and bad sitting posture

Good posture allows the muscles to do the minimum amount of work in keeping the body upright. The muscles do not get tired so readily, and *muscle fatigue* is thus reduced. The symptoms of muscle fatigue are aching muscles, a slowing down of movement and clumsiness.

Food, digestion and diet

Food is needed by the body for three purposes. It is the source of *energy* and warmth, it is used for *growth* and repair; and to *protect* the body, keeping it healthy. The very large number of substances which we eat as food all contain one or more materials which the body needs. These components of food are known as *nutrients*, and there are six main types. *Carbohydrates* and *fats* are the nutrients mainly used to provide energy and warmth. *Proteins, mineral salts* and *water* are the nutrients used for body building. *Vitamins* are the protective nutrients.

DIGESTION

Some of the nutrients contained in the food are not in a suitable form for the body to absorb, as they will not dissolve in water. Such nutrients must be *digested*, being converted into simpler, *soluble* substances. Most carbohydrates, fats and proteins need digesting, while minerals and vitamins are already soluble. The digestion and absorption of food occurs in a long tube called the *alimentary canal*. Food is pushed along this tube by squeezing movements of the walls, known as *peristalsis*. The process of digestion involves breaking down the food by *chemical* changes. These chemical changes will occur only slowly at body temperature (37°C) so special *catalysts*, called *enzymes*, are present in digestive juices. These act on the food and speed up digestion. Movements of the walls of the alimentary canal churn up the food, and mix it with the digestive juices.

The *alimentary canal* is a continuous tube, opening at the mouth and the anus, and divided into several regions. The mouth opens into the *buccal cavity* where food is broken into small pieces by the teeth and rolled about by the tongue, so that it is mixed with *saliva*, a digestive juice secreted into the mouth by three pairs of salivary glands. Food is *swallowed* by movement of the pharynx (throat). A flap called the epiglottis closes over the entrance to the windpipe stopping food from 'going down the wrong way'.

The swallowed food passes down the *oesophagus*, being lubricated and digested by the saliva as it travels. The oesophagus passes through the thorax and enters the abdomen through a hole in the diaphragm. The tube now widens forming the *stomach*, in which food remains for up to six hours. The stomach walls produce a very acid juice, called *gastric juice*, which converts the food into a soup-like liquid called *chyme*. Peristaltic movements of the stomach wall churn up the food, and are particularly noticeable when the stomach is empty, just before normal meal times. *Alcohol* is absorbed through the stomach wall, and quickly passes into the blood, particularly when the stomach is empty.

The chyme passes into the first part of the small intestine, called the *duodenum*. Two alkaline digestive juices enter here; *bile* from the liver, and *pancreatic juice* from the pancreas, a gland lying below the stomach. The second part of the small intestine is a very long narrow tube, called the *ileum*. Its walls produce *intestinal juice* which completes the digestion of the food.

The end-products of digestion are *glucose* sugar from carbohydrates, *amino-acids* from proteins, and *fatty acids* from fats. These end-products are all soluble in water and are absorbed through the wall of the ileum, together with minerals and vitamins. The ileum wall has finger-like projections inside, called *villi*, which increase its absorptive surface. Most of the digested food is absorbed into the *blood* in the capillary networks of the villi, while the fatty end-products pass into the *lymph* vessels, one in the centre of each villus.

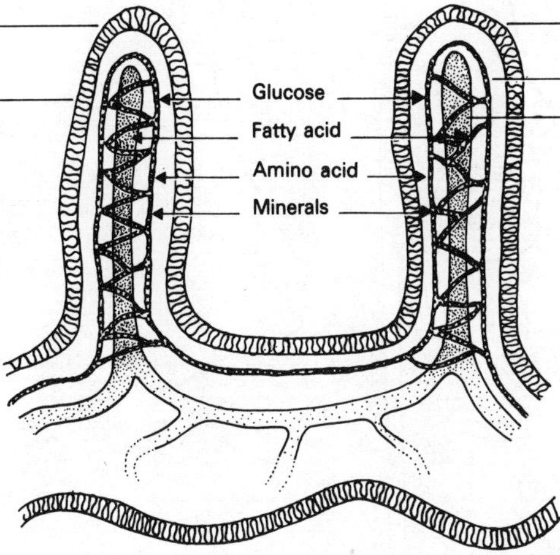

13.5 Section through ileum wall to show villi

The *blood* takes the absorbed food straight to the *liver*, the blood capillaries in the villi all joining up to form a *hepatic portal vein*.

In the first part of the large intestine, a wide tube called the *colon*, water is absorbed from the food remains. That part of the food that cannot be digested is called *roughage*, and eventually becomes the *faeces* which pass down the second part of the large intestine, the *rectum*, and are eliminated at the *anus* by the process of *defaecation*.

The *liver* has several other functions in addition to producing bile, stored temporarily in the gall bladder before passing down the *bile duct* to the duodenum. The liver receives all the food which has been absorbed into the blood through the ileum wall, and controls its *distribution*. A certain amount of food remains in the blood to be taken to the tissues, while surplus glucose is changed into storage materials. It either forms *glycogen*, stored in the liver and muscles, or is converted into *fat* and stored together with other fats under the skin, or round the organs. Surplus amino-acids cannot be stored, but are broken down to provide energy, the amine group being converted to the waste product urea, and removed by the kidneys.

DIET

A *balanced* diet contains all six main nutrients in adequate amounts for energy, growth, reproduction, and protection of the body. Each type of nutrient should be present in the food eaten at every meal.

Malnutrition is the result of having a diet which is inadequate

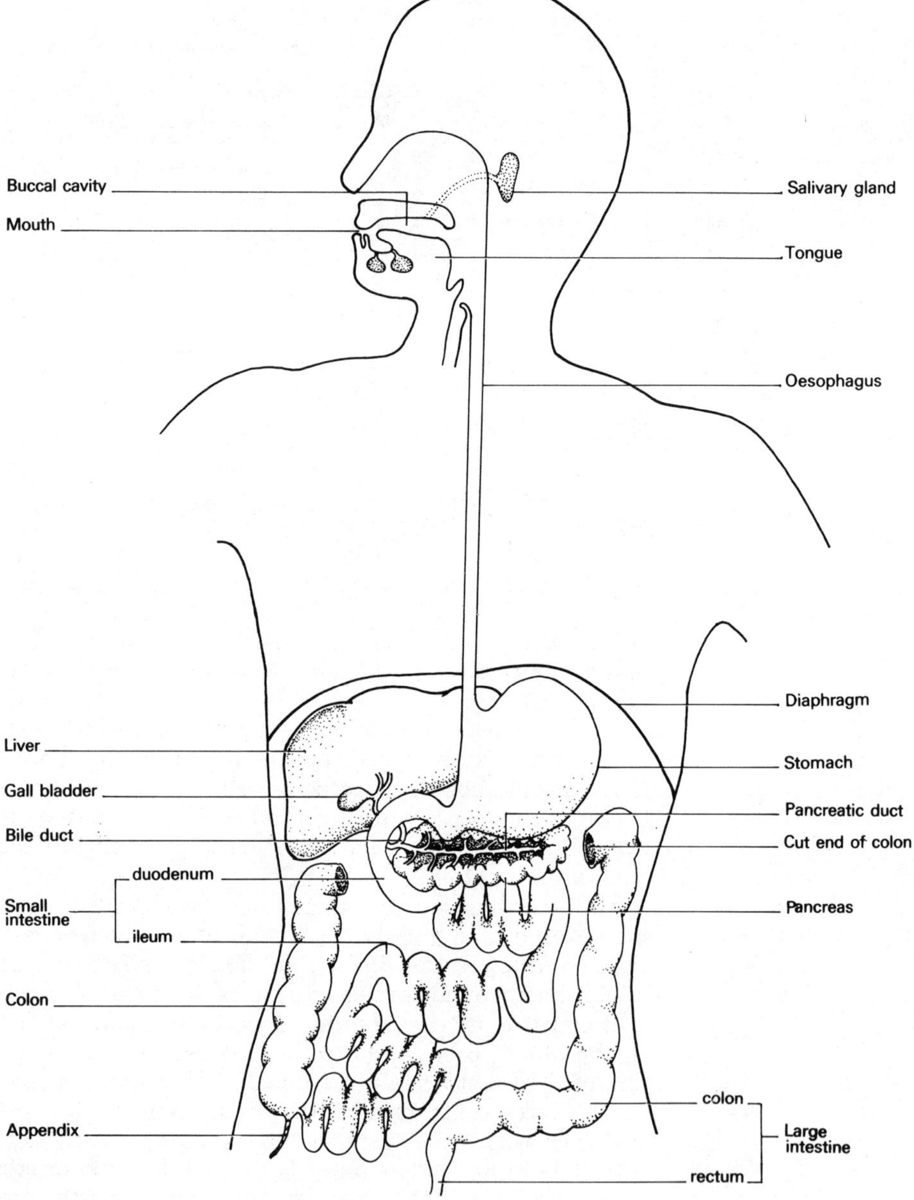

Buccal cavity
Mouth
Salivary gland
Tongue
Oesophagus
Diaphragm
Liver
Stomach
Gall bladder
Pancreatic duct
Bile duct
Cut end of colon
duodenum
Small intestine
Pancreas
ileum
Colon
colon
Appendix
Large intestine
rectum

13.6 Alimentary canal (opposite)

or not balanced. If all the nutrients are present, but in inadequate amounts for the body's needs, then *under-nutrition* and, eventually, *starvation* result. If one particular nutrient is lacking, then a *deficiency disease* may occur. *Rickets* is due to a shortage of Vitamin D; *scurvy* to a shortage of Vitamin C; and *anaemia* to a shortage of the mineral iron. Equally if too much of any one nutrient is present in the diet, malnutrition occurs. *Overweight* or *obesity* is a form of malnutrition found now in 80% of the adults in most developed countries, largely because people eat more carbohydrate than the body can use up in producing energy. Obesity is a major cause of much ill-health, increasing the likelihood of coronary heart disease, diabetes, and many other diseases, and resulting in death at an earlier age than would otherwise be expected.

Overweight can be treated by adopting a *slimming diet*, containing less than the required amount of energy-producing foods, so that the body will use up its stored fat. *Reducing* the amount of *carbohydrate* is the usual method of slimming. The amount of fat should not be reduced, or enough fat-soluble vitamins will not be obtained.

NUTRIENTS IN COMMON FOODS

Carbohydrates (starch and sugar) occur in bread, potatoes, cereals, cake, biscuits, sweets and chocolates. *Fats* occur in butter, cheese, egg-yolk, meat fat, milk, and margarine. *Proteins* occur in meat, eggs, fish and cheese.

Minerals. Calcium, for hardening bones and teeth, occurs in milk. *Iron*, needed for the red blood pigment, occurs in green vegetables. *Fluoride*, which reduces tooth decay, occurs in drinking water in some, but not all, areas.

Vitamins. These are a number of substances which are required in very small amounts in the food. Only one of these, Vitamin D, can be made by the body. It is made in the *skin* by the action of ultra-violet rays. *Vitamin A* gives resistance to skin and eye diseases. It increases the ability to see in dim light, and a shortage causes the skin, particularly on the backs of the arms and legs, to become rough and horny. *Vitamin D* is concerned in hardening bones and teeth. Both these two vitamins are fat-soluble, occurring in fatty foods such as butter, margarine, eggs, and fish oils.

Vitamin B which keeps the digestive and nervous systems functioning effectively, and helps the body to obtain energy from food, occurs in meat, liver, wholemeal bread, and marmite. *Vitamin C* helps wounds to heal, gives resistance to infection and keeps gums healthy. It occurs in fresh fruit and green vegetables. As it is rapidly destroyed by cooking, vegetables should be placed in already boiling water and cooked for the minimum time. Citrus fruits (grapefruit, lemons, and oranges) are a very good source of Vitamin C.

TEETH

Unhealthy gums and teeth are one of the causes of *bad breath* (halitosis). Food particles which remain between the teeth are broken down by bacteria in the mouth and produce substances which have unpleasant smells and which attack the teeth (causing decay, or *caries*) and the gums (causing *gingivitis* and *pyorrhoea*).

To keep the teeth healthy, they should be *brushed* from the gums to the tips of the teeth, inside and outside, to remove food caught between the teeth, and to massage the gums. They should be brushed after every meal if possible, and always at the end of the day, so that food does not remain on the teeth overnight.

Regular visits to the *dentist* will ensure that tooth decay is checked in its early stages. Tough *fibrous foods* (apples, carrots, celery) remove sticky food remains from the teeth, and help to keep them healthy. *Fluoride* treatment is helpful in preserving teeth from decay, if it is not already present in the drinking water.

13.7 Vertical section through a human tooth

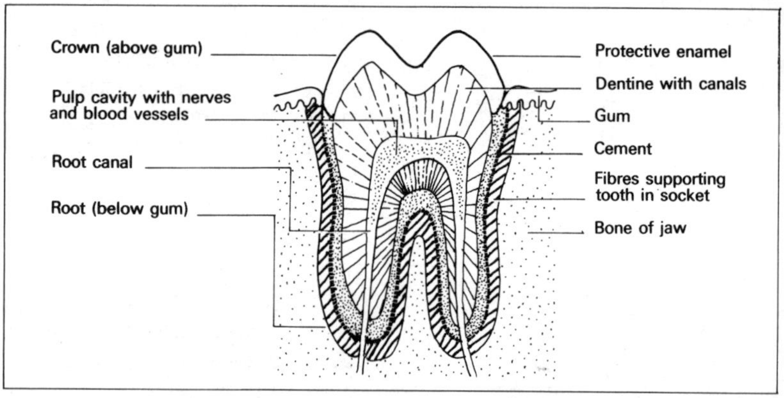

Respiration and breathing

Respiration is the process by which the body obtains a supply of *energy* for doing its work. It obtains the energy by breaking down energy foods, such as glucose sugar. The type of chemical change occurring in the breakdown of food to release energy is *oxidation*, for which oxygen is needed. The oxidation of energy foods is brought about by means of *respiratory enzymes*. The *waste* products produced during respiration are *carbon dioxide* gas and *water*.

$$\text{Energy food} + \text{Oxygen} \xrightarrow[\text{enzymes}]{\text{respiratory}} \text{Energy} + \underset{\text{dioxide}}{\text{carbon}} + \text{water}$$

This process is often called *tissue respiration*, as it occurs in every living cell of the body tissues. Each living cell must have a constant supply of energy food and oxygen, which are brought by the *blood*. The waste product, carbon dioxide, is removed by the blood.

The oxygen required is obtained from the *air* and must be brought into the body, so that it can pass into the blood, while carbon dioxide moves in the opposite direction. This process is known as breathing, or *gaseous exchange*. The two gases oxygen and carbon dioxide are exchanged across a respiratory surface provided inside the *lungs*.

The two lungs, and the system of tubes connecting them with the outside air form the *respiratory system*, and all the organs involved are contained in the head, neck, and thorax (chest).

Air can enter and leave the body through the nostrils or the mouth. The nostrils open into *nasal passages* in the nose, which are lined by a membrane secreting mucus. *Inflammation* of this

13.8 Human respiratory organs

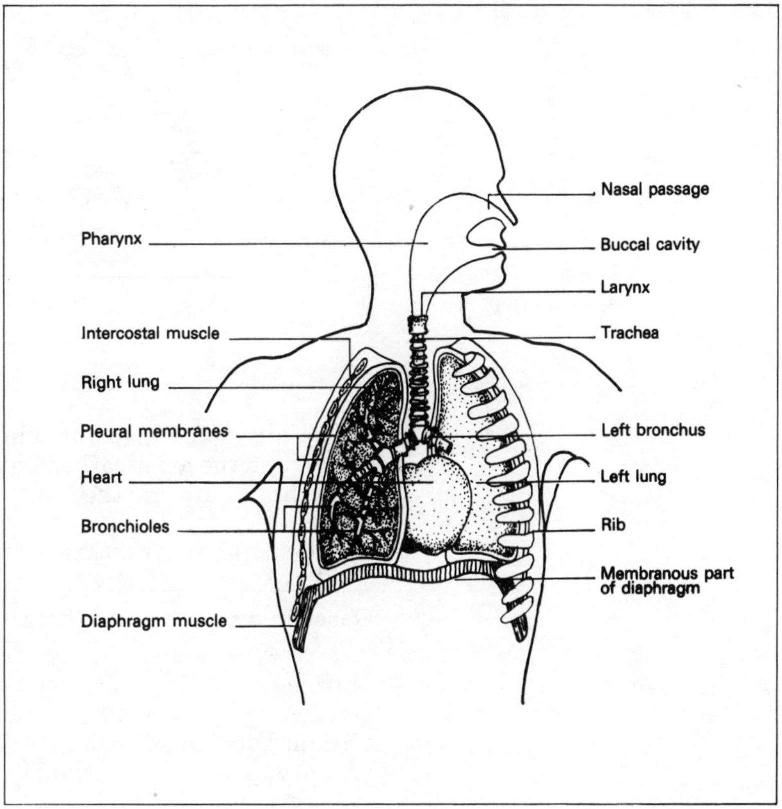

membrane by an infection may cause catarrh, or bad breath. As air passes over the membrane it is warmed, moistened, and has most of the dirt particles removed from it by the mucus. Air passing in through the mouth is similarly warmed and moistened, but less effectively. Breathing in through the *nose* protects the delicate lining of the lungs to a greater extent than mouth-breathing. The nasal passages lead into the *pharynx*, from which air enters the *larynx* (voice box) through an opening called the *glottis*. The larynx contains the stretched vocal cords which produce sounds as air passes between them. The larynx leads into the *trachea* (windpipe) which is held permanently open by C-shaped rings of cartilage. The trachea divides to form two *bronchi*, one leading to each lung. Like the nasal passages, these tubes are all lined by a wet *mucus membrane* from which small *hair-like* processes project. These beat outwards towards the throat pushing up mucus and dirt particles, which would otherwise get into the lungs. *Tobacco* smoke poisons these hair-like structures, and stops their protective action.

The lungs are made up of groups of tiny air spaces called *alveoli*, each group being connected to the bronchus by a fine branching tube or *bronchiolus*.

The wall of each *alveolus* is very thin, and contains a rich network of blood *capillaries*. The inside lining of the alveolus is covered by a thin film of *water*. *Oxygen* from the air in the alveolus dissolves in the water, and moves by diffusion through the alveolar wall into the blood. Carbon dioxide diffuses in the opposite direction.

13.9 Functional unit of the lung

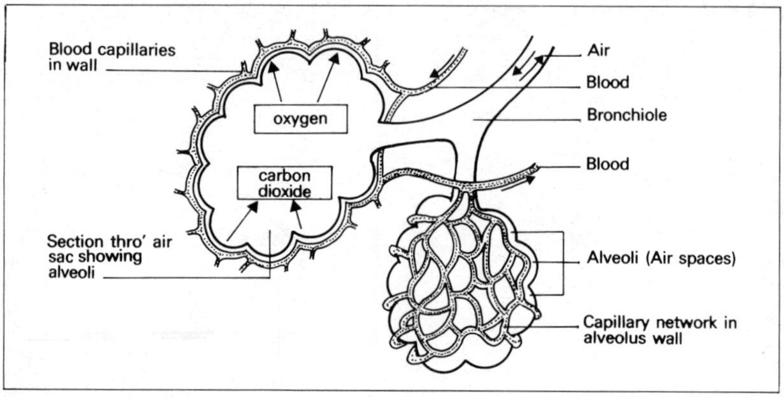

The air in the alveolus must be changed by *breathing movements*, and the air breathed out will have a different composition from that of air breathed in.

COMPOSITION IN VOLUMES PER CENT

Gases in air	Air breathed in	Air breathed out
Nitrogen	78	78
Oxygen	21	17
Carbon Dioxide	0.03	4
Water vapour	variable	increased

INSPIRATION OR BREATHING IN

To bring air from outside into the lungs the *chest cavity* must *increase* in size. This will lower the pressure inside the lungs, and air will enter until the pressure inside the lungs is as great as the pressure outside. The lungs are elastic, and will stretch to hold the increased volume of air.

To increase the chest cavity, the *diaphragm* muscles contract. The diaphragm forms the floor of the chest but bulges upwards into it, being pushed from below by the liver and stomach. The centre part of the diaphragm is composed of tough membrane with a ring of muscle round the edge. When this muscle contracts the diaphragm has a smaller diameter, and flattens, increasing the chest cavity from top to bottom.

13.10 Diaphragm action in breathing

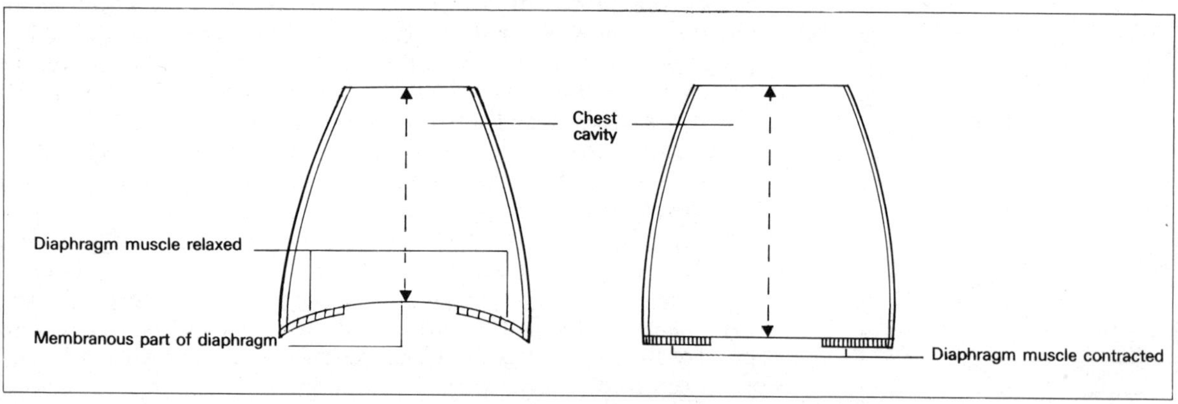

The *intercostal* muscles between the ribs also contract, and lift up the ribs so that they are horizontal, instead of sloping downwards. This lifting movement pushes the breastbone forward, thus increasing the circumference of the chest.

13.11 Action of intercostal muscles in breathing

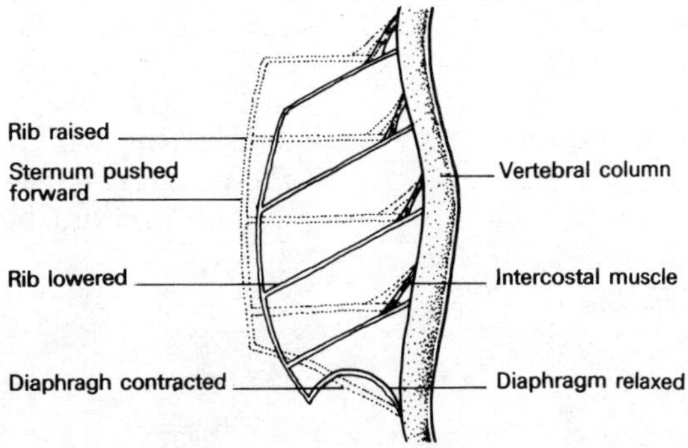

EXPIRATION OR BREATHING OUT

To force air out of the lungs after gaseous exchange has occurred, the *diaphragm* muscles relax, so that it again bulges up into the chest cavity. The intercostal muscles relax, and the ribs are lowered. The *chest* cavity thus becomes *smaller*, and the air inside the lungs is forced out by the increased pressure upon it.

SMOKING AND HEALTH

If tobacco smoke is inhaled, solid particles in the smoke and droplets of tar enter the trachea and bronchi, and are deposited in the air sacs of the lungs where they accumulate.

It has been shown that among people dying of lung cancer (30,000 each year) there is a higher proportion of heavy smokers, particularly cigarette smokers, than in the population generally, and deaths from lung cancer are increasing each year. *Giving up smoking* at any time reduces the chance of dying from lung cancer. Women who smoke during *pregnancy* produce babies up to 0·23 kg (8 oz) lighter, and are more likely to miscarry or have a still-born child.

The circulatory system

The body needs to *move* substances from one place to another, and does so by its *vascular* (or circulatory) system. The heart pumps blood through tubes called *blood vessels.* The substances that the blood is carrying must pass through the walls of the blood vessels to reach the living cells.

BLOOD

Blood consists of a pale yellow watery liquid called *plasma* in which large numbers of small *blood cells* float.

The majority of these cells are *red*, giving the blood its characteristic colour. A few of the cells are white. *Red* blood cells are small, circular, biconcave discs filled with the purple pigment *haemoglobin*, a compound containing *iron.* Haemoglobin takes up *oxygen* gas, becoming bright red, and is then called *oxyhaemoglobin.* Red blood cells wear out in about three months, so the body must produce them continuously in the red *marrow*, which occurs in the centre of the *bones*. When the concentration of haemoglobin in the blood is below normal, the condition is called *anaemia*. One cause is a shortage of iron in the diet. *White* blood cells are slightly larger than the red ones. They have a less regular shape, and contain a *nucleus*. They are able to move independently, and can squeeze out of the fine blood vessels into the tissues. *Blood platelets*, which are very small floating fragments, also occur. The blood *plasma* also contains a number of substances which are *dissolved* in it. It contains salts, soluble food materials, waste substances, blood proteins (fibrin), hormones, and antibodies.

13.12 Blood smear

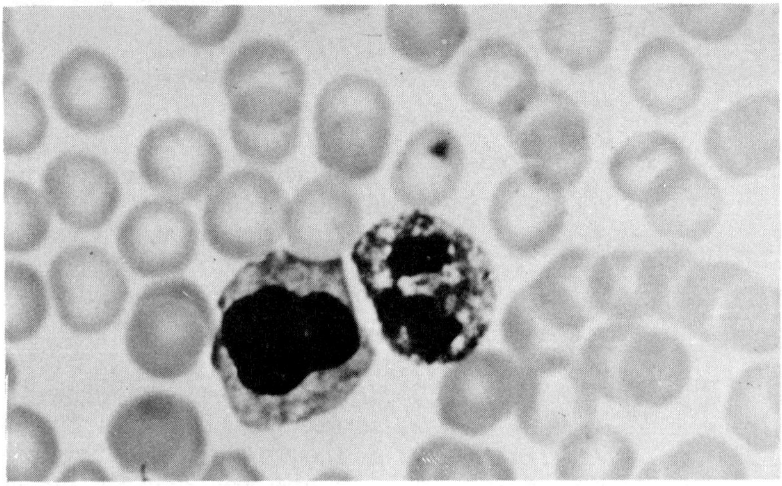

13.13 Blood cells

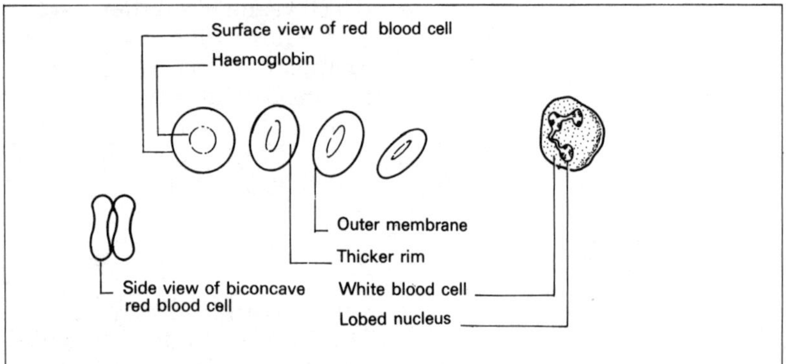

FUNCTIONS OF BLOOD

The blood takes up *oxygen* in the lungs, by means of its haemoglobin, and carries it to all the living cells of the body. *Carbon dioxide*, which the cells produce as a waste-product during respiration is carried by the blood to the lungs. Carbon dioxide is carried partly by the haemoglobin, and partly as salts (bicarbonates) in the plasma. Blood carries the absorbed *food* from the small intestine to all the living cells of the body. *Waste* materials produced in the tissues from protein, are carried to the liver, where they are changed into *urea*, and then carried to the *kidneys*. *Hormones* are chemicals which control the activity or growth of various organs. *Endocrine* glands secrete these hormones directly into the blood, and this type of gland has no duct. The blood carries the hormones to the particular parts of the body where they produce their effects. *Heat*, which is produced in tissues that are doing work (particularly the muscles and liver), is evenly distributed by the blood, and surplus heat is lost from the blood in the skin capillaries. The *white blood cells* protect the body from disease (see Chapter 15). The *blood platelets* and *fibrin* cause clotting of the blood if a blood vessel is damaged.

BLOOD VESSELS

The blood vessels are of three kinds, arteries, veins, and capillaries. *Arteries* carry blood from the heart, and have thick muscular walls. Blood moves through them with a jerky movement, known as the *pulse*, which is caused by the heart beat, and occurs about 70 times per minute. *Veins* carry blood to the heart and have thinner walls, through which the colour of the blood can be seen. The blood flows smoothly through the veins, which have pocket-like *valves* on their inside walls, to prevent blood from flowing backwards.

13.14 Vein showing a valve

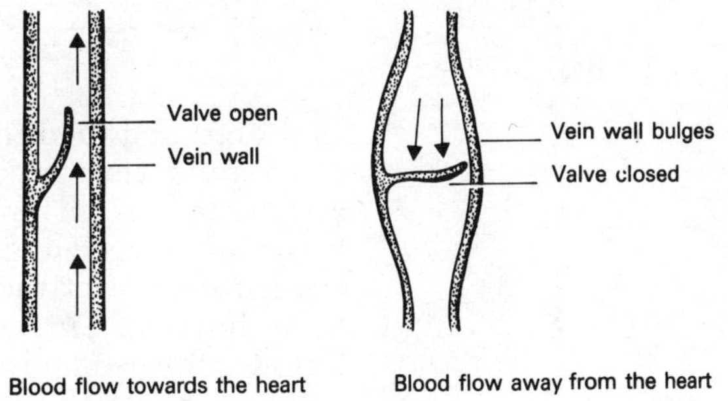

Capillaries are very fine blood vessels which form *networks* in the tissues, and link the smaller arteries with the veins. It is through the capillary walls that substances are exchanged between the blood and the living cells of the tissues.

THE HEART

The *heart* is a hollow organ whose walls are composed of muscle, and which acts as a *pump*, driving the blood through the blood vessels. The heart muscle contracts regularly and continuously, about 70 times a minute, throughout life. There are four *cavities* in the heart, two upper *auricles*, and two lower *ventricles*. The right and left sides of the heart are completely separated by a *septum*. The right auricle opens into the right ventricle, and the left auricle into the left ventricle. The openings are guarded by *valves*, which allow blood to pass in one direction only, from auricle to ventricle.

Circulation of blood through the heart. The blood entering the *right auricle* by the *caval veins* comes from the body tissues to which the blood has given up its oxygen, thus becoming deoxygenated. It passes into the *right ventricle* as the heart muscle

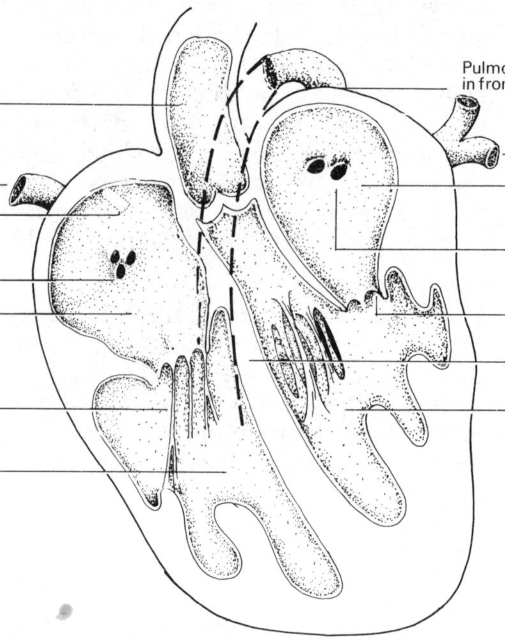

13.15 Human heart—front wall removed

contracts, and then through the *pulmonary arteries*, which rise out of the right ventricle like a chimney, before branching into arteries to the two lungs. In the lungs, the blood picks up oxygen, becoming oxygenated, and returning in the *pulmonary veins* to the *left auricle* of the heart. Contraction of the auricle forces blood into the *left ventricle*, through the valve. From here it is forced into the main artery, the *aorta*, which gives off branches to all parts of the body. In the heart, *deoxygenated* blood is confined to the *right* side, and *oxygenated* blood to the *left*, so that two streams of blood pass through the heart simultaneously. The *pulmonary* stream goes from the heart to the lungs and back, and the *systemic* stream from the heart to all the body systems, and back.

Heart disease is the most frequent cause of death in Britain today. Contributary causes to the occurrence of heart disease are overweight, and lack of exercise. Loss of energy, breathlessness after exertion, and depression, are frequently due to *anaemia*, which is a common cause of ill-health in women.

Excretion

Excretion is the removal of the *waste products* produced during the body's activities (metabolism). If these waste products accumulated in the tissues and organs, the body could not function efficiently, and ill-health and finally death would occur. Waste materials which must be completely removed are *carbon dioxide*, and *urea* formed from the nitrogen waste of protein breakdown. The *liver* converts the poisonous nitrogen compounds into urea, which is less poisonous. *Excess* water or mineral salts must also be removed for the body to maintain an exact *balance* between its salt content and its water content.

13.16 Circulation of the blood

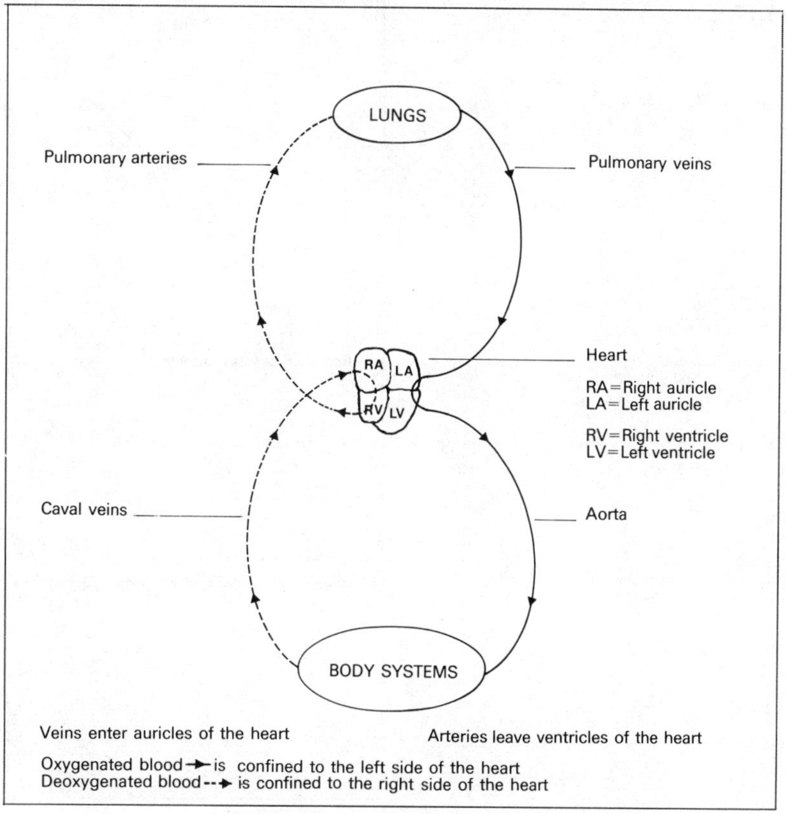

Three organs in the body function as excretory organs. The *lungs* remove carbon dioxide and some water vapour, which pass out of the blood into the air sacs of the lung, and are removed when breathing out. The *kidneys* filter a liquid out of the blood, which becomes the *urine*, which is mainly a solution of urea and mineral salts in water. The renal artery, which is a branch from the aorta, brings blood to the kidney, while the blood returns in the renal vein, which joins a caval vein. From each kidney, the urine flows down a tube, the *ureter*, opening into the *bladder* in which urine is stored, to be expelled at intervals, when the walls of the bladder contract.

The *skin* also removes some of the surplus salts and water during sweating. In hot weather, when sweating increases to lose more heat from the body, less water and salt are removed in urine. In cold weather, a greater volume of urine is produced as sweating decreases.

Regulating the body temperature

The human body maintains a fairly *constant temperature* in spite of wide variations in the temperature of its surroundings, and so is able to remain active in a variety of climatic and weather conditions.

The body is constantly producing *heat*, and even when at rest the body temperature would rise 1°C each hour if no heat loss occurred. When the body is active, and heat is produced by the muscles, a further increase of 1°C per hour would occur. Muscles also produce heat during *shivering*. (Erector muscles also contract

13.17 Excretory organs—kidneys

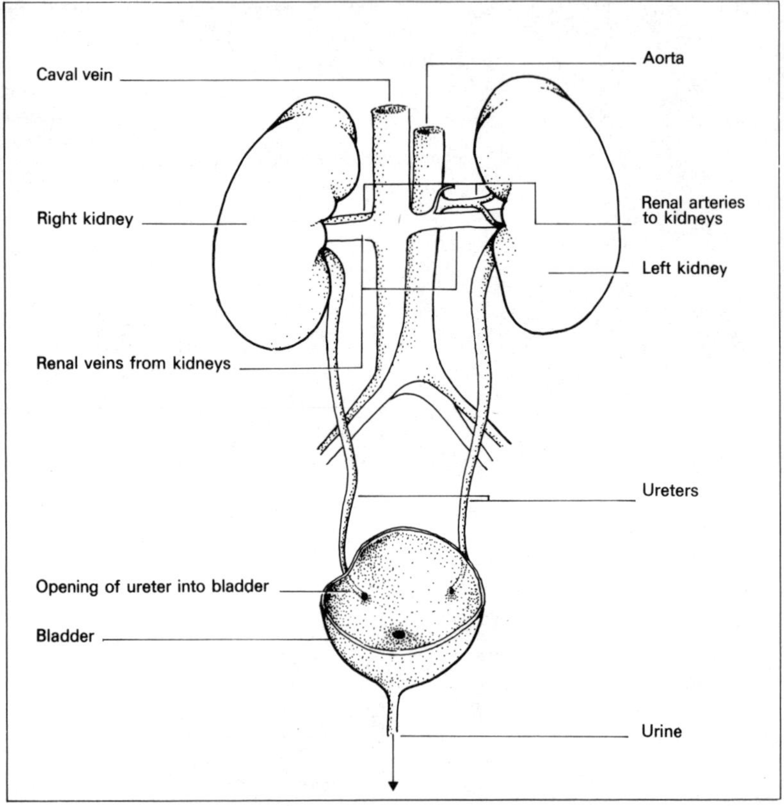

causing 'gooseflesh'.) The body will *absorb* heat from its surroundings, where sunshine, or space heaters have made the atmosphere hotter than the body.

The body *loses* heat by radiation from the skin when the blood capillaries in the dermis are dilated. This brings more blood to the surface, so that the skin looks flushed. The skin is separated from the atmosphere by a layer of *convecting air*, which is warmed by the skin, and is therefore less dense than atmospheric air. Starting from the feet, there is a layer of air 1-2 cm thick which passes up against the body surface its thickness increasing as it rises to form a plume 1 m above the hair, i.e. a *convection current* occurs (see Chapter 14). *Evaporation* of sweat requires *latent heat*, which it takes from the skin. If sweat is wiped away instead of evaporating, it does not cool the body. As sweating increases, the blood capillaries round the sweat glands dilate, increasing the blood flow. With an air temperature of 20°C *convection* accounts for 36% of the total heat loss from the body at rest; *radiation* 45%; and *evaporation* 19% of the total.

At the base of the brain there is a *heat control centre*, acting as a thermostat, to keep the body temperature fairly constant at 37°C. This temperature is maintained by a *balance* between heat loss and heat gain. The brain thermostat is connected through the nervous system with the blood vessels of the skin, and with the sweat glands. As the body temperature rises above 37°C, heat is lost by convection and radiation from the skin, and by increased sweating. As the body temperature falls below 37°C the skin blood vessels contract, so that heat from the blood is no longer radiated, convection is reduced, and the sweat glands stop producing sweat. The body produces more heat to increase its temperature by voluntary muscular movements, or involuntary shivering. The *hair* is not sufficiently thick on most parts of the skin to trap a layer of air, which would act as an insulator. This method of reducing heat loss only occurs in other mammals which have a complete covering of hair.

If the body temperature increases, and heat loss by sweating cannot occur, because the humidity is too high to allow evaporation of sweat, then *heat fatigue* will occur (see Chapter 14).

The nervous system

All the body systems must be controlled, so that they work together, i.e. are *co-ordinated*. The *nervous* system and the *hormones* bring this about, the nervous system acting rapidly, while hormones are usually slow-acting. The controlling centre of the nervous system is the *brain*, assisted by the *spinal cord*. These two organs make up the *central nervous system*. The brain is found inside the cranium of the skull, the spinal cord being a continuation of the brain which runs down the centre of the vertebral column. The central nervous system is composed of very soft tissue, and needs to be protected by surrounding bone. From the brain and spinal cord pairs of *cranial* and *spinal nerves* emerge. The *nerves* consist of bundles of nerve fibres, which connect either with a *sense organ*, or with a *muscle* or *gland*. Nerve fibres linking a sense organ with the central nervous system are *sensory*, and carry messages from the sense organ. Nerve fibres linking a muscle or gland with the central nervous system are *motor* fibres, and carry messages to the muscle or gland.

Sense organs pick up information, reacting to changes in the surroundings, or in the condition of the body. Sense organs are therefore known as *receptors*. The eyes receive light reflected from surrounding objects, and the ears pick up sounds. The nose and tongue have receptors sensitive to chemical substances in the air and food. The fine branched nerve endings in the dermis of the skin are receptors which give the sensations of touch, temperature and pain.

The *brain* receives and sorts the information arriving along sensory nerve fibres from the sense organs, and decides on the best response. This decision is influenced by memories, which the

13.18 The parts of the nervous system

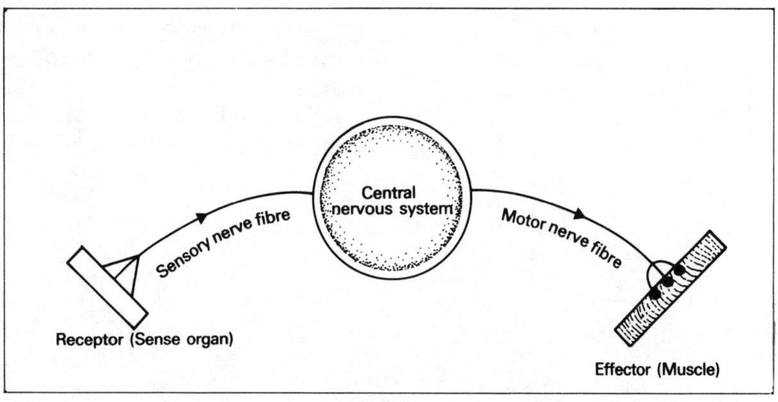

brain has stored, and intelligence. Messages then pass along motor nerve fibres to muscles or glands (the *effectors*) which then behave in the way determined by the brain.

When a hairdresser is working, information about the client's hair reaches the brain from the eyes, and skin sense organs (seeing and feeling the hair). The muscles of the hands contract or relax to control the tools used to carry out the hairdressing procedures.

13.19 Human brain (section)

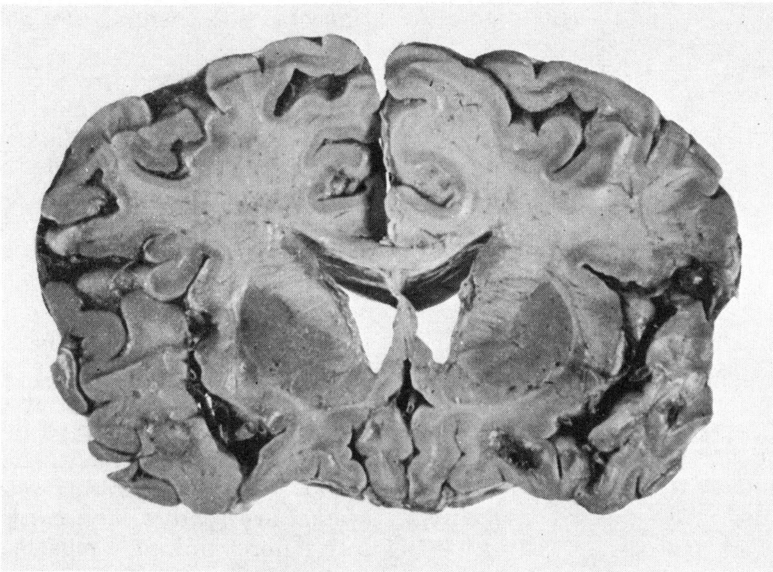

Such actions are *voluntary*, being the result of conscious effort. There are some actions carried out by the body over which there is no conscious control. These are *involuntary*, or *reflex actions*. Reflex actions are usually concerned with protecting parts of the body from injury. *Blinking* is a reflex action, as the eye-lids close if dangerous objects come close to the eye. Bright light shining into the eyes causes the *pupil* to *contract*, letting less light in, as very strong light damages the eye. *Coughing* if food particles get into the windpipe is a reflex action, to prevent suffocation by blocking the air passages.

The healthy functioning of the nervous system is adversely affected by *alcohol* and some *drugs*. Alcohol and barbiturates cause lack of co-ordination and faulty judgement. Amphetamines cause restlessness and irritability. Psychodelics (L.S.D. and cannabis) cause disturbances of feeling, thinking, and perception.

Vitamin B promotes the health of the nervous system, and so does sufficient *rest* and *relaxation*.

Multiple choice questions

1 A hairdresser should adopt a good standing posture because it

a prevents loss of balance *b* reduces muscle fatigue
c prevents heat fatigue *d* causes muscle atrophy

2 The two nutrients from which the body obtains energy are

a carbohydrates and fats *b* proteins and vitamins
c mineral salts and water *d* vitamins and iron

3 The vitamin which helps wounds to heal and keeps the gums in a healthy condition is

a Vitamin A *b* Vitamin B *c* Vitamin C *d* Vitamin D

4 The blood vessels which are called arteries

a only take blood from the lungs
b take blood from the heart
c always carry oxygenated blood
d contain valves to stop back-flow

5 When living cells break down glucose sugar to obtain energy the process is

a excretion *b* peristalsis *c* expiration *d* respiration

6 During digestion chemical changes in the food materials are brought about by

a hormones *b* enzymes *c* antibodies *d* nutrients

7 The white blood cells are able to

a destroy invading germs *b* carry oxygen round the body
c cause the blood to clot *d* remove waste products

8 Co-ordination of the body's activities is brought about by the

a circulatory system *b* vascular system
c muscular system *d* nervous system

9 If the temperature of the body rises above 37°C, it will lose heat by means of the following physical processes

a radiation, evaporation, and convection
b shivering, radiation, and hydrolysis
c evaporation, conduction, and shivering
d convection, contraction, and conduction

10 The main excretory organs of the body are

a hair follicles and pores *b* lungs, skin, and kidneys
c liver and rectum *d* sweat glands and bladder

14 Comfort in the Salon

To be comfortable for both clients and staff, the *air* in the salon must have certain properties relating to its temperature, pressure, and composition. Hot *water* for shampooing must also be available at a suitable temperature at all times.

Composition of the air in the salon

Air is a mixture of several gases. Although it is a *mixture* its composition remains fairly constant whether the air is inside the salon or outside, and wherever the salon occurs geographically, so that the *percentage composition* by volume of air can be stated. The composition of air is:

Nitrogen 78%; *oxygen* 21%; *carbon dioxide* 0·03%; *rare gases* approximately 1%; *water vapour*, a variable amount; *pollutants* (including gases like sulphur dioxide, soot particles, bacteria and spores) in variable small amounts. The gases which form the major part of the air are *nitrogen* (approximately four-fifths) and *oxygen* (approximately one-fifth). These gases are similar in that both are colourless and odourless, and of almost the same weight. Both gases dissolve in water, oxygen being a little more soluble than nitrogen. They differ because oxygen is very *reactive*, while nitrogen is *inert*. Oxygen is said to be reactive because it combines very readily with a large number of substances, i.e. it readily undergoes chemical changes. Nitrogen does not combine easily with other substances, so it does not allow substances to burn in it. Thus, once all the oxygen in the air has combined with a burning substance, the flame will go out, as nitrogen does not *support combustion*. The presence of oxygen in the air can be shown by *burning* substances in it. If a candle burns in an enclosed volume of air, it will continue to burn until all the oxygen has been used up, when the flame will go out. If the air is enclosed by means of a water seal, water will rise to take the place of the oxygen used up in burning, and its volume can be measured (see Experiment 1).

The presence of oxygen in the air is necessary for the *respiration* of plants and animals, including man. The *carbon dioxide* present in air comes from the burning of fuels and the breathing of plants and animals. The amount of carbon dioxide in the air might be expected to increase, but carbon dioxide is removed from the air by green plants which use it to produce their food by the process of *photosynthesis*. However, if carbon dioxide production in modern urban societies continues to rise as population increases and more fuel is burned, and if the green areas are cut down and replaced by buildings, the increased amount of carbon dioxide may have an effect on the *world climate*, as it increases air temperatures. Temperatures are already very slightly higher in cities than in rural areas.

The amount of *water vapour* present in the air is known as the *humidity*. It occurs as a result of the evaporation of liquid water from a wide variety of sources, from burning some fuels, and from people during respiration and perspiration. Certain substances absorb water vapour from the air, and so reduce the humidity. Such substances are *hygroscopic*, and include hair, wool, common salt (sodium chloride), caustic soda (sodium hydroxide), and calcium chloride. Other substances give off water vapour into the air, e.g. washing soda (sodium carbonate) and borax (sodium borate), which give off some of the water vapour contained in their crystals, forming a coating of white powder which is the *anhydrous* form of the chemical. These substances are said to be *efflorescent*. The presence of water vapour in the salon air can be shown by placing a beaker of *ice* in the room. Water vapour from the air *condenses* on the outside of the cold beaker, and so becomes visible.

Impurities in the form of sulphur compounds are produced by burning fuels and so are present in larger amounts in industrial areas. The amounts of soot and ash are also higher in industrial areas unless such areas have been designated 'smokeless zones'.

Atmospheric pressure

Because air is composed of molecules, it has *weight*. The air stretches above us for at least 320 kilometres at sea-level, its weight producing a force of 10·1 Newtons on every cm^2 of the surface it rests on. The atmospheric pressure can be demonstrated by its effect on a tin from which most of the air has been removed. As the air pressure outside is no longer equalled by air pressure inside, the walls of the tin are forced inwards, so that the tin will crumple (see Experiment 3). Slight changes in atmospheric pressure are caused by changes in the *humidity* of the air, and by the *altitude*, i.e. height above or below sea-level. Increasing the humidity decreases the atmospheric pressure, as the density of water vapour is less than that of air. Moist air is lighter than dry air, and therefore has a lower pressure. Increasing the altitude decreases the atmospheric pressure as the atmosphere becomes 'thinner', i.e. there are fewer molecules to produce weight.

BAROMETERS

The instrument used to measure atmospheric *pressure* is the *barometer*. The *mercury* barometer is used in science laboratories. It consists of a long glass tube which has been filled with mercury, and then inverted into a container of mercury. The atmospheric pressure will push the mercury up the tube, while the weight of the mercury column will resist the upward thrust, so that when the two forces are equal the mercury column has a height of 76 cm at sea-level. The tube is fitted into a case with a scale, so that the height of the mercury column can be read.

14.1 Mercury barometer

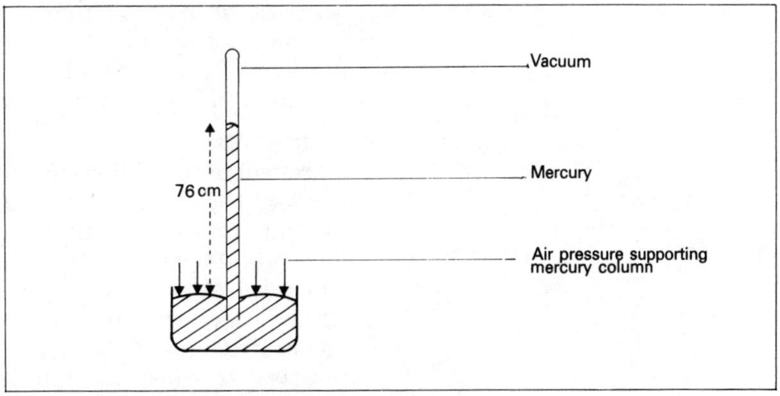

The *anaeroid* barometer is used in homes and shops. This type of barometer uses the changes in volume of an evacuated metal box produced by changes in the air pressure. When the air pressure is high the box is compressed, so that its volume is less. Lower air pressure causes the box to expand. These *volume changes* in the box are magnified by a system of levers to which a pointer is attached. The pointer moves over a dial with a pressure scale marked on it.

14.2 Aneroid barometer

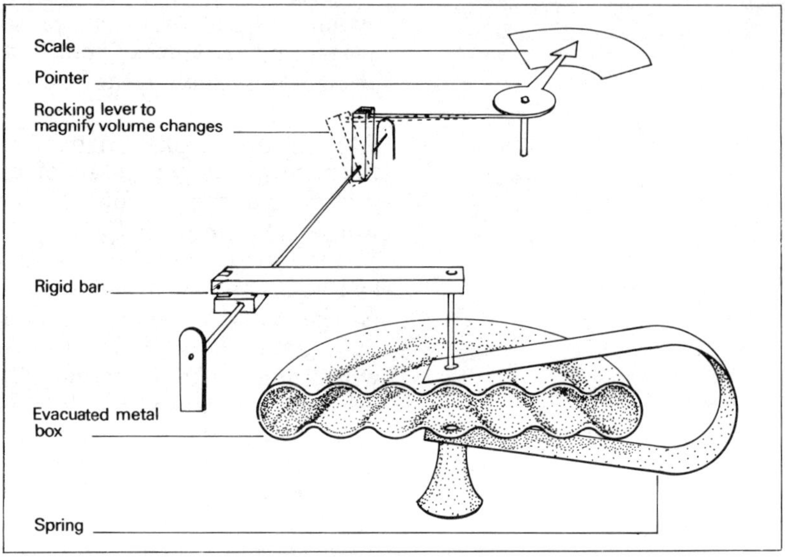

The atmospheric pressure will only cause air to move into the lungs during breathing if the air pressure inside the lungs is lower than atmospheric. Thus, if the atmospheric pressure becomes reduced, less air will enter the lungs, and less oxygen will be available for tissue respiration.

Air temperature

A suitable *temperature* must be maintained in the salon for comfort. As clients have wet heads, their bodies lose heat because of the *cooling* effect of *evaporation*, so the salon temperature needs to be at least 21°C. In cold weather some form of *artificial* heating is required to maintain this temperature. The salon temperature normally fluctuates during the day, becoming steadily *warmer* as it gains heat from hot water, dryers, people, etc. Some heat will also be lost through the colder walls, windows and ceiling. The temperature of the salon air must therefore be continually checked by a *thermometer*.

THERMOMETERS

A thermometer is an instrument used to measure temperature by *comparing* the hotness of a substance with that of melting ice or boiling water. It consists of a glass capillary tube with a *bulb* at one end containing a liquid. The *liquid* is either mercury or coloured alcohol which *expands* on heating, rising up the capillary tube. The tube or *stem* carries a scale divided into a number of *degrees*. The scale has two *fixed points* where the liquid rises to when the bulb is immersed in melting ice, and in boiling water. These are the lower and upper fixed points respectively. The distance between these points is divided into 100 divisions on the *Celsius* scale, each division being 1 degree Celsius (1°C). The temperature scale originally in everyday use was the *Fahrenheit* scale with a lower fixed point at 32°F, and an upper fixed point at 212°F. Thus 180°F lie between the two fixed points. At —40° both these scales *correspond*.

14.3 Laboratory Thermometer
Salon Wall Thermometer

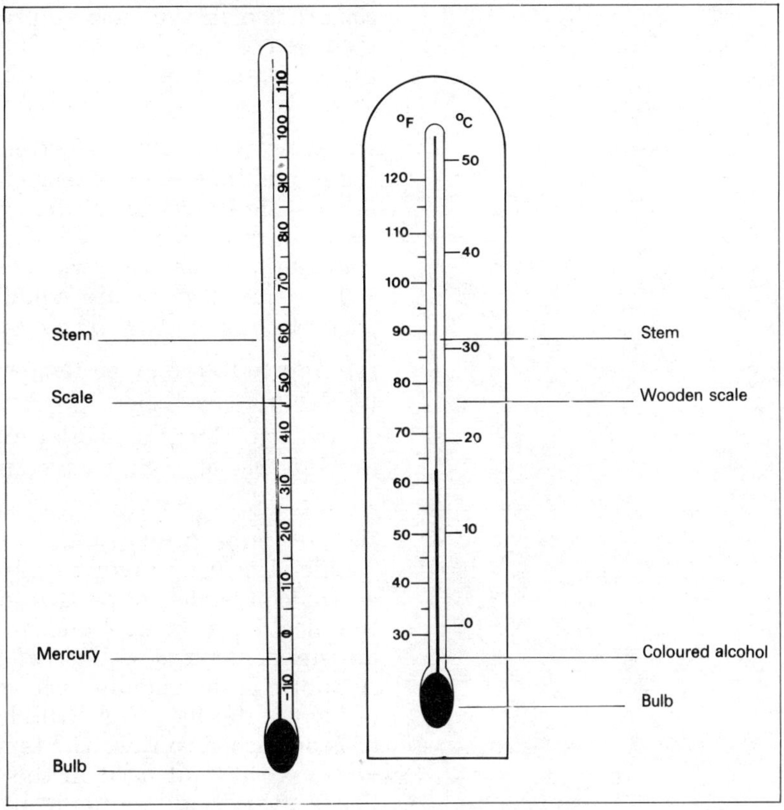

Comparison of Temperature Scales

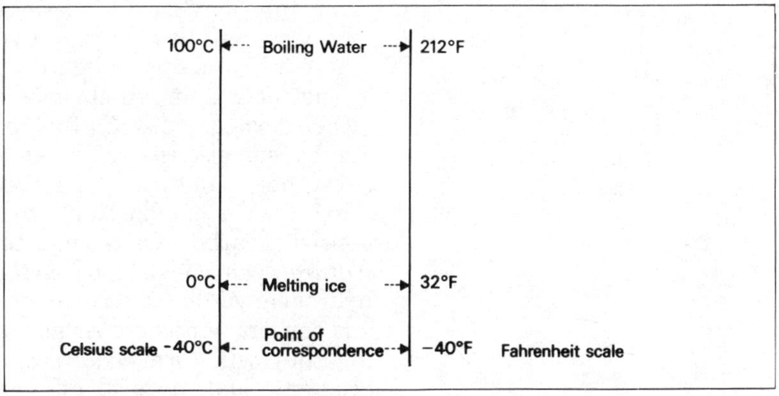

Laboratory thermometers contain *mercury* and are graduated in the *Celsius* scale, commonly having a range of —10°C to 110°C. These thermometers give an accurate temperature reading provided the whole bulb is immersed in the substance when reading its temperature, and the eye is level with the top of the mercury. *Salon wall* thermometers contain either mercury or coloured alcohol, and are supported by a wooden scale, usually with Celsius temperatures on one side, and Fahrenheit temperatures on the other.

Clinical thermometers are a special type used for taking the *body* temperature. They contain *mercury* and have a very narrow temperature range from 35°C to 45°C. As the temperature must be read with the thermometer out of the mouth, there is a *constriction* in the stem to prevent the mercury falling, unless the thermometer is shaken. Clinical thermometers must be rinsed in *cold* water. Hot water causes the mercury to expand so much that it breaks the thermometer.

TO CONVERT ONE TEMPERATURE SCALE INTO THE OTHER
Fahrenheit and Celsius temperatures may be converted into the other scale by means of a temperature *graph* (see Experiment 4), or by an *arithmetical* method. The *simplest* arithmetical method uses the fact that the two scales correspond at —40°, and that 100 Celsius degrees are equal to 180 Fahrenheit degrees, the proportion being 5 : 9. The method is as follows:

(1) *Add* 40 to the given temperature
(2) *Multiply* by either $\frac{9}{5}$ (to obtain a *larger* number) for °C to °F or $\frac{5}{9}$ (to obtain a smaller number) for °F to °C
(3) *Subtract* 40, giving the converted temperature.

Salon space heating

Artificial heating involves the production of heat in *appliances* by the conversion of *fuels* into *heat energy*, and the *transfer* of that heat from the appliance into the salon. The heat produced is measured in units, called *calories*, or in *British thermal units*. A calorie is the amount of heat needed to raise the temperature of 1 g of water by 1°C. A British thermal unit (Btu) is the amount of heat needed to raise the temperature of 1 lb of water by 1°F, and was the unit used in the past by heating engineers. As a Btu is a very small unit of heat, a *therm* is often used (e.g. by Gas Companies), where 1 therm is 100,000 Btu's. Eventually gas engineers will be changing over to a different unit, the joule (J), where a Btu is approximately 1055 J.

The *fuels* from which heat is obtained in the appliances are either burned, e.g. *solid* fuel, *oil*, and *gas*, or converted into heat energy, e.g. *electricity*. The fuels which are burned are all *organic* substances containing carbon, and therefore produce *carbon dioxide* as a combustion product. Solid fuels (coal and coke) consist of carbon. Oil is a mixture of *hydrocarbons* from petroleum. *Natural gas* consists of *methane*, a compound of carbon and hydrogen, while *town gas* contains both methane and the poisonous carbon monoxide. As gas and oil contain *hydrogen*, on burning they will form *water vapour* as an additional combustion product. Coal, natural gas, and oil are known as *fossil* fuels, because although they are obtained from the earth, they were originally derived from *living* things, and were transformed by heat and pressure within the earth. Coal was formed from trees; natural gas from plant remains in marshy conditions; oil from the remains of the shells of tiny marine animals (plankton). The *calorific value* of a fuel is the amount of heat it will produce when a given amount is completely burned. The calorific value of town gas is 500 Btu/ cubic foot, while that of natural gas is double this, being 1000 Btu/ cubic foot.

Heat can be *transferred* from an appliance in three possible ways, by *conduction*, *convection*, and *radiation*. In conduction, heat is passed from one molecule to the next, but the molecules themselves do not travel. This process usually occurs most rapidly in solids, although not all solids are good conductors of heat.

A number of substances including glass, plastic, cotton, wood, wool, and hair do not allow heat to travel through them quickly and are thus bad conductors of heat, or *insulators*. Metals are good conductors of heat, the best being copper, then aluminium.

During *convection* heat travels by the movement of heated molecules which obtain extra energy. It occurs in both liquids and gases. The stream of moving heated molecules is called a *convection current*. It can be demonstrated in water coloured by potassium permanganate crystals, and in air by cigarette smoke.

14.4 Convection current in water

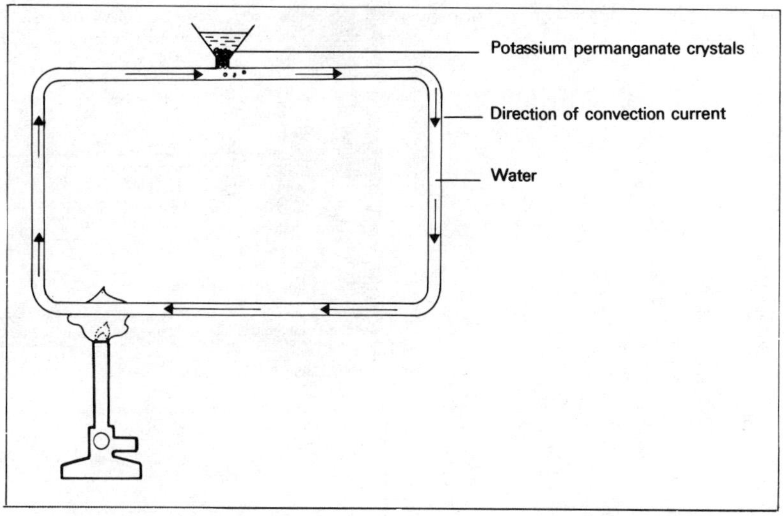

Convection current in air

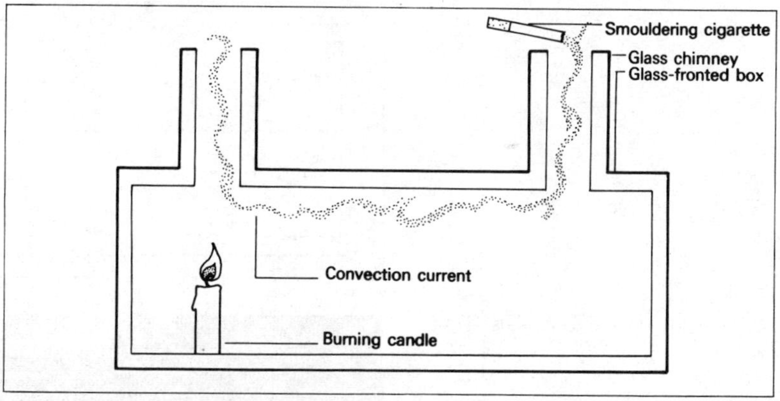

Radiation is the method by which heat travels in the form of *rays* through gases or space. Heat rays travel in straight lines. They do not warm the air or space through which they pass, but only objects in their path which *absorb* the rays. Objects which *reflect* the heat rays instead of absorbing them will not get hotter. It is the nature of the *surface* of an object which determines whether radiant heat is absorbed or reflected. A dull dark surface absorbs most of the heat, and reflects very little. A light coloured shiny surface (e.g. polished metal) absorbs very little radiant heat, reflecting most of it. All hot objects give out radiant heat. Those with a dull, dark surface radiate more effectively than objects with a light coloured shiny surface.

Heat produced in an *appliance* may heat the salon by *convection* or *radiation*, or both. Conduction of heat is not involved in salon space-heating.

SPACE HEATERS

Space heaters may be *portable*, i.e. they can be moved from place to place, or *fixed*. Heaters may also form part of a *central heating system*. *Portable* appliances are useful for supplying heat temporarily, or in an emergency. The *disadvantages* of portable heaters are that they may be a fire hazard if badly placed, and they are inadequate for all but a very small salon. Suitable portable appliances all use *full-price* electricity as the fuel, which makes them expensive to run.

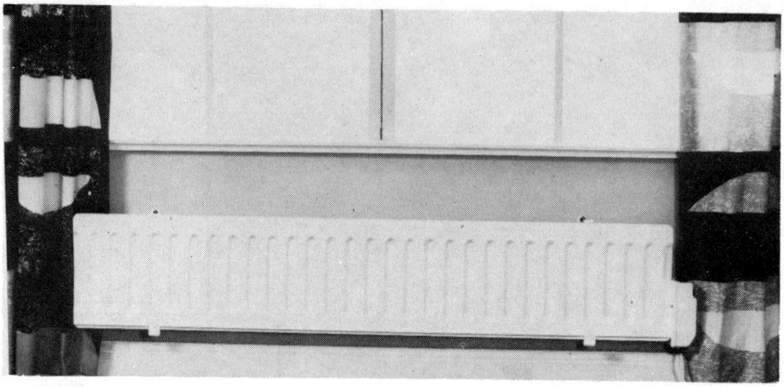

14.5 Oil-filled radiator—heats salon by convection

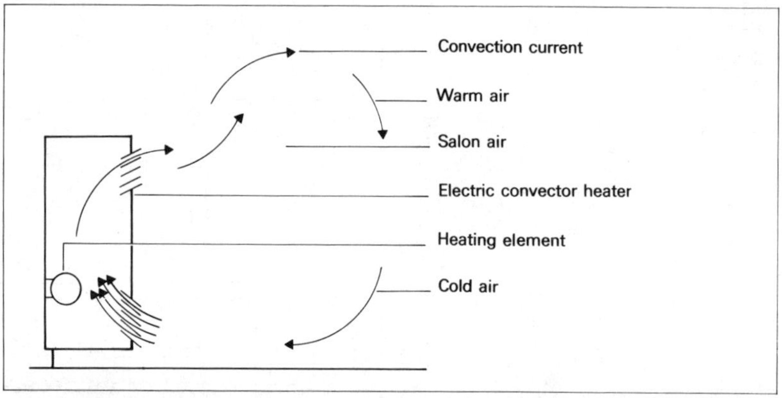

14.6 Electric convector heater

14.7 Electric fan heater—heats salon by convection

14.8 Radiant electric fire

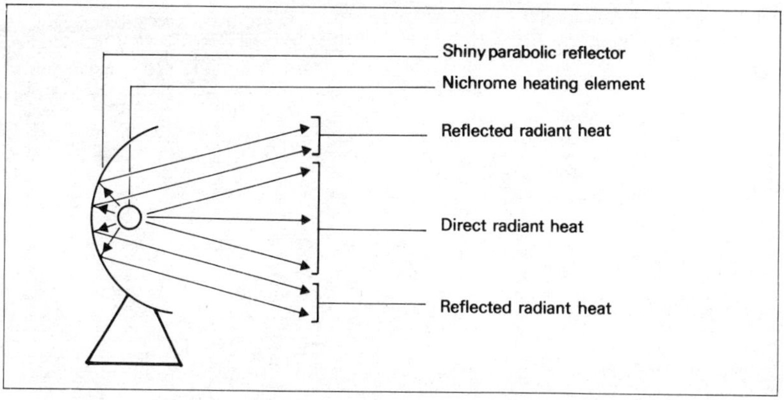

All these electric appliances have the *advantage* that they do not add *combustion gases* to the salon atmosphere.

Fixed appliances may be the best type in a salon of moderate size where there is no central heating. They are usually less expensive to run, as cheaper fuels such as gas or off-peak electricity are used. (*See Figs* 14.9-14.12)

14.9 Storage radiator—heats salon by convection

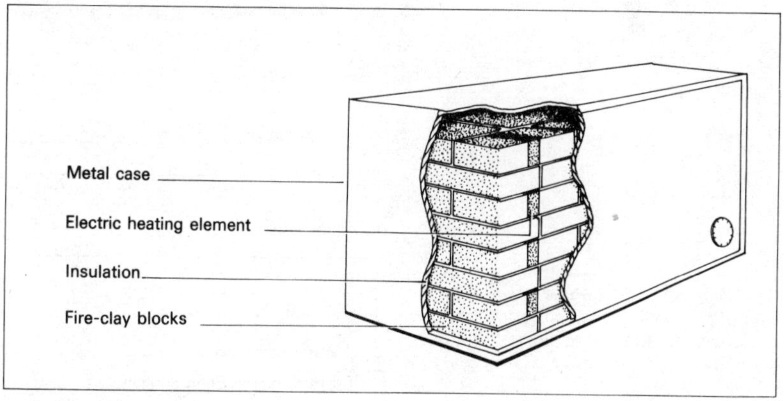

CENTRAL HEATING

For a large salon, central heating is likely to be a more efficient and economical method of space-heating than fitting a number of separate heaters which are independently controlled. There are three main systems of central heating.

1 *Hot water systems* consist of a boiler which heats the water which is then circulated by an electric pump through pipes to 'radiators'. 'Radiators' warm the salon by *convection*, and not by radiation. Most systems are fitted with a programmer which is a type of time-switch. This type of central heating usually provides *hot water* as well as *space-heating*. All types of combustible fuels may be used with this system, which is the cheapest form of central heating to run. The disadvantage is that radiators take up a lot of wall space which may be needed for other equipment in the salon. At least one radiator should be placed under the window to heat the colder air as it enters the salon.

2 *Warm air systems* have a heater which warms air which is then circulated by a fan through a system of *ducts*. These open at *grilles* a few inches above the floor level, so that warm air is blown out into the salon. Some of these systems will provide hot

14.10 Infra-red wall heater—heats salon by radiation

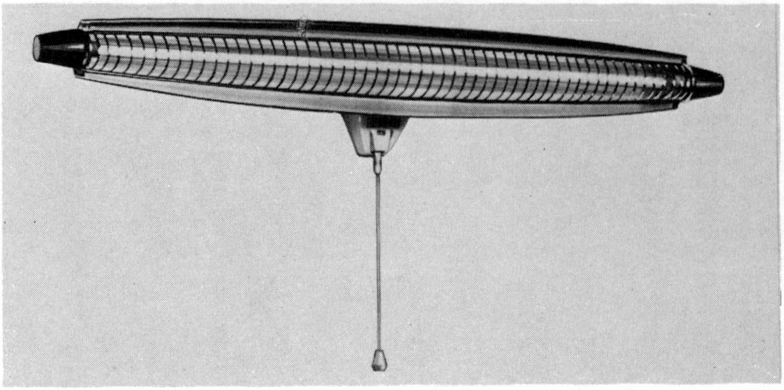

14.11 Gas radiant convector heater —heats salon by radiation and convection

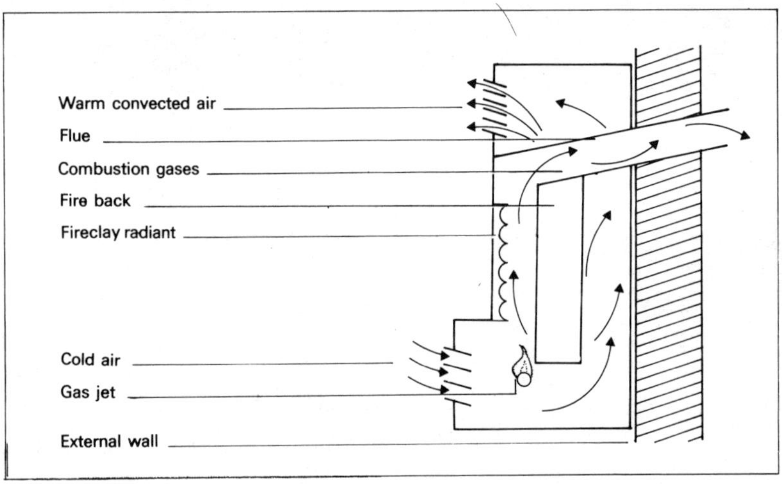

14.12 Balanced flue heater—heats salon by convection. The combustion products are unable to enter the salon

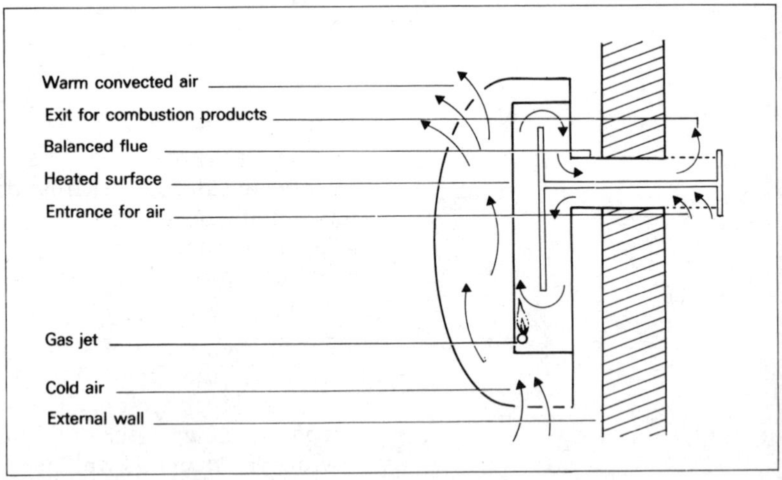

water. The fuels used may be gas, oil, solid-fuel, or off-peak electricity, and the system is usually controlled by a programmer. This type of central heating is rather expensive to run, but takes up very little wall space.

3 *Floor warming systems* comprise electric heating elements embedded in the floor while it is being laid. There is *insulation* below the elements to prevent heat loss downwards. *Off-peak* electricity is used to heat the floor overnight, and the heat is given off into the salon during the day. This system will provide

background heating only, as a wattage of more than 160 watts per square metre will make the floor too hot. The floor temperature does not exceed 26°C, but even so, most hairdressers find the heated floor tiring to their feet. A floor-warming system is also expensive to run, so that the disadvantages probably outweigh the advantages.

Salon humidity

During the working day, the *humidity* in the salon will increase as a result of evaporation of water from drying hair, wet towels, and sweat from the skin. Steam from hot water or using the steamer also increases the humidity. Water vapour in the air is increased when people breathe out. All these processes increase the *natural* humidity of the air, which depends on the weather. The higher the temperature of the air, the more water vapour it can hold before it becomes *saturated*. If air which is saturated with water vapour is cooled, it is no longer able to hold as much, so water *condenses* out of the air until it is again saturated at the new lower temperature. If air which is not saturated is sufficiently cooled, eventually the water vapour it contains will saturate it, so that if it is cooled any further, water will condense. The temperature at which air becomes saturated by the water vapour it contains is known as the *dew point*, and *condensation* occurs in the salon once the dew point temperature has been reached. The humidity is usually expressed as % *relative humidity.*

$$\text{Relative humidity} = \frac{\text{Actual amount of water vapour in air}}{\text{Amount of water vapour saturating air at the same temperature.}}$$

For comfort, the salon air should have a relative humidity of 40-50%, and the humidity should never exceed 70% even at the end of the day. Too *high* a percentage relative humidity is an indication of *inadequate ventilation* of the salon. Where salon humidity is too high, sweat will not evaporate to cool the body and maintain the normal body temperature of 37°C. If overheating occurs, this leads to *discomfort*, and eventually to *heat fatigue*. The symptoms of heat fatigue are headache, dizziness, tiredness, and irritability.

MEASUREMENT OF HUMIDITY

The instrument used for measuring humidity is a *hygrometer*, and three different types are used. A *hair* hygrometer is the simplest type as this gives a direct reading of the % relative humidity on a dial. The hygrometer has a long hollow metal cylinder attached to a circular dial. The cylinder has holes in it to allow access for the air, and contains several long degreased human hairs fixed at the outer end. At the dial end these hairs are attached through a spring to a pointer which moves over the dial. A change in *length* of the hairs allows the spring and pointer to move. As the hairs are *hygroscopic* they absorb water vapour from the air. The higher the humidity, the more water vapour they absorb. As they take in water, they lengthen and the pointer moves over the scale.

Regnault's hygrometer is used to determine the *dew point* temperature of the air by observing the temperature at which a *mist* (dew) appears on a highly polished metal surface when the

14.13 Hair Hygrometer

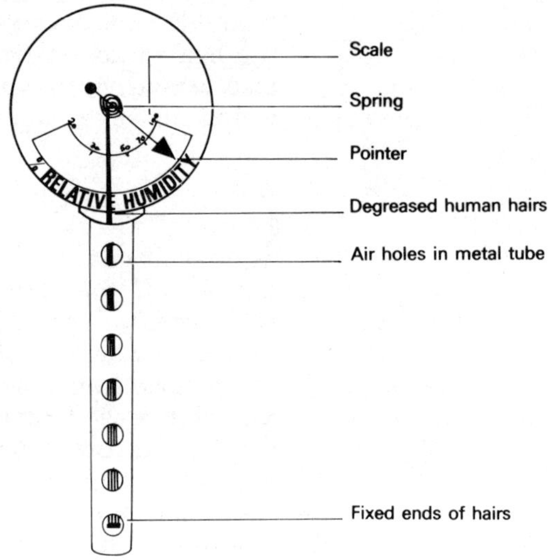

air is cooled. Air bubbles are drawn through *ether* in the hygrometer by connecting it to a *pump* or aspirator. The air current speeds up the rate of *evaporation* of the ether, which takes *latent heat* from its surroundings, thus *cooling* the silvered surface of the hygrometer, and the outside air in contact with it. When the temperature is reduced to the dew point of the air, the silvered surface mists over. The pump is then shut off, and the ether allowed to warm up. The temperature at which the mist disappears again is also noted, and the average of the two temperatures is taken as the dew point. Using suitable *tables*, the relative humidity can be obtained from the dew point temperature.

14.14 Regnault's Hygrometer

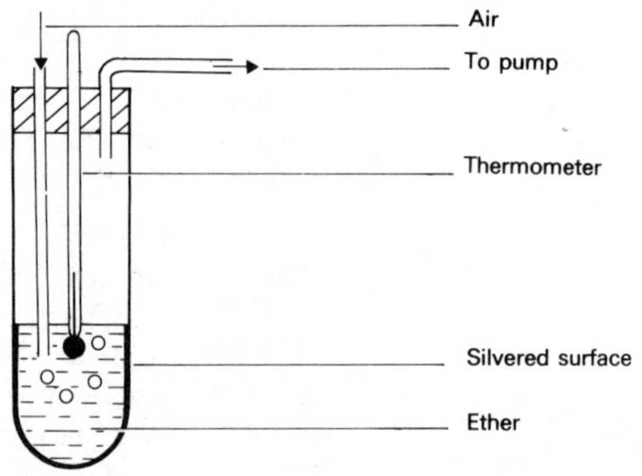

The *wet-and-dry bulb* hygrometer consists of two thermometers one of which has its bulb covered with wet muslin. The *dry-bulb* thermometer measures the air temperature, and if the air is completely *saturated* with water vapour, the wet bulb thermometer will give the *same* temperature reading. If the air is not saturated, water will *evaporate* from the wet muslin round the thermometer bulb. The wet-bulb temperature will then be *lower* than the dry-bulb temperature because of cooling due to evaporation when latent heat is absorbed. The drier the air, the greater

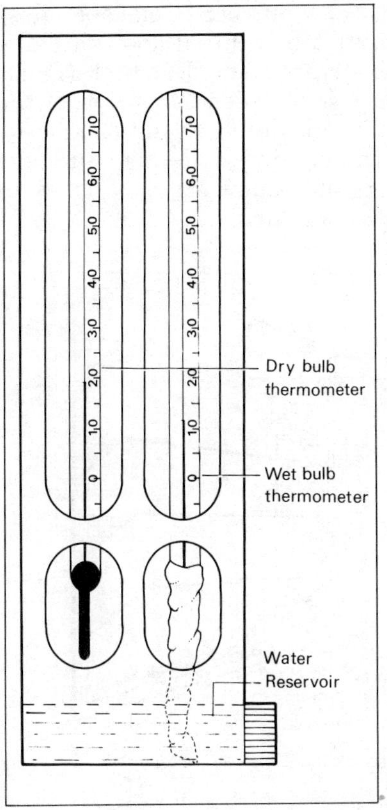

14.15 Wet-and-dry bulb hygrometer

the rate of evaporation, and the greater the temperature difference between the two thermometers, called the wet-bulb depression. Using suitable tables, the *percentage humidity* can be obtained from the wet-bulb depression. (Meteorological Office Hygrometric Tables Part II H.M. Stationery Office.)

CONDENSATION

Condensation due to high humidity can be a problem in the salon. It can be reduced by providing *thermal insulation* so that the air does not cool down sufficiently to reach the dew point temperature. Roof insulation, polystyrene ceiling tiles, and double-glazed windows are all methods of thermal insulation which can be used in the salon. Good *ventilation* will also reduce condensation by keeping the humidity low. *Hygroscopic* furnishing fabrics which absorb water vapour from the air, e.g. woollen carpets or upholstery, also help to reduce humidity.

Ventilation

Ventilation is the process by which *stale* air is replaced by *fresh* air. It is the means of keeping the composition of the salon air stable, and preventing too great a rise in temperature. The people in the salon alter the composition of the air in a number of ways; reducing its oxygen content, and increasing its carbon dioxide, water vapour and bacterial content, by their breathing and perspiration. If the air is replaced too rapidly, *draughts* result. Air movement increases the rate of evaporation of water from a client's wet hair, cooling the head to cause discomfort. *Over-ventilation* also means that a good deal of heat, which must be replaced by space-heating appliances, is lost, thus increasing heating costs. A balance between space-heating and ventilation must be maintained for comfort.

Diffusion is one of the processes concerned in ventilation. All gases attempt to distribute themselves evenly throughout the space they occupy. This is possible because the molecules of a gas are always moving. If water vapour is being produced by a steamer at one end of the salon, the water vapour molecules will spread out until they are evenly spaced, moving from the region of high to low concentration.

Convection Currents due to the upward movement of heated molecules which expand and so become less dense, and the downward movement of denser cooling molecules, contribute to ventilation.

In a salon, ventilation will occur by diffusion and convection provided suitable entrances for fresh air and exits for stale air are provided. This is known as *natural* ventilation, as all air movement occurs by natural *physical* processes. If the movement of air is assisted by fans, it is known as *artificial* ventilation.

NATURAL VENTILATION

Exits for stale air are placed high in the room as stale air, which is warm and less dense, will rise towards the ceiling. *Entrances* for cold fresh air will be at a lower level. Apart from open doors and windows, a number of special devices which allow some *control* over natural ventilation and increase comfort are available.

Louvred windows which consist of a number of movable glass strips (similar to a Venetian blind) can be fitted above a plate-glass window, or door. Each glass strip is pivoted, so that when it is in a sloping position, air can pass between the strips. If the highest part of the strip is on the inside, fresh air enters the salon. If the highest part is on the outside, stale air will leave through the louvres. Thus this type of window may be used as an inlet for fresh air or an outlet for stale air.

14.16 Louvred window

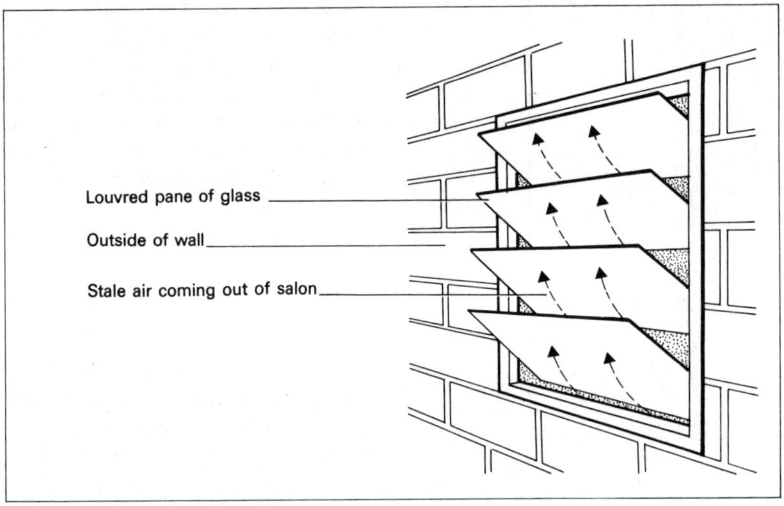

Hopper inlets are windows which are hinged at the bottom and open inwards, being held by metal guards at the sides. These are similar in effect to louvred windows, and may be fitted above internal doors in a salon.

14.17 Hopper inlet

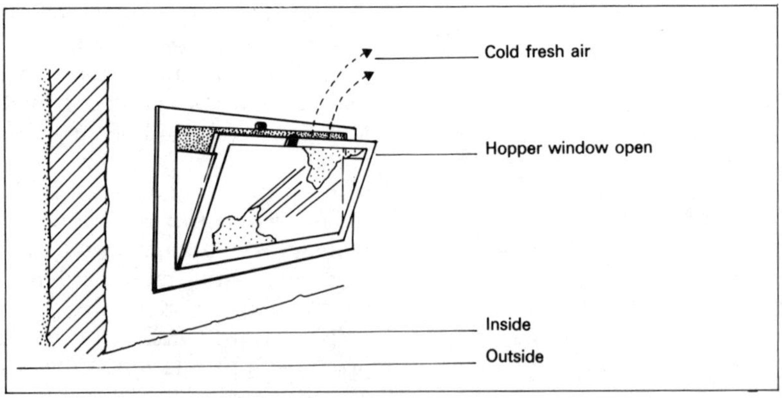

Cooper's discs consisting of two glass circles, each perforated by a number of holes, can be fitted into windows. The inner glass circle can be rotated so that the holes coincide, and allow air to pass through.

Ventilating bricks can be let into an outside wall at a high level to allow the escape of stale air. However, even when devices to aid natural ventilation are present, it remains an inadequate means of ventilating most salons, so that *artificial* ventilation is *necessary* to give a comfortable atmosphere.

ARTIFICIAL VENTILATION

Air can be moved *mechanically* by means of a *fan* driven by an *electric motor* which converts electrical energy into mechanical energy to turn the blades.

14.18 Cooper's disc

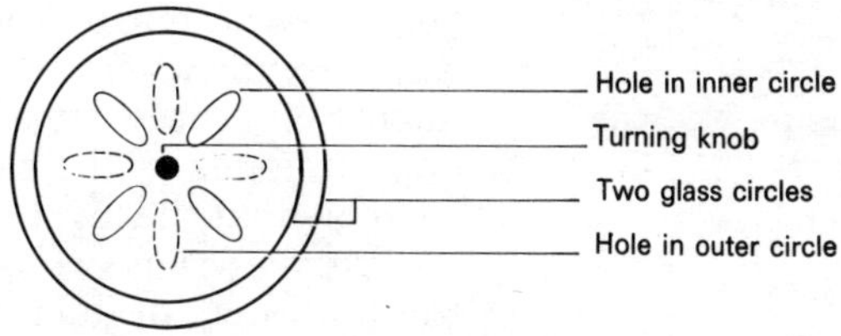

THE ELECTRIC MOTOR

An electric *current* flowing through a wire produces a *magnetic field*. This is stronger when the wire is wound into a *coil* round a *soft iron* core. An electric *motor* contains such a coil, (the *rotor*), which is made to rotate between the two opposite poles of a *permanent magnet*. An electric current is passed through the rotor, which becomes an *electromagnet*. The effect of the interaction between the magnetic fields of the permanent magnet and of the electromagnet, results in a *repulsion*, making the coil *rotate*. To keep the rotor turning always in the same direction, the direction of the electric current passing through it must change every half-turn of the rotor. A *split-ring commutator* is used for this purpose. The two free ends of the wire in the rotor are connected to one of the semi-circular plates of the split-ring.

14.19 An electric motor

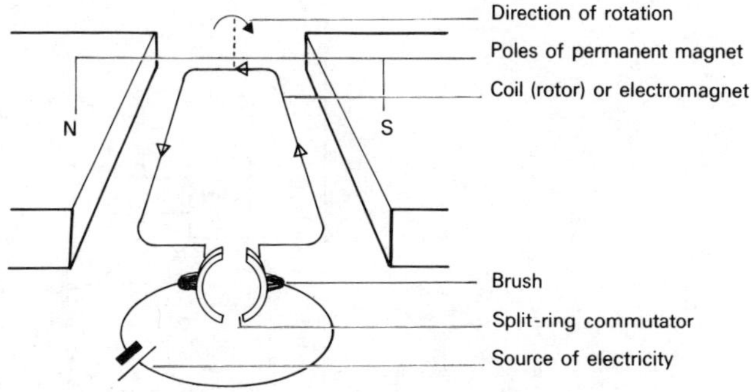

These plates rotate with the coil, and the electric current is passed to them from the *carbon brushes*. Every half turn, the commutator halves interchange brushes.

Extractor fans may be fitted into an outside wall, or in a window. An electric motor is connected to a shaft extended to form several blades. The *rotation* of the rotor turns the shaft, and movement of the blades drives *stale* air out of the salon. The speed of

14.20 An extractor fan

rotation of the blades can be altered to increase or decrease the rate of ventilation. Most fans have a *thermal cut out*, which should switch off the current if the blades stick. These fans are cheap to run, and should be installed in every hairdressing salon which has no other means of artificial ventilation.

Extraction systems. Larger salons have a *fan* which is usually on the roof of the building, connected with the salon by *ducts* terminating in *grilles*. Through these, *stale* air leaves the salon, being driven out by the fan. *Fresh* air enters by natural means, e.g. through windows. The position of inlet and outlet points is important; the most efficient arrangement is for them to be at opposite ends of the salon. The aim is to cause the greatest air movement at the level of the occupants without causing draughts.

Plenum systems consist of a fan drawing a current of fresh air into a system of ducts which open at grilles in the salon. Stale air leaves by natural ventilation through suitable openings.

Combined systems where air is moved into and out of the salon by mechanical means, are possible for large salons.

Air-conditioning

Control of the *temperature* and *humidity* of the air, and the removal of *pollutants* occurs during air conditioning. Air is brought into and out of the salon by mechanical means, using large fans, and its condition is altered by the air-conditioning plant, which contains filters, heaters, and humidifiers.

After the conditioned air has circulated through the salon it is withdrawn, and can be re-circulated. It is mixed with fresh air, and passes through the air-conditioning plant again. Air-conditioning is essential in hot climates, but as it is expensive it is only found in a few large salons in this country.

14.21 Air-conditioning plant

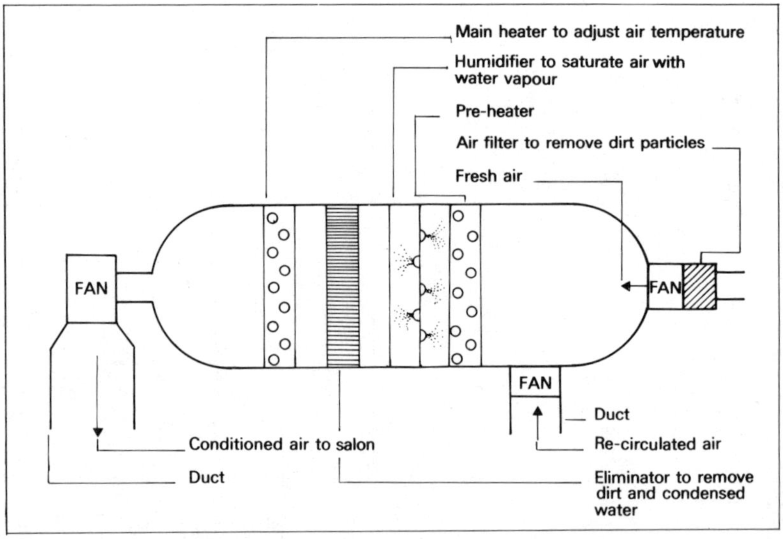

Water heating

The *temperature* of the water used for *shampooing* is important for the comfort of the client. The usual temperature of a supply of hot water is 60°C. This temperature will not produce scale in boilers where the water is hard, yet it is hot enough for laundering towels and gowns, and for cleaning the salon. For shampooing it can easily be cooled to 40°C by mixing with cold water. The quantity of hot water required in the salon will vary from day to day, so the method of heating the water must be adaptable in the interests of comfort and economy. Water heating is required all the year round. There are a number of appliances that can be used.

1 A *central heating* system can provide hot water as well as space heating, provided the hot water tank is of the *'indirect'* type, containing a central compartment, the *heat exchanger.* Hot water from the boiler circulates to the heat exchanger which heats the water for the taps in the outer part of the tank by *conduction.* This method gives a plentiful supply of hot water, and a programmer allows it to be produced with or without space heating, so that it can be used throughout the year.

2 *Immersion heaters* consist of an electric heating element immersed in the hot water tank. The heating element is fitted into a metal tube filled with a material which is an electrical insulator, but a conductor of heat. A thermostat cuts off the electricity to the element when the water reaches a preset temperature, usually 60°C. If the immersion heater is fitted

14.22 Central heating hot water system

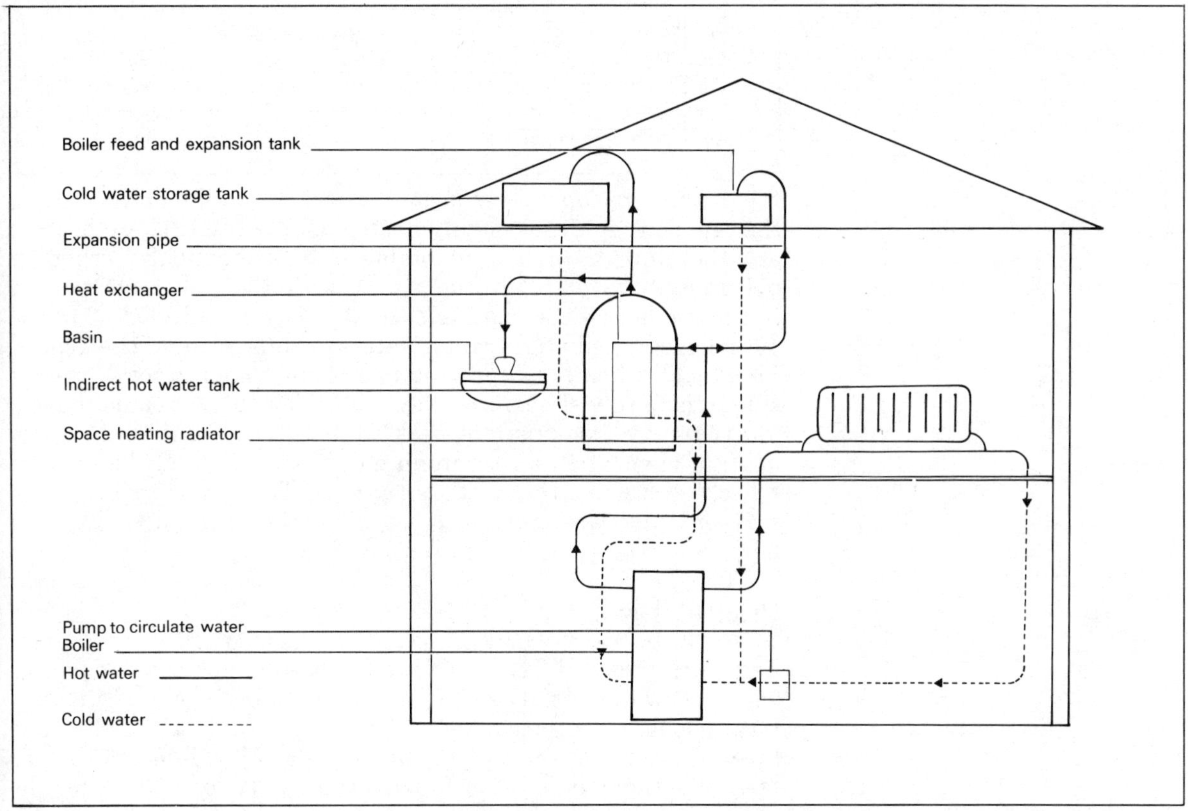

vertically at the top of the tank, it will provide a small amount of hot water there quickly, the less dense hot water floating on top of the cold water. As water is a *bad conductor* of heat, the warmth spreads downwards only slowly. If the heater is fitted *horizontally* near the bottom of the tank it will heat all the water evenly but slowly. As water at the bottom is heated, it will rise by *convection*. A *two-element* heater can be fitted which uses *off-peak* electricity at night. Both elements are vertical and fitted from the top of the tank, but one is longer than the other. The water is heated overnight, and used during the day. With immersion heaters, it is essential for the hot water tank to be completely *lagged* with a thick layer of heat-insulating material, preventing heat loss and reducing costs. Although the off-peak type of heater is less costly, it is not so adaptable, as a fixed amount of hot water is always produced, regardless of the quantity required on different days.

14.23 Immersion heater

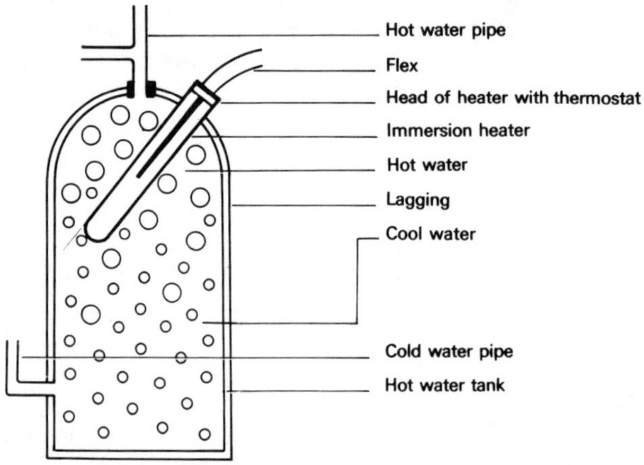

3 *Instantaneous water heaters* warm the water on its way to the tap, so that water is only heated as it is used. These heaters are therefore a highly adaptable and economical method of obtaining hot water. The fuel they use is either gas or electricity. In the *gas* heaters, a small *pilot* light burns continuously but the main burners only light when water is running out of the heater. *Single point* heaters supplying one basin, or *multipoint* heaters supplying a row of basins are available. The heaters must have a *flue* to remove combustion gases. In the *electric* heaters there is a heating element like that in an electric kettle, and the current switches on when the water is running. These heaters are much smaller and less conspicuous than the gas instantaneous heaters.

Practical work

1 TO FIND THE VOLUME OF OXYGEN PRESENT IN AIR

Take a trough and fix a candle to the bottom by means of melted wax. Put water into the trough to a depth of 5 cm, and invert a large gas jar over the candle. With a Chinagraph pencil mark the level of the water on the outside of the gas jar. Remove the gas jar, light the candle, then replace the gas jar over it. After the candle flame goes out mark the new water level in the gas jar. Remove the gas jar and fill it with water up to the first mark you made. Using a measuring cylinder find the volume of this water, which is equal to the volume of air originally in the gas jar (A). Fill the gas jar up to the second mark you made and find this

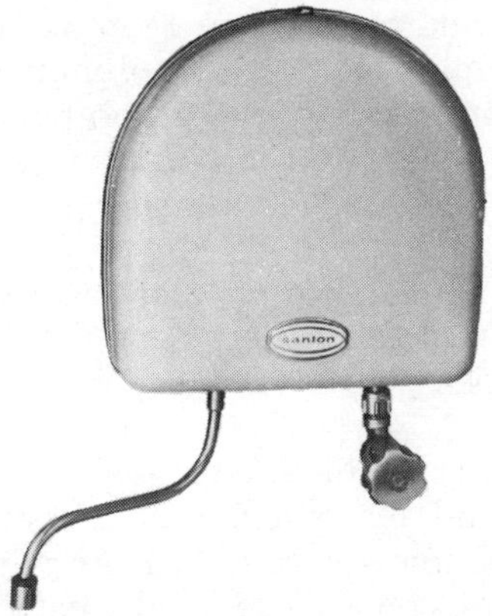

Electric instantaneous heater

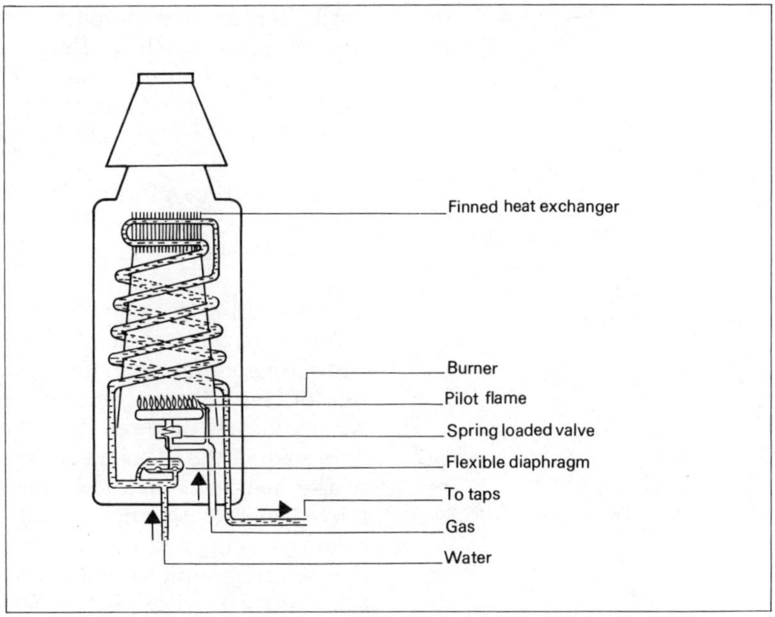

14.24 Gas multipoint instantaneous heater

volume (B), which is equal to the volume of air left in the gas jar when the candle flame went out. The difference between the two volumes (A-B) is the volume of oxygen used up (C). Find the % of oxygen in the air from the expression: $\frac{C}{A} \times 100$

Note. The result will probably be low because the candle flame goes out before all the oxygen is used up.

2 TO DEMONSTRATE ATMOSPHERIC PRESSURE

Take a tall narrow tin can with completely air-tight seams and a narrow opening with a tightly fitting cork. Remove the cork and place a little water in the can. Support the can on a tripod and gauze, and heat it with a bunsen flame until the water boils and steam comes out from the top. Turn off the burner, place the cork firmly in the opening at the top of the can, and leave it to cool down. As the steam inside the can has driven out much of the air, when the steam condenses a partial vacuum will be produced, so that the air pressure outside the can is greater than the pressure inside. The walls of the can will thus be pushed inwards.

3 TO PREPARE A TEMPERATURE CONVERSION GRAPH

Take a large beaker, and two-thirds fill it with tap water. Support it on a tripod and gauze, and place two thermometers in the water, one being a Celsius, and the other a Fahrenheit thermometer. Take the temperature of the water with both thermometers, and write down the readings at the top of two columns on a sheet of paper. Place a bunsen with a small flame under the beaker, so that the water is heated slowly to its boiling point. As it is heating, take the temperature every half minute with both thermometers simultaneously, and record your readings in the columns as before. Prepare a graph from the two columns of temperature readings, using the shorter side of the graph paper for the Celsius temperatures. Do not join up the points on the graph, but rule a straight line which goes through as many points as possible.

The *accuracy* of your graph can be checked by plotting two points using the known fixed points on the scales, i.e. 0°C/32°F and 100°C/212°F, and joining these two points.

4 TO COMPARE THE INSULATING QUALITY OF MATERIALS

Take four 250 ml (cm³) beakers and place a 6 inch Celsius thermometer in each. Pack the thermometer round firmly with one of the following materials; polystyrene pieces, hair, cotton wool, glass wool lagging. Use a different material in each beaker, and ensure that the thermometer bulb is 5 cm from the bottom of the beaker. Place the beakers in a trough of hot water, and leave them for two minutes. Lift up each thermometer in turn to read the temperature, and replace it quickly. Leave for a further five minutes, and take another temperature reading. The lowest temperature indicates the best insulator.

5 TO SHOW THAT WATER IS A BAD CONDUCTOR OF HEAT

Take a test-tube, and half fill it with water. Place in it a piece of paraffin wax that has been weighted by lead shot. Using a stand and clamp, support the tube so that it is almost horizontal. Heat the water at the top, using a small bunsen flame. Note that the water will boil at the top of the tube, while remaining too cool to melt the wax at the bottom.

6 TO SHOW HOW THE SURFACE AFFECTS THE ABSORPTION OF RADIANT HEAT

Take two squares of metal, and place a short Celsius thermometer in the holder behind each. One square should have a shiny metal surface and the other a dull black painted surface. Support each metal square vertically by means of a stand and clamp, and place them so that each is equidistant from a bunsen burner (approx. 20 cm). Clamp a piece of metal piping over the bunsen flame to provide a source of radiant heat. Take the temperature of both thermometers simultaneously every half minute and record your readings. A higher temperature means that more radiant heat has been absorbed.

14.25 Radiation experiment

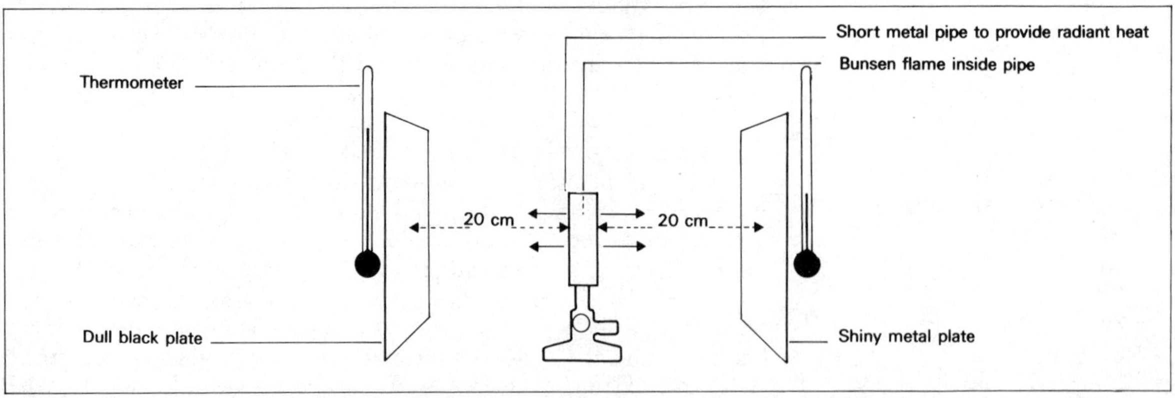

Multiple choice questions

1 An instrument used to measure the humidity in the salon is
a an anaeroid barometer *b* a hair hygrometer
c a clinical thermometer *d* a mercury barometer

2 The water used for shampooing hair will not cause discomfort to your client if its temperature is
a 10°C *b* 40°C *c* 60°C *d* 90°C

3 A balanced flue heater has the advantage that
a the space heating is by radiation
b humidity in the salon is increased
c flue gases do not enter the salon
d it air-conditions the salon

4 The pipes connecting with a salon basin hot tap lead out of the top of the hot water tank because
a hot water rises by convection
b the hot tank is of the indirect type
c hot water is pumped to the top of the tank
d the tank has a lagging jacket

5 As hairdressing proceeds in a salon the air changes becoming
a cooler and saturated *b* staler and drier
c warmer and denser *d* warmer and more humid

6 If your gas bill states that you have been supplied with 450 therms, the number of British thermal units your gas appliances have given is
a 4·50 *b* 45 *c* 450,000 *d* 45,000,000

7 The method by which heat from the sun travels through space and air is
a radiation *b* convection *c* insulation *d* conduction

8 When the salon air is cooled below its dew point temperature it will contain less
a oxygen *b* nitrogen *c* water vapour
d carbon dioxide

9 The physical processes on which natural ventilation depends are
a humidity and condensation
b conduction and radiation
c diffusion and convection
d evaporation and condensation

10 A device which contains both a permanent magnet and an electromagnet is likely to be
a a time-switch *b* an electric motor *c* a thermostat
d an immersion heater

15
Hygiene in the Salon

Hygiene is the science and practice of maintaining *health*. In the salon, this is achieved by scrupulous *cleanliness* of the salon itself, the hairdressing staff, and the tools and equipment used on the clients. The *diseases* which can be passed from person to person are caused by tiny living organisms (*micro-organisms*) called *pathogens* (germs). These are the organisms which must be destroyed, or prevented from multiplying and spreading to other people. However not all micro-organisms are pathogens, i.e. disease-producing; many are harmless.

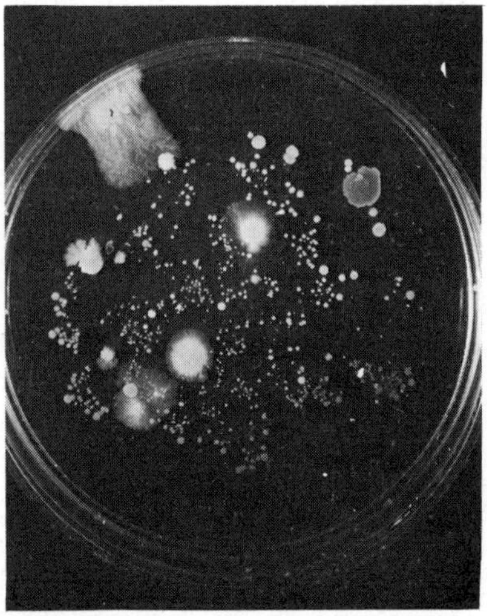

15.1 Agar plate from infected fingers

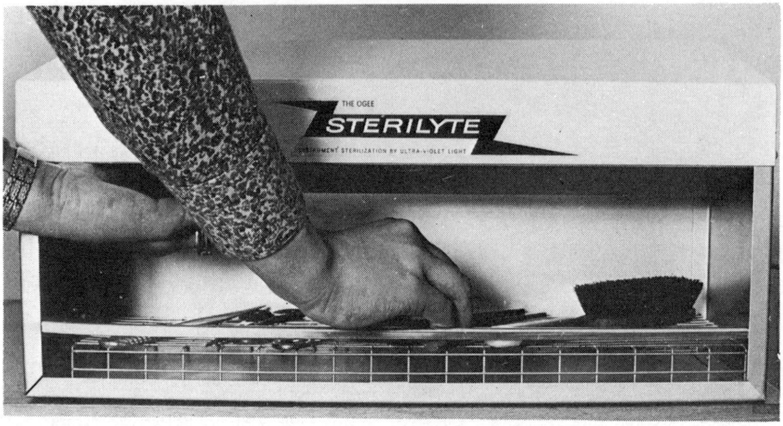

The conditions in a salon will normally favour the spread of pathogens for three reasons; the *clients*, the high *temperature*, the high *humidity*. Large numbers of people enter each day thus continually introducing micro-organisms on the clothing, skin, and hair and in the air they breathe out. Thus salon air and surfaces are being continually *reinfected*. *Dust* particles from clothes, *droplets* from the nose and throat produced by coughing and sneezing, and 'rafts' *of skin* rubbed off by friction, all carry large numbers of micro-organisms.

These micro-organisms are either *fungi*, *bacteria*, or *viruses* (see chapter 16). The fungi are either *yeasts* or the spores of *moulds*, and very few are pathogenic. Yeasts grow most abundantly on the scalp, on the greasy areas of the face, and between the toes. Fungal spores occur on the clothing and hair. Enormous numbers of *bacteria* occur on the skin, particularly on the face, neck, armpits and groin.

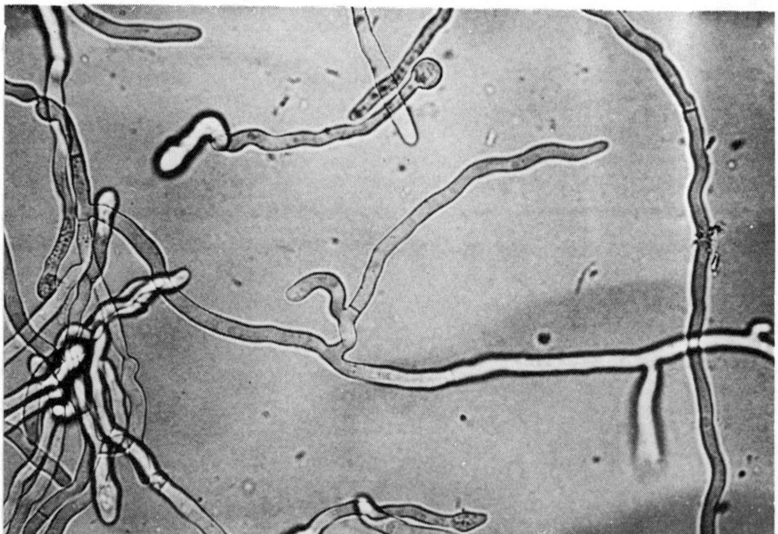

15.2 Fungal hyphae

Some bacteria are pathogens, but many are harmless. Among the pathogenic bacteria are *staphylococci* and *streptococci*. These two types of bacteria are responsible for most septic infections causing inflammation in any tissue. Staphylococci divide to form groups or *bunches*, while streptococci form *chains*. Bacteria are

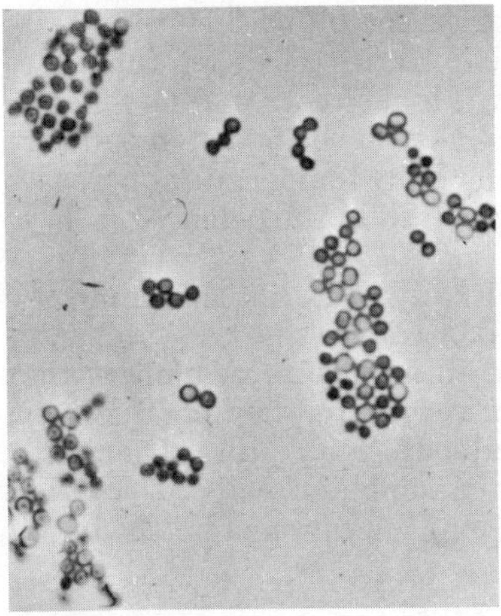

15.3 Staphylococci

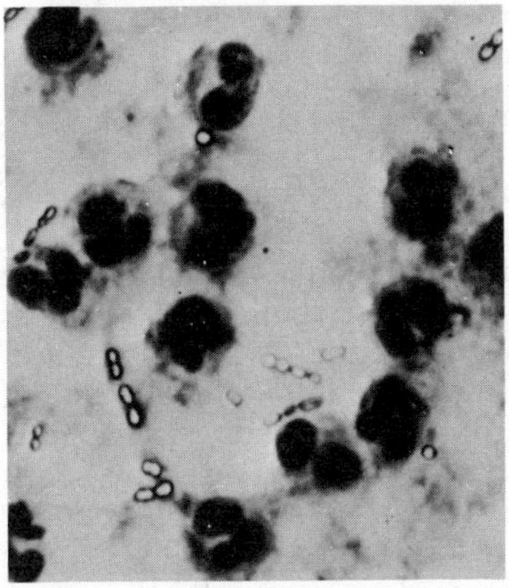

Streptococci

15.4 Wart virus particle

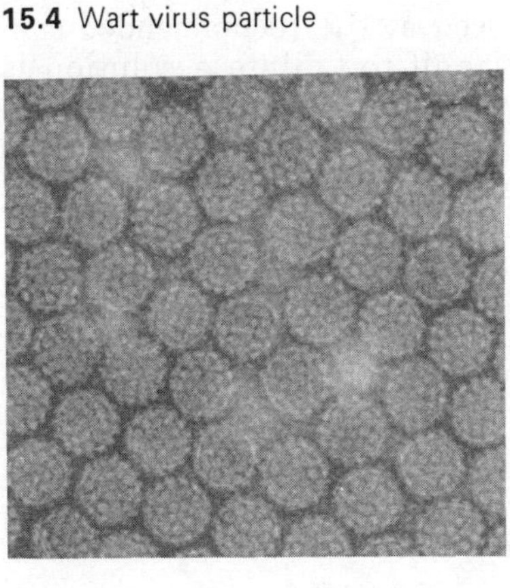

present on skin particles, clothing and droplets from the nose and mouth, and there is a constant transfer from one person to another by contact, and convection currents in the air.

Viruses leave the nose and mouth in droplets of mucus and thus can survive for a short time out of the body. To infect, they must be breathed in by another person almost immediately.

The *temperature* of the salon, which is kept fairly high to keep clients with wet heads feeling comfortable, aids the survival of micro-organisms in the air and on the salon surfaces. Pathogenic bacteria grow best at *body* temperature (37°C), so the warmer the salon, the longer they survive.

The high *humidity* in the salon provides a moist atmosphere which all micro-organisms require. The humidity will be higher as the temperature increases, and as ventilation becomes less effective, since warm air holds more water vapour than cool air. Thus the salon provides conditions in which micro-organisms will thrive, namely a food supply (the people present), oxygen and moisture (from air), and a favourable temperature.

How pathogens enter the body

Pathogenic micro-organisms will enter the body, and thus cause disease, through *breaks* in the *skin*, by being *breathed* in, or by the *mouth*. Areas of skin which are rubbed, chapped, cut, or scratched provide points of entry. Pathogens present in the air which is breathed in attack the lining of the nose, throat, and deeper air passages. Infected fingers, cups, food and drink, carry pathogens to the mouth and so into the digestive system.

Methods by which the body resists infection

The body has its own *defence* mechanism for resisting any attack by pathogens. The *white blood cells* play a major role in this *resistance* to disease. One type move to the site of infection, and engulf and destroy the invading pathogens (phagocytosis). The white cells then die and form *pus*. Another type of white blood cell produces chemical substances called *antibodies* which destroy pathogens and the poisonous substances, *toxins*, which some of them produce. The antibody destroys the pathogen by sticking to its surface, and causing it to *burst*, or making a number of pathogens *clump* together. This defence method is known as the *immune reaction*. A *specific* antibody is produced in response to each type of pathogen. These antibodies may remain in the blood for a considerable time after the first infection by the causal pathogen. Any further attack by this same pathogen will be immediately dealt with by the existing antibodies, so that the person is *immune* to the disease it causes. Different antibodies persist for different lengths of time, so the length of the immune period varies with the pathogen. This is known as *active* immunity, since people make their own antibodies in response to an attack by the pathogen. *Active artificial* immunity can be given to a person by injecting a small amount of material from a pathogen, called a *vaccine*, which acts like the pathogen, causing the person to form the antibody. Immunity to polio, smallpox and influenza can be obtained by this method. *Passive artificial* immunity occurs when a person is injected with the *antibody* against a particular pathogen, not the pathogen itself. Immunity to diphtheria is obtained by this means.

When a pathogen attacks the body, the blood flow to the site of infection increases. The blood capillaries dilate, so that more heat is brought to this region and it looks red, i.e. *inflammation* occurs. The body retains more heat, so that the body temperature rises, and produces *fever*. The higher body temperature increases the rate of the chemical changes involved in the defence mechanisms.

The body of a healthy person normally contains small numbers of pathogens which are kept in control by the body's defence mechanisms. If pathogens invade in such large numbers that the body's defences are overcome, they enter the blood stream, are carried all round the body, and a *disease* results. The pathogens continue to multiply in the tissues and cells, destroying them and interfering with the normal functions of the body.

Disinfection

There are a number of ways in which pathogens can be *destroyed* or *inactivated*, some of which are more effective than others. The three main methods employ *chemicals*, *heat*, and *ultra-violet* radiation respectively, and the process is called disinfection.

CHEMICAL DISINFECTION

Chemical disinfection is carried out by three groups of substances, antiseptics, disinfectants, and sterilizing agents.

An *antiseptic* is a chemical which prevents pathogens from *multiplying*, but does not necessarily kill them. The simplest antiseptic is *soap* or *detergent* and *hot* water. A 1% solution of *Cetrimide* (Cetyl trimethyl ammonium bromide) which is one of a group of quaternary ammonium compounds, is a good antiseptic for use in the salon, but it is inactivated by soaps and soapless detergents. Another antiseptic is *Hexachlorophene* (a diphenyl), which is one of the few not inactivated by soap or soapless detergents, and so can be used to 'medicate' them (see chapter 3). There are now legal limitations on its use. Certain of the *essential oils* act as antiseptics, e.g. sandalwood, rose, and bay oils. These mainly act against the fungal micro-organisms. *Hydrogen peroxide* acts as an antiseptic, the oxygen it liberates destroying some of the micro-organisms. Certain mild antiseptics are added to hairdressing lotions as preservatives, as they prevent the growth of moulds and bacteria, e.g. *Salicylic acid, Nipagin.*

A *disinfectant* (germicide, bactericide) is a chemical which *kills* most pathogens when it is used at the recommended *concentration*, and for a sufficient *time*. If too dilute a solution is used, or the time is too short, it acts as an antiseptic, i.e. does not destroy the pathogens, but only prevents them from multiplying. *Examples* of disinfectants are ethanol, formalin (40% formaldehyde solution), phenolics (from coal tar), xylenol, and chlorine bleach. *Chlorine* reacts with water to form a very reactive compound called *hypochlorous acid*, which readily gives off oxygen. This free oxygen is responsible for the bleaching property, and for the destruction of pathogens. Hydrochloric acid is produced by chlorine bleach, which makes it unsuitable for use on surfaces which are attacked by acid, including the skin. Chlorine is used to destry the micro-organisms in drinking water. *Sterilization* is the *total destruction* of all micro-organisms, and their *spores*, in the substance treated. *Formaldehyde* is a chemical sterilizing agent. This is liberated as a gas inside one type of sterilizing cabinet in which a 5% formaldehyde solution is heated by an electric element.

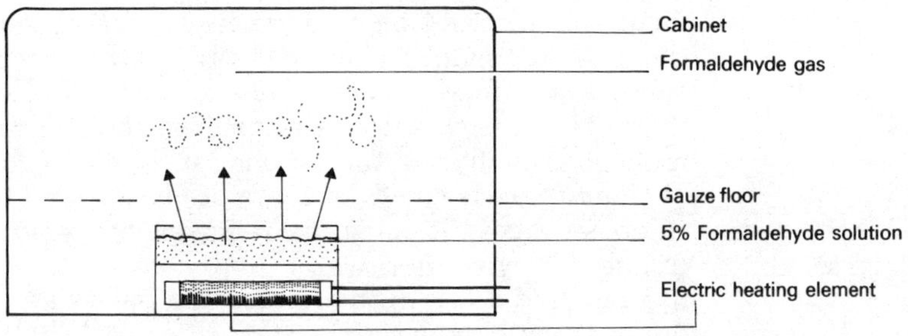

15.5 Formaldehyde sterilizing cabinet

DISINFECTION BY HEAT

Heating to 70°C will destroy many micro-organisms. This treatment is applied to milk during *pasteurisation*. It does not however, kill most *spores*, which are more resistant than the active micro-organisms.

Boiling water will destroy pathogens provided the object is boiled for at least 15 minutes. Towels, gowns and overalls, etc., should be moved around, so that the boiling water reaches all surfaces.

Steam under pressure results in a temperature higher than 100°C, and is produced in an *autoclave*. This is a very effective means of rapid sterilization and is used in hospitals, and to prepare sterile first-aid dressings.

Burning will destroy micro-organisms, and is the method used for infected dressings, hair, etc., which must be hygienically disposed of. A *flame* is also used to sterilize the platinum wire loops used in transferring micro-organisms to *Agar plates* before culturing them.

DISINFECTION BY ULTRA-VIOLET RADIATION

Ultra-violet rays will destroy pathogens. Strong *sunlight* and quartz *mercury vapour* lamps produce these rays. One type of salon *sterilizing cabinet* contains a mercury vapour lamp to produce these rays. Ultra-violet rays produce skin *burns*, so care must be taken not to subject the skin of the hands to them for any length of time. Ultra-violet rays from lamps may be used for destroying micro-organisms on the skin as a form of treatment for skin disorders, e.g. boils, and as a means of obtaining a tan. Ultra-violet rays can damage the eyes, as well as the skin, so *dark glasses* must be worn, and the skin exposed to the radiation for a *limited time*.

Methods of controlling micro-organisms in the salon

In addition to the internal defence mechanisms of the body, there are a number of external methods for controlling micro-organisms in the salon.

1 Micro-organisms in the air will die more quickly if the humidity is reduced by *improving ventilation*, and their numbers will be reduced if the people using the salon cough or sneeze into a *handkerchief*.

2 Salon *surfaces* will pick up a large quantity of micro-organisms which have settled out of the air as *dust*. Tiny fragments of skin and hair and their attendant germs form 87% of the dust in a salon. They will stick to the greasy smears left on surfaces by fingers. Where dust settles in dark corners, on the floor or on the salon equipment, the micro-organisms will multiply rapidly, as the absence of light favours their growth. *Dust and grease* must not therefore be allowed to accumulate on salon surfaces. It must be removed by *washing* the surfaces frequently with hot water and detergent. The standards of hygiene laid down in the Health and Safety at Work Act require floors to be cleaned at least once a week by washing. This is quite inadequate for a salon, however, where all surfaces should be freed from dirt at least once every day. Apart from the large human skin element in dust, it will also contain fine grit brought in on the shoes of clients and staff, carbon particles from car exhausts, fibres from clothing, and pollen from flowering plants, to which some people have an *allergy* known as *hay-fever*. Dust or *dirt* is usually defined as matter in the wrong place.

The salon *floor* should have a surface in which dirt cannot lodge, and which can be easily swept and washed. Non-slip *thermoplastic* coverings coved at the wall have these properties. The brushes, mops, and cloths used in cleaning floors, should be frequently washed with boiling water and detergent.

Dressing-out tables are most easily cleaned if they have a hard plastic surface without grooves or a retaining rim in which dirt will be trapped. This type of surface can be washed down with hot water and detergent. Dust and splashes of lacquer or hair preparations can be removed from *mirrors* by cleaning them with methylated spirit or isopropanol, and then polishing the mirror with a clean dry duster.

The *seating* in the salon should be upholstered in a material which is easily cleaned, and to which hair does not stick. *Vinyl* upholstery fabric can be washed with detergent and water, and has a smooth surface. *Wool* upholstery fabric must be cleaned with a suction cleaner.

Hair and dust must be regularly removed from the *hairdryers* and the rest of the salon furniture.

Rubbish bins must be kept *covered*. The pedal type of opener stops micro-organisms being transferred to the hands. The bins should be emptied frequently, and washed with hot water and detergent regularly. The most suitable material for rubbish bins is *plastic*, as it is easily washed, and quiet in use.

3 *Washbasins and drains*

The salon *basins* and *lavatory* are connected with the *drains* in which micro-organisms from sewage and waste water flourish. Because of this connection with the rest of the drainage system, each basin has a *trap* in the waste pipe leading from the plug hole. This trap consists of a *water seal* to prevent airborne pathogens and unpleasant smelling gases from the drains entering the salon. There are two common types, known as *S-traps* and *bottle traps*, both retaining some water each time the basin is emptied.

15.6 S-trap

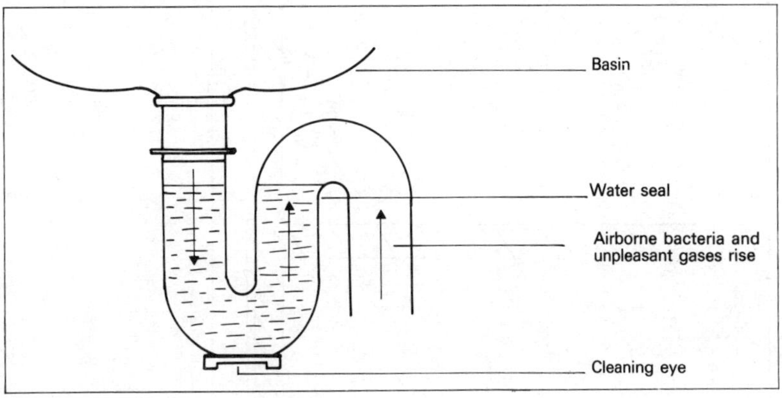

Bottle trap

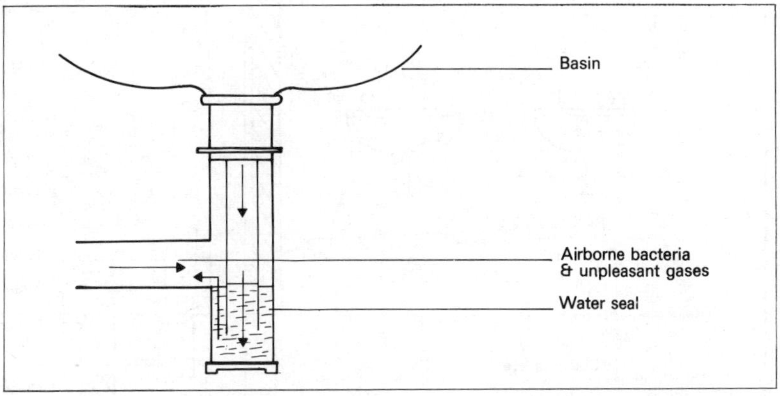

The trap has a removable cap, or *cleaning eye*, at the base, so that the water forming the seal can run out, and any solids deposited can be removed. A *plastic filter* in the plug hole will prevent hair from getting into the trap and blocking the waste pipe.

Below the trap, the basin waste pipes run into a *waste water pipe* which empties outside the building into a *gulley trap* (drain) below ground. The gulley trap is a short pipe, covered at ground level by a protective grating, while below it is bent into an S-bend with a *water seal*. From here, it opens into a large underground *inspection chamber* which is covered by an air-tight *drain cover*.

The *lavatory* waste passes through a *water seal* at the base of the lavatory pan, into a *soil pipe*, which runs down the outside of the building, opening at the bottom into the inspection chamber. The top of the soil pipe, which is above the highest window in the building, is open to allow the escape of unpleasant smelling gases.

From the inspection chamber all the waste passes into the *main drain*, leading to the *sewer* in the road.

The basin waste pipes and the gulley trap can be treated with *sodium carbonate* (washing soda) and boiling water. This will remove grease in which the micro-organisms could be held, and will also kill any pathogens.

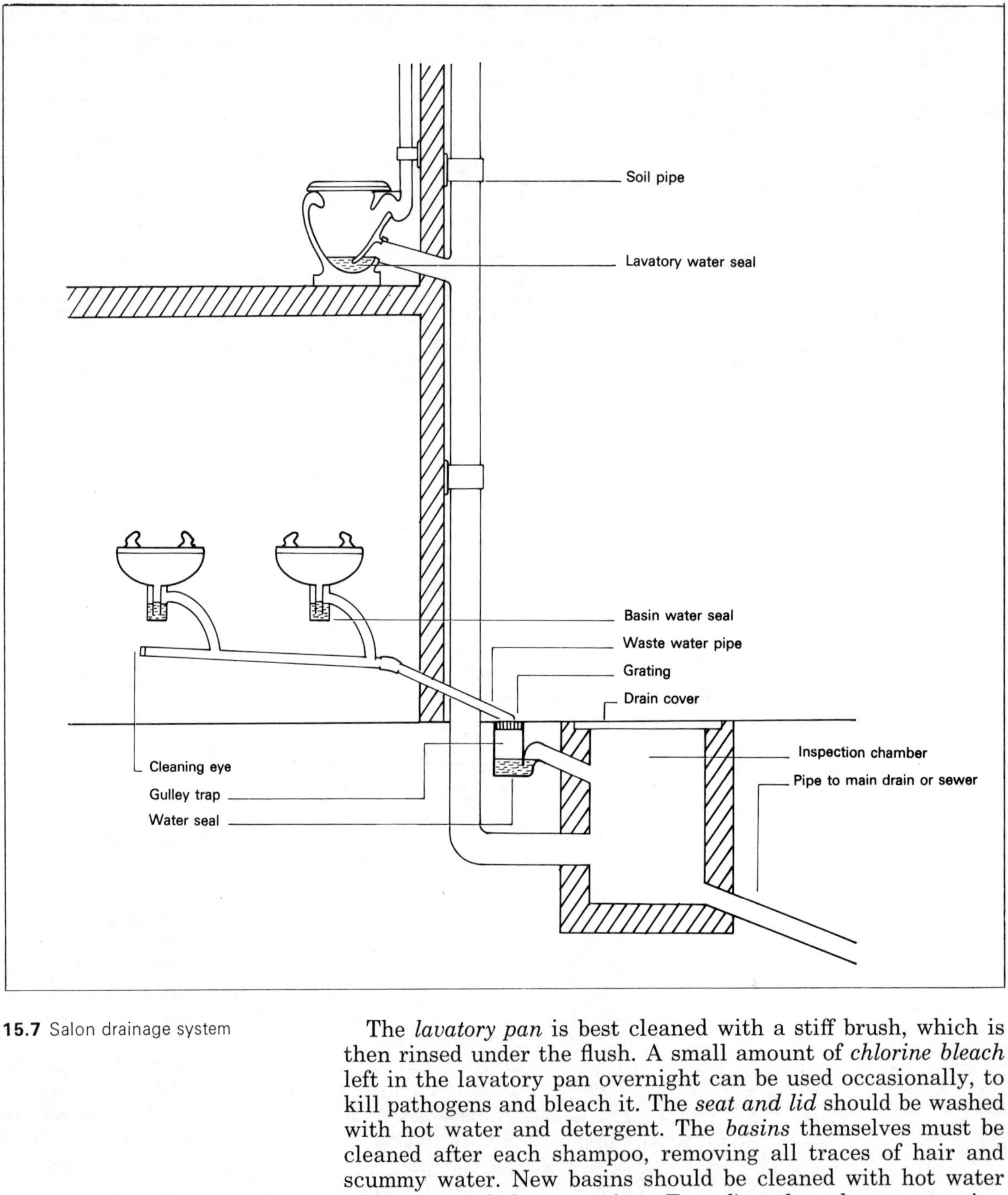

15.7 Salon drainage system

The *lavatory pan* is best cleaned with a stiff brush, which is then rinsed under the flush. A small amount of *chlorine bleach* left in the lavatory pan overnight can be used occasionally, to kill pathogens and bleach it. The *seat and lid* should be washed with hot water and detergent. The *basins* themselves must be cleaned after each shampoo, removing all traces of hair and scummy water. New basins should be cleaned with hot water and a *neutral detergent* (e.g. Teepol) rather than a scouring powder, as the abrasive will damage the porcelain surface, leaving small pits in which micro-organisms can collect.

4 *Tools and equipment*
As a hairdresser's equipment is used on each client, it is necessary to ensure that pathogens are not picked up from one client and passed on to the next during the hairdressing service. To keep *tools* free from infection, a hairdresser should have two

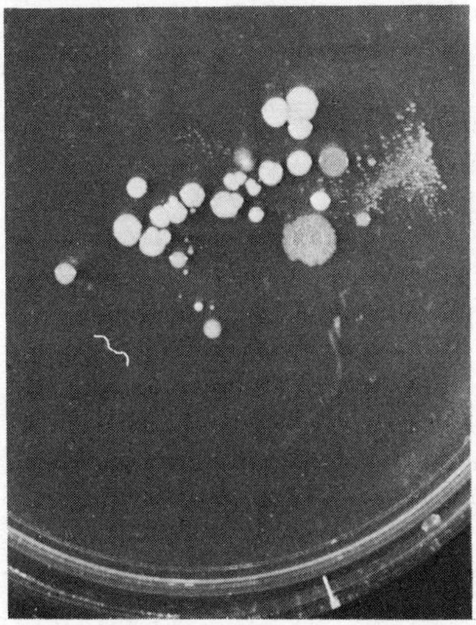

15.8 Agar plate from neck of gown

sets, one in use, and the other kept in the salon *sterilizer*, to be used for the next client. The set in use should be placed on a clean *paper towel* on the dressing-out table. Tools should never be placed in overall *pockets* where they can pick up micro-organisms from handkerchiefs, or dust trapped in the seams. After a known infection all tools must be thoroughly disinfected. *Sharp* tools like razors and scissors may be wiped over with ethanol or methylated spirit, and brushes and combs placed in the *sterilizing cabinet*, or an antiseptic solution, such as 1% *Cetrimide* solution.

Each client should have clean *towels*. A towel which has been used for a previous client and then dried, but not washed, would be a likely source of infection. The warmth supplied when drying the towel would allow any pathogens to multiply, so this practice is very unhygienic. If each client is not provided with a clean *gown*, then a clean disposable *neck strip* should be provided. This will prevent the neck of the gown coming into contact with the client's skin and either picking up or passing on pathogens.

Disposable *ear covers*, either strips of tissue, or fresh pieces of cotton wool, are more hygienic than the plastic variety of ear protection. If these are used, they should be placed in the sterilizing cabinet for an adequate length of time before being used on another client.

Hair nets and rollers should also be placed in the sterilizing cabinet from time to time.

Personal hygiene

A hairdresser needs to maintain a high standard of personal hygiene because she comes into very close contact with her clients. Personal hygiene involves the *cleanliness* of skin, hair, and clothing.

The *skin* needs to be *washed* all over daily to remove the layer of sweat, sebum, and dead epidermal cells, on which micro-organisms present on the skin surface feed. The substances produced by this action have unpleasant smells, particularly those from the *sweat* produced by the *apocrine glands* in the armpits. Apocrine sweat is a milky fluid containing small amounts of organic substances (proteins, sugars). *Deodorants* which remove smells, and *antiperspirants* which reduce sweating, in addition to washing, are helpful in this connection. *Make-up* should be removed from the skin, particularly at night. Because cosmetics are fatty emulsions, they can be removed by cold cream or by soap and water. Stale make-up adheres to cold cream, so the mixture can be wiped off with a tissue. Soap will emulsify fatty cosmetic materials so that they can be rinsed away. Astringents, which tighten the skin and close the pores, may be applied to oily, but not to dry skins. Cold water, witch-hazel, ethanol, and after-shave lotions all act as astringents. Because *faeces* contain large numbers of micro-organisms many of which are pathogens, you should always *wash your hands* after using the *lavatory*. The hands should also be *washed* before preparing and eating *food*.

The *hair* must be shampooed regularly to remove the coating of sebum to which dirt and micro-organisms have become attached. *Brushing* the hair stimulates the sebaceous glands and spreads the sebum evenly over the hair shaft. It also removes dust and dandruff, and ensures that small animal parasites do not get established on the scalp. The *brush* used should be *washed* frequently in warm water and detergent and its bristles should have rounded ends so that they cannot scratch the scalp and allow pathogens to penetrate the skin.

CLOTHING

The hairdresser's *clothing* serves two main biological purposes. It helps to keep the body at its normal *temperature*, aiding heat loss if the body becomes too warm, and heat retention if the body temperature falls. It also provides *protection* from weather, chemicals, and micro-organisms. The properties of clothing depend largely on the *textile fibre* of which they are composed. The most important properties of a fibre are its ability to absorb water, conduct heat, and trap air. The less *absorbent* a fibre, the more quickly it *dries* after laundering, but the less easily it absorbs sweat. Fibres which *trap air* will help the body to retain *heat*, as air is an insulator. Fibres can be *textured* to put air spaces into them, e.g. Crimplene.

Textile fibres are of two main types. *Natural* fibres are those that occur in nature, being obtained from plants or animals. *Man-made* fibres are produced by forcing viscous liquid chemicals through fine holes in a nozzle, and then solidifying the filaments produced. The viscous liquid may be obtained by treating *wood pulp* with chemicals to form *regenerated* fibres, or new large molecules may be produced by *polymerization* from simple chemicals obtained from *oil* or *coal-tar*. These polymers are known as *synthetic* fibres. The properties of some common textile fibres are given in the table opposite.

15.9 Wool, viscose and polyester fibres

The *clothing* worn in the salon must allow *loss of heat* from the body readily, as the salon temperature has to be kept fairly high. It must be *absorptive* so that it will soak up the sweat produced then allow it to evaporate in order to cool the body and maintain its normal temperature. It must be *easily washed* and dried so that sweat, sebum, and micro-organisms can be removed frequently, without damaging the garment.

For *underwear* the most suitable fibre is *cotton*. Nylon is only suitable in cooler weather. It is non-absorbent and does not allow

Table of textile fibres

Name	Type	Water absorbency	Other names	Qualities of clothing made from the fibre	Laundering HLCC process
Wool	Natural (sheep)	High		Light, warm, sweat absorbent. Attacked by moths. Does not hold its shape.	[7]
Cotton	Natural (plant)	Moderate		Allows heat loss, so cool in a warm atmosphere. Hard-wearing.	[2]
Flax	Natural (plant)	Moderate	Linen	Allows heat loss, so cool in a warm atmosphere. Creases. Expensive.	[2]
Silk	Natural (insect)	Moderate		Light, warm, sweat absorbent. Expensive.	Dry clean
Viscose	Man-made regenerated	High	Sarille Vincel Rayon	Light, warm, sweat absorbent. Weak when wet, otherwise hardwearing. Creases.	[5]
Acetate	Man-made	Moderate	Dicel	Like cotton but not as strong. Creases. Develops static electricity, attracts dirt.	[6]
Triacetate	Man-made	Low	Tricel	Like cotton but not as strong. Crease resistant. Develops static electricity.	[6]
Nylon	Man-made synthetic	Low	Bri-nylon Enkalon	Very strong. Stretches. Develops static electricity so attracts dirt. Hot in a warm atmosphere. Dries quickly.	[3] white [4] coloured
Polyester	Man-made synthetic	Very low	Dacron Terylene Crimplene	Very strong. Warm. Crease resistant. Develops static electricity.	[3] white [4] coloured
Acrylic	Man-made synthetic	Low	Acrilan Orlon Courtelle	Soft, warm and light. Fairly strong. Does not absorb sweat. Mothproof. Keeps its shape.	[6]
Moda-crylic	Man-made synthetic	Low	Teklan Dynel	Flameproof. Develops static electricity. Used in wigs.	[6]

the body to lose heat. *Stockings* and tights are made of nylon because this fibre is elastic, hard wearing, and easily laundered. *Overalls* must be made of a fibre which is washable, dries quickly, keeps its shape, is hardwearing, and protects the clothing below from water splashes or lotions. If the overall is pale in colour, dirt will be more readily noticed and it is therefore more likely

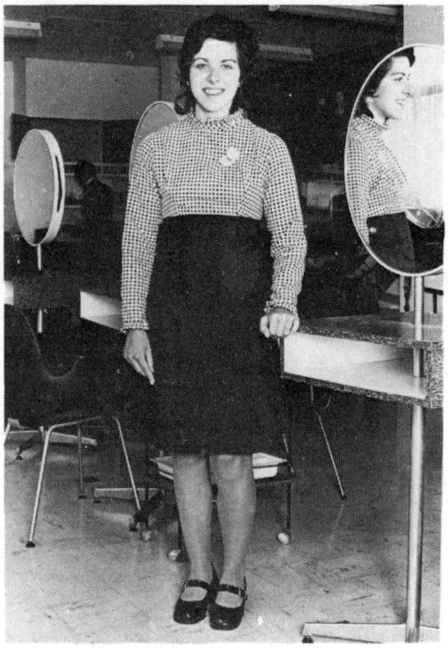

15.10 Suitable hairdressing overall

to be washed frequently. The style chosen for the overall should allow air to circulate round the body and permit easy movement. *Nylon* has many of the required properties for use in overalls, but it has the disadvantage that it may retain body heat and increase sweating. *Cotton* is cooler in wear, and is suitable for overalls provided the fabric is treated to make it crease-resistant, water-repellant, and drip-dry. *Blends* of cotton with man-made fibres such as polyester are also suitable for overalls.

Apart from the *cleanliness* of her person, the hairdresser should maintain a high standard of *health* by having a suitable *diet*, and enough *exercise* and *rest*, so that the body is able to *resist* attack by pathogens. If a hairdresser develops an infectious disease she should stay away from work until normal good health has been regained.

Practical work

1 TO FIND THE SOURCES OF MICRO-ORGANISMS IN THE SALON

You require a number of sterile nutrient agar plates which have been previously prepared. Leave the lid covering each plate until you are ready to use it, and replace the lid very quickly after transferring your material to it. The material tested may be obtained from any salon source. The material may be picked up on a platinum wire loop, which has been previously sterilized in a flame. Where fabrics or skin are being tested for micro-organisms they may be gently pressed onto the agar plate. After placing your material on the plate, write an identification on the lid with a chinagraph pencil. The plate will then need to be incubated at 37°C so that any micro-organisms which have been introduced will grow rapidly, feeding on the nutrient agar. Observe each plate again after a few days incubation, and note which salon sources provided the largest number of micro-organisms.

Suggested sources of micro-organisms

1 The neck-band of a gown which has been in use.
2 The plug hole of a basin after shampooing.
3 Hair clippings.
4 Fingers.
5 Dust from the salon floor.
6 A page of the appointment book.
7 Used comb.
8 Dirt from under finger nails.

Care should be taken after incubation, as some of the micro-organisms could be *pathogenic*. It is best to observe them *without removing the lid.*

2 TO FIND THE EFFECTIVENESS OF THE STERILIZING CABINET

Take two filter papers and place on each clippings of hair which have not been washed before cutting. Take two sterile nutrient agar plates which have been prepared previously. Transfer the hair from one of the filter papers to one of the agar plates, mark to identify it, and place it ready for incubation as a control. Place a second filter paper and hair into the sterilizing cabinet, and leave it there for the time specified by the manufacturer, then remove it and, without touching it, slide the hair on to the second agar plate. Mark the lid to identify the plate, and place it ready for incubation. After a few days incubation, examine both plates and compare the amount of microbial growth. There should be much less from the hair which had been placed in the sterilizer.

3 TESTS ON TEXTILE FIBRES

Using a pair of tongs, hold small tufts of a series of different textile fibres in a small bunsen flame for a few seconds, and then remove them from the flame. Notice how readily each one will ignite, and if it burns, whether it continues to do so on removing it from the flame, i.e. if it is self-*extinguishing*. Note any smell which is produced, and the nature of the material left after burning. Fibres to test are hair, wool, silk, cotton, viscose, nylon, polyester (Terylene), modacrylic, and acrylic (Courtelle). Put your observations down in a table of results:

Name of fibre	Inflammable	Self-extinguishing	Melts	Smell	Material left
	(Yes or no)	(Yes or no)	(Yes or no)	(Describe)	(Describe)

Multiple choice questions

1 To remove both greasy finger marks and splashes of hair lacquer, a salon mirror should be cleaned with
a carbon tetrachloride *b* cetrimide solution
c neutral detergent *d* isopropanol

2 Salon basins have a trap below them in order to
a prevent hairs blocking the waste pipe
b prevent the return of airborne pathogens
c make disinfection of the drains possible
d allow dirty water to run away quickly

3 To provide a surface which can be kept free from germs the salon floor should be covered with
a thermoplastic tiles *b* wood blocks
c nylon carpet squares *d* an all-wool carpet

4 Cotton is the best fibre for underclothing worn in the salon because it is
a absorbent and traps air
b absorbent and does not trap air
c non-absorbent and does not trap air
d non-absorbent and traps air

5 A synthetic fibre with properties which make it suitable for salon overalls is
a rayon *b* acetate *c* flax *d* nylon

6 Which of the following micro-organisms is usually the cause of a septic condition in which pus is formed?
a yeast *b* staphylococcus *c* fungal spore *d* virus

7 Which of the following rays are produced by a non-chemical type of sterilizing cabinet
a ultra-violet *b* cosmic *c* infra-red *d* ultra-sonic

8 The simplest antiseptic solution for salon use is
a hot water and detergent *b* hot chlorine bleach
c hydrochloric acid *d* essential oil

9 A hairdresser's tools should never be put in her overall pocket because
a frictional electricity will form
b pathogens may be picked up by them
c sharp tools may damage the overall
d they are more difficult to find quickly

10 One method by which the body protects itself from attack by harmful micro-organisms is by producing
a antibiotics *b* toxins *c* antibodies *d* vaccines

16 Diseases of the Skin and Scalp

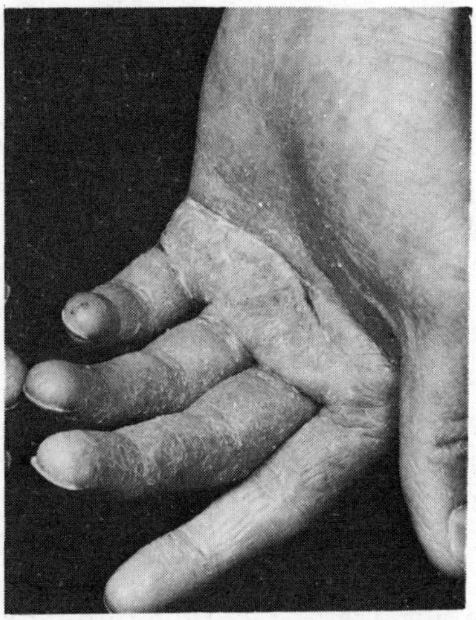

Diseases of the skin and scalp usually arise because there is both a *causal agent* and a *predisposition* to succumb to the disease. The *causal agent* may come from outside the body. It may be a living organism or pathogen, an irritant chemical, a weather condition, or something causing mechanical damage. The causal agent may also come from inside the body, as in the case of growth or physiological disorders, allergy, or inherited defects. *Predisposing factors* are those which lower the *resistance* of the skin, and so make it more susceptible to attack by the causal agent. Age may be a predisposing factor, many diseases being more prevalent in particular age groups, e.g. ringworm and impetigo in childhood (when the skin is less protectively acid) ; acne in adolescence. Sex has a predisposing effect in some cases, e.g. acne and seborrhoea are more prevalent in males.

Infectious diseases are caused by a living organism called a pathogen, which can be passed on to another person in whom it may also cause the disease.

Non-infectious diseases are not caused by pathogens, but by one of the other causal agents, and cannot be passed on to others. Predisposing factors may be present in both infectious and non-infectious diseases.

Infectious diseases

There are four groups of *pathogens* which may attack skin and hair: fungi, small animal parasites, bacteria, and viruses.

Fungal diseases

Fungi are a group of non-green *plants* some of which live as *parasites*, taking their food from another living organism which may be a human *host*. The fungi which attack human skin consist of a network of fine branched threads. The individual threads of the fungus are called *hyphae*, and the network of hyphae is a *mycelium*. (*See Fig.* 15.2.) Digestive enzymes are produced by the hyphae to digest the host tissues. The digested tissue is then absorbed by the mycelium and used as food. Some fungi reproduce by forming tiny *spores* which float about in the air, or are present in dust. Other fungi spread by small pieces of hypha becoming free, reaching a new host, and growing to form a new mycelium. Diseases caused by fungi include ringworm and athlete's foot.

SCALP RINGWORM (*Tinea capitis*)

This disease is caused by fungi which infect the dead tissue of the *epidermis* and *hair shafts* of the scalp. It occurs most frequently in younger children and is very contagious, often giving rise to epidemics in schools or families. The infection begins with the occurrence of a pink patch on the scalp which after a few days develops into a circular area covered with *grey scales* and short *broken hairs* about 2 mm long. The patch spreads rapidly as the mycelium extends in the epidermis. This disease is detected by examining the scalp under *ultra-violet* radiation from a Wood's light in a dark room. Hairs and skin infected by the fungus fluoresce with greenish-blue light.

Scalp ringworm is *transmitted* when small pieces of infected hair or epidermis get on the scalp of another person, either through close contact of children's heads when playing, or via hats, towels, pillows, or hair brushes.

If the hairdresser discovers the presence of ringworm on a child's head when she is cutting the hair, she must quietly point it out to the adult with the child, finish cutting the hair, then carefully sweep up and burn, or otherwise dispose of, all hair trimmings. She must place all the tools used in the sterilizing cabinet, and disinfect and wash the gown and towels used, and her own overall. In this way it will be impossible to transfer infected hair to anyone else. The disease is *treated* by an oral *antibiotic* called *griseofulvin*. When taken, the antibiotic circulates in the blood and is taken up by the keratin of the epidermis and hairs and destroys the fungus in them. This antibiotic replaces the older treatment of *epilation* followed by treatment of the scalp with a fungicide.

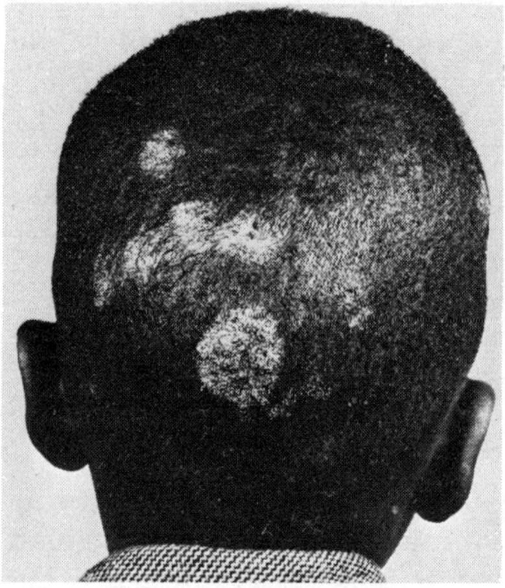

16.1 Scalp ringworm

BODY RINGWORM (*Tinea corporis*)
Ringworm fungi may attack the skin, usually of the face, neck, or hands, producing red circular patches. Blisters appear which ooze and form crusts. It is treated by a fungicide cream or griseofulvin.

BLACK-DOT RINGWORM
This is a rare form of scalp ringworm where the bald circular patches are not scaly but appear to contain black dots. These dots are the tops of the broken hairs just visible in the follicles.

HONEYCOMB RINGWORM (*Favus*)
This rare form of ringworm may occur on the body or scalp, and infects the skin and hair. Yellow crusts develop on the scalp, and permanently bald areas may result. The yellow crusts are saucer-shaped and up to 1 cm in diameter, with the hairs sticking up through them. The disease is more likely to occur in children.

ATHLETE'S FOOT (*Tinea pedis*)
This is one of the commonest fungal diseases, particularly in men. The fungus attacks the skin between the *toes*, usually starting between the fourth and fifth, to form sodden white patches. The skin may become red and blister. It may itch or feel sore. The patches later dry, becoming scaly, but after a resting period the disease breaks out again. The infection may spread on to the soles of the feet. The disease is *transmitted* in places where people walk with bare feet, as in swimming baths, showers, and changing rooms. It is *treated* by applying a fungicide cream. The feet should be kept as cool and dry as possible to reduce sweating as warm damp conditions encourage fungal growth.

Small animal parasites

An attack on the body by small animal parasites is known as an *infestation*. Those attacking the skin and scalp live on the outside of the body and are therefore *ectoparasites*. They possess biting and/or sucking *mouthparts* which enable them to feed on their host. Their *legs* usually end in claws for gripping the host, and their *eyes* are usually reduced as vision is not important for their survival. Some of these animals spend their entire life on the body, so personal disinfestation is needed to destroy them. Others visit the host periodically when feeding, so disinfestation of furniture and buildings is also required.

THE HEAD LOUSE (*Pediculus capitis*)
The head louse is a small *insect* which infests the human scalp causing the disease *pediculosis capitis*. An average infestation is twenty to thirty insects and usually starts behind the ears. It is a very *irritant* condition. The adult head lice are grey and about 2 mm long. The body consists of head, thorax, and abdomen, the head having a pair of antennae, and biting and sucking mouthparts to obtain blood from the scalp on which they feed. The thorax has three pairs of jointed legs ending on a claw to grip the hair, but no wings are present. Each insect lives four to five weeks.

The females lay *eggs* on the hair close to the scalp. The lower part of the egg has some adhesive which cements it firmly to a hair. The eggs are white and oval being 1 mm long, and are called '*nits*'. After a week the eggs hatch, and a young louse emerges from each egg. They moult three times during the next week, becoming adult after the third moult. The female lice then begin to produce eggs. Head lice are *transmitted* by contact with an infected person, as lice can survive only a short time away from the body. Recently there has been an increase in the incidence of *pediculosis capitis,* about 1·5 million people being affected in Great Britain, particularly young girls. When head lice bite the scalp the insect's saliva produces *irritation* which induces scratching. Germs may enter these breaks in the skin to produce *secondary* infections such as impetigo. Lice can carry other infections, e.g. typhus fever is transmitted by louse bites.

Pediculosis is *treated* by applying a preparation containing *insecticide* to the roots of the hair for five days, the last application being left on for one week. The insecticide used may be *Benzene hexachloride* (BHC) or *Malathion* (now the use of DDT is discouraged) as both are effective in killing both adult lice and nits. The dead nits remain cemented on the hairs and must be removed by combing the hair with a fine comb, or by a special shampoo treatment.

16.2 'Nit' attached to a hair
Adult head louse

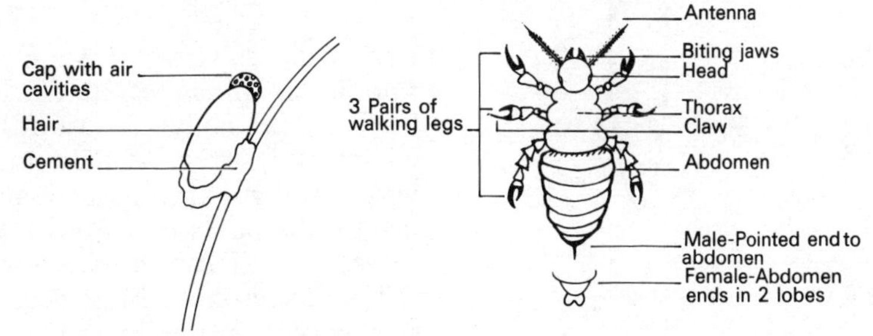

THE BODY LOUSE (*Pediculus humanus*)

Body lice infest the body living among the underclothes, and cause the disease *pediculosis corporis.* The bites can be seen as small red spots, often with dried blood in the centre. The eggs are usually cemented to the clothing, and the life history is similar to that of the head louse. The clothing of an infested person must be treated with insecticides or fumigated to kill the lice. This disease is uncommon in countries with a good standard of hygiene.

THE ITCH MITE (*Sarcoptes scabiei*)

Mites are small eight-legged animals related to *spiders.* They are not insects, which have six legs. An infestation by the itch mite causes the disease *scabies.* Scabies does not involve the face and scalp but can occur anywhere else on the body. Itch mites are very tiny animals. The females, which are much bigger than the males, are only 0·36 mm by 0·26 mm. They have rounded white bodies from which the eight short legs project. The mites feed on the horny layer of the epidermis which they bite with a pair of toothed jaws. The female mites use their jaws and first two

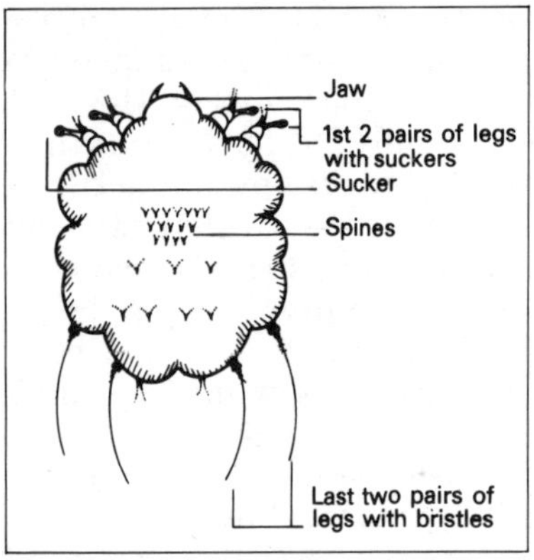

16.3 Female itch mite

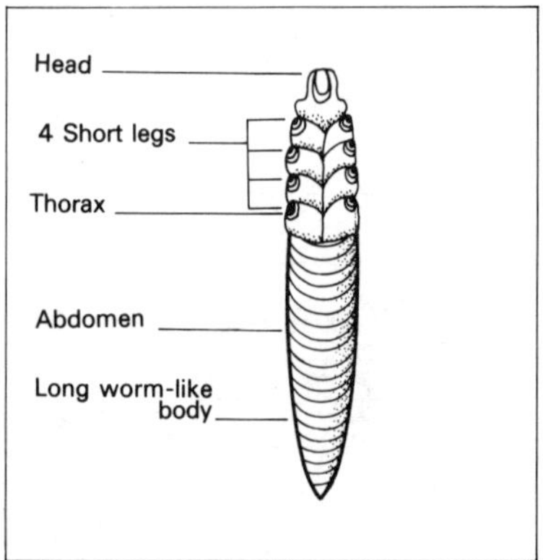

16.4 The face mite—Demodex

pairs of legs for digging *burrows* in the epidermis, particularly between the knuckles and in the folds of the wrist and elbow. The female lays *eggs* in the burrows. The eggs are smooth, white, glossy, and very small being only 0·17 mm by 0·09 mm, and they hatch in three to four days. The *larva* emerging from the egg resembles the adult, but has only three pairs of legs. They leave the burrows and creep into a hair follicle in which they moult twice, becoming adult about ten days after hatching.

Scabies is a condition characterized by intense *itching* particularly at night. Scratching frequently results in *secondary* infections, e.g. boils and impetigo. The disease is *transmitted* by close contact with an infected person, or with infected articles such as sheets and blankets. It is *treated* by giving the patient a hot bath and then applying a 25% *benzyl benzoate* emulsion to the whole body except the head. A second application is made a few days later.

THE FACE MITE (*Demodex folliculorum*)
This is a very small *mite* with reduced legs and a long body which occurs in the hair follicles that produce abundant sebum, and is therefore often associated with blackheads. It occurs mainly in follicles of the eyelashes, nose, and chin, and is found in most adult humans. The mite feeds on the fatty sebum.

THE COMMON FLEA (*Pulex irritans*)
The flea is an *insect*, its six legs being very long and ending in hooks. The body is laterally compressed, and there are no wings as it uses its long legs for *jumping* movements. It has biting and sucking mouthparts which it uses to take a periodic meal of blood from the host. Flea bites show as groups of small red spots which itch as the saliva of the flea is irritant.

The female fleas lay small oval pearly eggs $\frac{1}{2}$ mm by $\frac{1}{3}$ mm in size, which are sticky and adhere to the dust or *rubbish* in which they are laid. *Larvae* hatch from the eggs as small white grubs which feed on the surrounding rubbish. They die if they become very dry. The larva moults three times then changes into a pupa which darkens becoming brown in colour. The adult flea hatches out of the pupa and must find a host in order to feed. The infestation is *transmitted* by the fleas jumping from one person to another. It is *treated* by thorough washing of clothes and bedding and the removal of dust and rubbish where fleas may be breeding. Antiseptic may be dabbed on the bites. Fleas can carry the pathogens causing plague.

Bacterial infections

Bacteria are very small living organisms that can only be seen under a microscope. They have a characteristic shape either spherical (*coccus*), rod-shaped (*bacillus*), or spirally coiled (*spirochaete*).

Like all living things bacteria require food, water, oxygen, and warmth, and given these conditions they *reproduce* by dividing into two every twenty to thirty minutes. In the absence of the required conditions they form *spores* which can survive unfavourable conditions of cold, dryness, and absence of food. Both bacteria and spores are killed by prolonged *heating* at temperatures above

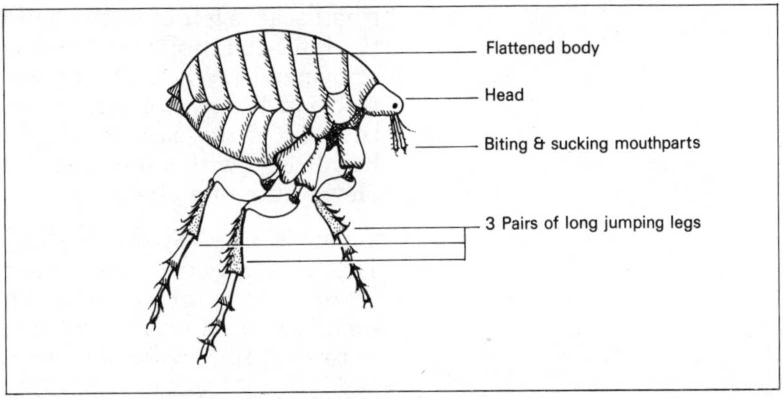

16.5 The flea

70°C, or by *ultra-violet* radiation. The *skin* has a large population of bacteria (one estimate is 530,000 bacteria per mg of scurf) some of which are harmless, while others cause *disease* if they manage to penetrate into the deeper layers of the skin. There is a constant transfer of bacteria from one person to another by contact, or on tiny 'rafts' of shed skin which are carried by air currents.

Bacteria which cause disease produce poisons called *toxins* which often cause the symptoms of the disease. Bacterial diseases are treated by *antibiotics* which destroy the bacteria very effectively without harming the person.

IMPETIGO

This is a skin infection caused by *streptococci* and *staphylococci*, the bacteria entering through a *break* in the *skin* where chapping or scratching has occurred. *Blisters* form in the outer layer of the epidermis. The clear fluid inside the blister thickens and dries to form a *yellow crust*. The disease usually attacks children particularly on the face, neck, and ears, and requires medical attention. The crusts are removed by bathing with cetrimide *antiseptic*, and an *antibiotic* ointment is then applied.

BOCKHARDT'S IMPETIGO

Staphylococci form tiny inflamed spots (*pustules*) at the opening of the hair follicles on the scalp. A hair protrudes from the centre of each pustule. The condition occurs in young children, and may follow pediculosis. The whole scalp may be affected. The disease is treated by an antibiotic solution, and ultra-violet radiation.

16.6 Bacteria

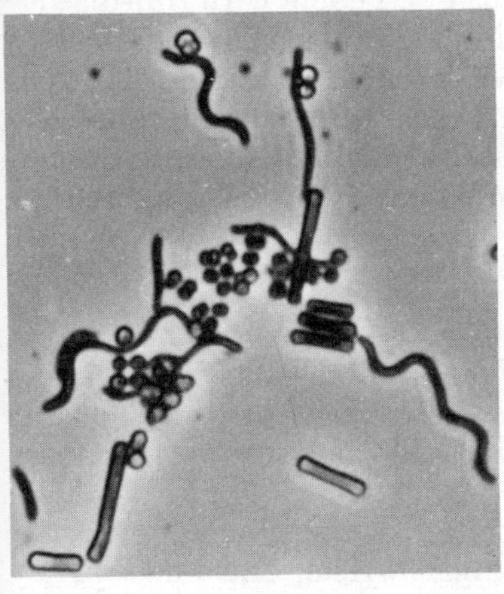

BOILS

Boils are due to the infection of hair follicles by *staphylococci*. A *faruncle* involves infection of only one hair follicle, a *carbuncle* occurs when a number of adjacent follicles are infected at the same time. Predisposing factors are poor general health, and rubbing of the skin by clothing. Bacteria multiply in the follicle and white blood cells move there to attack them. There is an increased blood flow to the infected area giving a red *inflamed* lump. *Pus* develops as the white blood cells destroy bacteria and die themselves, and forms the 'head' of the boil. The boil eventually bursts releasing pus, blood, and bacteria on to the skin. A small scar is left after the boil heals as the dermis is damaged by the infection. Boils are treated by giving *antibiotics* by injection or by mouth. When a boil *bursts* all dressings and materials used to clean the skin must be *burned* as they are infective. Avoid rubbing of the skin by tight clothing. Boils can develop if a hairdresser with a sore throat due to a bacterial infection coughs on the skin of a client.

BARBER'S ITCH (*Sycosis barbae*)
This is a *staphylococcal* infection of the hair follicles of the *beard*, and is a form of *folliculitis* producing pustular spots round each hair. It is *transmitted* by infected shaving brushes, razors, or towels. It is *treated* by antibiotics.

CONJUNCTIVITIS
This is inflammation of the *conjunctiva*, the very thin skin covering the front of the eye. The condition can be caused by a bacterium, and makes the eyes look red and sore. It can be *transmitted* by infected towels, and neither hairdressers nor clients should come to the salon if they are suffering from this highly infectious condition. It is *treated* by an antibiotic lotion.

Virus infections

A *virus* is a living organism responsible for disease which can grow only within the living cells of a suitable host. It is considerably smaller than a bacterium; too small to be visible under a light microscope, though visible using the electron microscope. A virus must pass, usually fairly directly, from an infected living cell to another living cell. Viruses are not usually killed by antibiotics. In many ways the damage produced by a virus in the skin is similar to that which results from a burn or scald. Viruses, unlike bacteria, are not thought to produce toxins. The body produces *antibodies* to destroy the invading virus, and these remain in the blood, giving future immunity to the disease.

COLD SORE (*Herpes simplex*)
This disease is caused by a virus infecting the *epidermal* cells of the *lips*. It begins as a red itchy spot which develops *blisters*. The blisters form a *crust* from under which moisture may ooze. The sore usually heals completely in a few days. Cold sores will break out again during feverish illnesses, strong sunlight, or cold winds, all of which act as irritants. People with this disease are usually infected in early childhood and retain the virus in their lips and saliva all their lives. With each attack of herpes there is enough virus set free from the cells to stimulate the body to make antibodies, so that the sore heals, but there is no permanent cure. The disease is *transmitted* by kissing, and by infected cups, toys, etc.

WARTS (*Verrucae*)
A wart is a small *epidermal* growth caused by a virus. The virus induces rapid division of the *prickle* cells, increasing the thickness of the *horny* layer. Warts usually grow outwards except on the foot, where the wart grows inwards and pressure on it causes pain.

Plane (or juvenile) warts are small growths which often occur in large numbers on the face, hands, wrists, and knees. They often disappear spontaneously due to the body developing immunity to the virus. *Plantar* warts are flat growths on the sole or heel of the foot. When the horny layer is scraped away the *papillae* show up as bleeding points; a diagnostic feature of these warts. The infection is *transmitted* to others in places where people walk with bare feet, e.g. at swimming baths. The *treatment* is to destroy that part of the skin which is infected by the virus. A 25% alcoholic solution of *podophyllum* resin, or *solid carbon dioxide*, is used, or the wart can be destroyed by *diathermy* or electrocautery.

16.7 Section through a wart

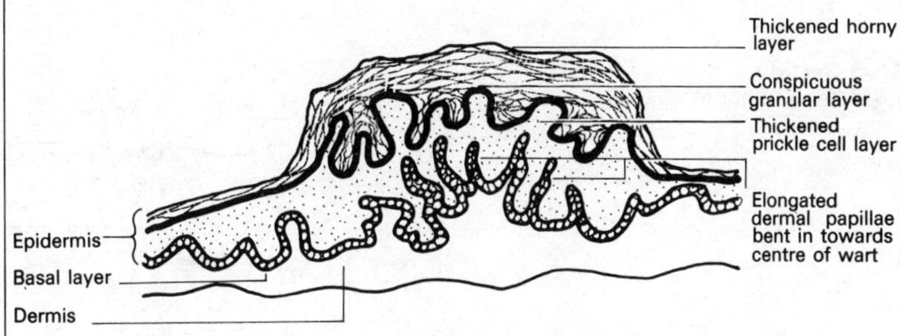

Non-infectious diseases of skin and hair

These diseases may be grouped according to their *primary cause* which may be physiological, genetic, chemical irritation, mechanical damage, or the weather.

Diseases having a physiological cause

DANDRUFF OR SCURF (*Pityriasis*)

The topmost dead layer of the *epidermis* is constantly flaking off as new cells are produced by the basal layer below. On the scalp these flakes of dry dead skin cells become trapped in the hairs, and will accumulate if the hair is not brushed and combed regularly. This condition is *Pityriasis simplex.* If the secretion of *sebum* by the scalp is large, the skin flakes get a greasy covering and stick together to form larger flakes, which characterises *P. steatoides.* Vigorous brushing or massaging of the scalp, which stimulates the sebaceous glands, should be avoided where this condition occurs. Fungi and bacteria have been found associated with the flakes of dandruff, so that medicated shampoos (see Chapter 3) containing an antiseptic may be used, although their effectiveness in preventing dandruff is uncertain. *Selenium sulphide* which is also used as a treatment for dandruff, causes the production of very small scales of dead skin which are less obvious. This compound damages the eyes, and if used continuously can cause dermititis.

GREASY HAIR AND SKIN (*Seborrhoea*)

This condition is due to *over-activity* of the *sebaceous* glands. It is more common in adolescence, and is often accompanied by pityriasis and acne, and sometimes by hair loss. The *treatment* for greasy hair is to wash it not oftener than once a week, using *cetrimide* as a shampoo for three or four weeks. Then use a *soapless shampoo* for three months before using cetrimide again. (*N.B.* Cetrimide is damaging to the *eyes.*)

ACNE

This is no longer thought to be a bacterial disease, but is now known to be due to *over-activity* of the *sebaceous* glands, the sebum becoming trapped in the duct. A plug of sebum builds up in the hair follicle to form a *blackhead* (comedo). The outer part of the white sebum plug goes black as a result of *oxidation.* The gland may become inflamed, and the blackhead develop into a 'spot' or *papule.* Acne occurs mainly where the number of sebaceous glands is large, i.e. on the forehead, nose, chin, neck, and back.

16.8 Section of skin showing typical blackhead of acne

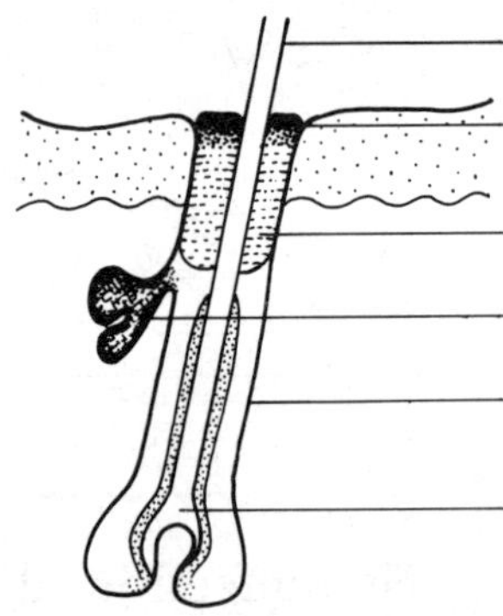

Male sex hormones stimulate the sebaceous glands to become more active. The treatment for acne is to *prevent blockage* of the follicular openings and to *reduce* the *secretion* of sebum. Creams making the skin peel and thus unblocking the ducts contain *salicylic acid.* Sunlight stimulates the blood flow to the skin and more liquid sebum is produced. The *ultra-violet rays* increase the growth rate of the skin so that the surface peels. *Washing* frequently will prevent the build-up of sebum on the skin. *Oestrogens* (female sex hormones) will reduce the secretion of sebum, and may be prescribed as a treatment for severe cases of acne. The drug *Tetracycline* affects the constitution of sebum and prevents the follicle becoming clogged.

HYPERIDROSIS

This condition of *excessive sweating* is often localised, occurring in the hands, feet, and armpits. Decomposition of the sweat by bacteria present on the skin surface may produce an unpleasant smell. The unpleasant effects of excessive sweating can be reduced by applying a lotion containing 3% of *tannic acid* or *salicylic acid*, or a powder composed of 3% salicylic acid in *talc.* Most antiperspirants for under-arm use contain aluminium chlorhydrate.

Genetic diseases

These skin diseases are due to some *inherited* abnormality.

PSORIASIS

Psoriasis is the most common inherited skin disorder, being present in 2% of the population. It is a scaly condition of the skin which often affects the scalp, elbows, and knees. It consists of thick patches of hard, dry, *silvery scales* below which the skin is *red.* Its onset may be sudden or gradual. It does not normally itch; any itching is usually because the patient is worried about the condition. As the disease is not infectious, normal hairdressing processes can be carried out. The skin of people with psoriasis tends to be *drier* than normal so frequent shampooing is inadvisable. The scalp should be massaged as little as possible as this increases the rate of cell division which builds up the scales. Substances called *chalones* have been extracted from skin epidermis which slow down the rate of cell growth in the germinating layer of the skin. It may become possible in the future to use chalones as a treatment for psoriasis. *Ultra-violet* radiation will improve this condition, but it cannot be cured.

ECZEMA

This skin condition is characterised by red *patches*, itching, blisters, crusts, and scaling. The patches may ooze, and occur in folds of skin at the joints e.g. wrist and elbow. Eczema is due to an *allergy* which has a *genetic* cause. It is treated by applying a *hydrocortisone* cream to the patches.

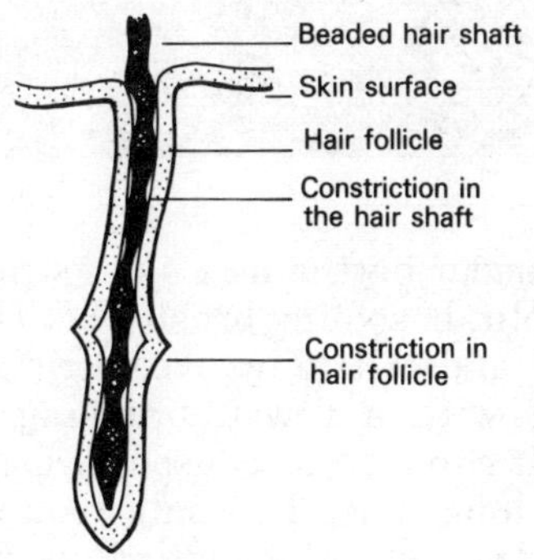

16.9 Section of scalp showing Monilethrix

MONILETHRIX

This is a rare hereditary condition of the hair due to *uneven* formation of *keratin* as the hair shaft grows in the follicle. The hairs have a *beaded* appearance as the shaft is constricted at intervals along its length.

Diseases due to chemical or mechanical damage

DERMATITIS

Dermatitis means '*inflammation* of the skin' and is caused by an external skin *irritant.* This may be a *primary* irritant if it causes dermatitis at its first contact with the skin, or a *sensitizer* if it produces dermatitis only in people who have previously been in contact with the irritant. Mechanical damage to the skin such as bruising, friction, or water-logging, lowers the normal resistance of the skin to irritant chemicals. The symptoms of dermatitis range from a mild reddening (*erythema*) to considerable blistering, oozing, and swelling, beginning a few hours after contact with the irritant. Any swelling subsides after a few days and the skin flakes off. *Chemicals* which cause dermatitis are acetic acid, ammonium hydroxide, aluminium salts (in antiperspirants), ammonium thioglycollate (in cold wave perming lotion), sodium lauryl sulphate (in shampoo), lanolin, formaldehyde resin (in nail lacquer), and eosin (red dye in lipstick). The commonest cause of dermatitis however are the *para-dyes*, so that a patch test should be carried out on every client before the first application of this type of dye. Occasionally the *perfume* included in a cosmetic preparation will cause dermatitis. To ensure that dermatitis does not occur the skin must be protected from all irritant chemicals. Immediately stop using any new cosmetic which may contain the irritant. Non-irritant cosmetics are available which are ideal if the skin appears to be sensitive. The hairdresser should always wear *rubber gloves* when applying para-dyes or perming lotion. If dermatitis occurs do not wash the skin with soap and water, and get medical advice.

Hair damage

Three conditions can arise in *hair* as a result of *mechanical* and *chemical* damage.

SPLIT ENDS (*Fragilitas crinium*)
If the hair becomes very dry and brittle the free end of the shaft may split. This condition is caused by perming and dyeing the hair too frequently, using shampoo which is too concentrated, over-vigorous brushing of fine hair, and excessive backcombing. Split ends cannot be repaired, but must be cut off. The hair requires treatment with *oily conditioners*.

16.10 Split end ×410

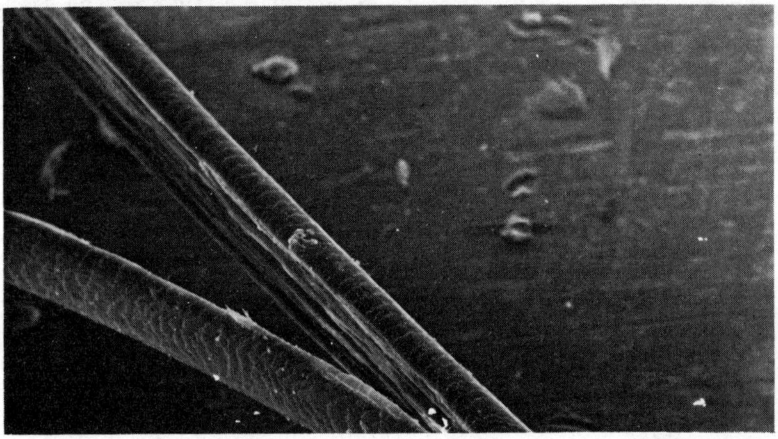

TRICHORRHEXIS NODOSA
In this condition rough swellings occur on the hair shaft which are regions where the cortex has split, becoming brush-like. This occurs when the hair becomes dry and brittle by over-perming, etc., when over-vigorous rubbing with a towel, brushing or combing, will cause the splitting. It can also be caused by using tight elastic bands to draw back long hair. The hair requires treatment with *oily conditioners*, and careful handling, as the hairs readily break at the weak places.

16.11 Hair shaft showing Trichorrhexis

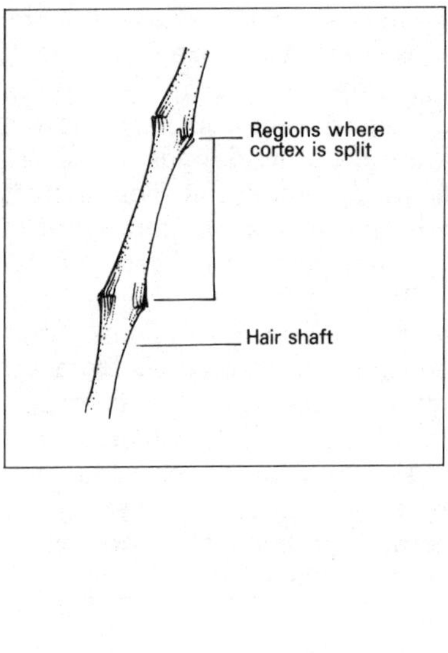

KNOTTED HAIR (*Trichonodosis*)
Sometimes hairs become knotted or looped just above the skin. This may be due to rough tugging when brushing or combing the hair, or it may occur in hairs which have regrown after plucking or electrolysis has been carried out.

Disorders due to the weather

CHILBLAINS
These are bluish-red itching swellings on the fingers, toes, and lower part of the leg. They are most common in young children, and Vitamin B deficiency may be a predisposing factor. Improving the *circulation* by exercise, and wearing *protective clothing* in cold weather will help to prevent chilblains.

SUNBURN
The effect of exposing the skin to sunlight is that the ultra-violet rays cause *burning* and *tanning*. The amount of dark *pigment* (melanin) in the skin increases and the germinating layer *grows* faster so that the horny layer thickens. The burning effect produces redness (erythema) and the skin blisters. Later, the

outer layers flake off or 'peel'. The affected skin feels hot and is painful. Sunburn can be treated by applying *Calamine lotion*, which is a suspension of *zinc carbonate* having a cooling effect on the skin. Severe sunburn needs medical attention. *Sunscreens*, which cut out much of the ultra-violet radiation, will reduce both the burning and the tanning effect of sunlight. It is advisable to start sunbathing gradually for only a few minutes a day until a protective tan has developed. Sunscreens contain a mechanical barrier to ultra-violet rays such as talc, chalk, or zinc oxide. *Suntan* preparations contain *para-aminobenzoic acid* to filter out more damaging rays of shorter wave length, but allow through the rays of longer wave length which increase pigment formation.

Multiple choice questions

1 The medical name for an infestation by the head louse is
a scabies *b* psoriasis *c* pediculosis *d* pityriasis

2 A small bald patch on the scalp where the skin is scaly and a few broken hairs are visible indicates
a ringworm *b* alopecia *c* impetigo *d* canities

3 An example of a skin disorder which is caused by a virus is a
a freckle *b* wart *c* mole *d* boil

4 Which of the following skin diseases could be cured by treatment with an antibiotic ointment?
a seborrhoea *b* impetigo *c* herpes *d* dermatitis

5 The pathogen responsible for the occurrence of athlete's foot is a
a bacterium *b* insect *c* virus *d* fungus

6 The presence of thick scaly patches silvery in colour and occurring at the frontal hairline would indicate
a psoriasis *b* dermatitis *c* hyperidrosis *d* eczema

7 Seborrhoea occurring on the scalp is due to
a a small animal parasite *b* overactive sebaceous glands
c a primary skin irritant *d* underactive sweat glands

8 The diagnostic feature of the condition known as Fragilitas crinium would be
a a beaded hair shaft
b infection of a group of hair follicles
c brittle hair splitting at the ends
d a mixture of coloured and white hairs

9 An ingredient used in red lipstick which can cause dermatitis is
a resin *b* rosin *c* alum *d* eosin

10 A chemical which may be used as a treatment for extensive pityriasis is
a benzyl benzoate *b* griseofulvin *c* selenium sulphide
d salicylic acid

17 Safety in the Salon

The *legal* requirements for safety in the salon are laid down in the Health and Safety at Work Act of 1974. The requirements for safety include the *cleanliness* of the salon (see Chapter 4) and the provision of *washing* facilities and *drinking water.* The lay-out of the equipment must be safe, and there must be facilities for hanging overalls and outdoor clothing. The salon and any staircases must be *well-lit*, and windows and sky-lights kept clean. The means of *heating* must not produce fumes, and there must be effective *ventilation*. The minimum *temperature* of 16°C must be attained after the first hour, and a *thermometer* must be placed conspicuously to show the temperature. *Fire* exits and fire precautions must be up to the required standard. A *First-Aid* box or cabinet containing the necessary equipment must be clearly marked, and in a position where it is easily visible and accessible.

Fire hazards in the salon

Much of the *waste* produced in the salon is *inflammable*, so care must be taken to prevent it falling on to space heaters where it would ignite. *Cigarette* butts that have not been stubbed out fully, and are then thrown away amongst burnable rubbish, can start a fire, so ash-trays should not be emptied into the salon waste bin. Portable space *heaters* should be placed in positions where they are unlikely to be knocked over, or where inflammable furnishings are not close enough to ignite. Make sure that the guard required by law on radiant electric and gas fires is present. If the *gas* supply is cut off, all gas appliances (fires and water heaters) should be turned off immediately. When the supply is turned on, make sure that all *pilot lights* are ignited, as escaping gas can explode. Do not place towels or gowns over convector space heaters. If the air vents are covered *over-heating* will occur, and cause a fire. Do not use gloss paint on *polystyrene* ceiling tiles, as this makes them very inflammable. Do not use *inflammable liquids* for dry-cleaning, e.g. petrol. Do not *smoke* when using inflammable liquids, e.g. methylated spirit, acetone. Store only very small quantities of inflammable liquids, preferably at floor level on a metal tray or in a bin. Keep *aerosol-type* containers away from heat, and never burn or puncture them, because the contents are under *pressure*, and in some cases are also *inflammable*. The volatile liquids they contain will *vaporize* rapidly and expand on heating inside the can, causing it to explode.

The *Fire Service* should be consulted about fire exits and suitable fire extinguishers for the salon. All the salon staff should know what to do in the case of a fire which is out of control. Bring all the clients to an exit on the ground floor, so that they can leave the building quickly and safely. Do not allow anyone to return to the salon. Call the Fire Service by dialling 999, giving the address of the salon fully and clearly. Money is not required for an emergency call, and the Fire Service is free. After checking that everyone has left the salon, close all doors and windows. This helps to contain the fire by reducing the oxygen available, and prevents smoke from spreading.

Putting out fires

If a person's *clothing* catches fire, pull them on to the floor, and roll them in a blanket, rug, or thick coat. If your own clothing catches fire, roll on the floor to put out the flames.

To put out a fire you must deprive it of air (oxygen), heat, or material to burn. *Water* is a good extinguisher for many fires, as it cools well, but it must not be used for burning liquid fires where the liquid floats on water, or where an electrical appliance is on fire. Water conducts electricity, and you could electrocute yourself by using it on an electrical fire. *Dry sand* or a *thick rug* can be used to put out the flames from a burning liquid as they deprive the fire of air. They may also be used for an electrical fire, provided the electricity has been turned off first. *Fire extinguishers* may be used as a first-aid measure against minor fires. A fire of any size must be dealt with by the Fire Service. A suitable fire extinguisher for the salon should put out all types of small fires. It should be easy to use by people who are not fire-fighting experts, and must work reliably however long it has been kept since purchasing. It should not make a lot of mess in putting out a fire.

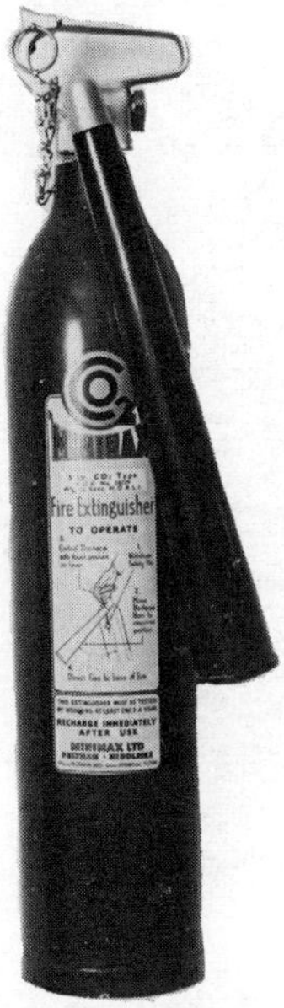

17.1 Carbon dioxide foam extinguisher

Types of fire extinguishers

A number of different types of fire extinguishers are available.

CARBON DIOXIDE FOAM EXTINGUISHERS

Hitting the knob at the top of the extinguisher pushes in a plunger which breaks a container holding *acid*. The acid reacts with *sodium bicarbonate* inside the extinguisher to produce carbon dioxide gas, which forms a foam with the *detergent* also present. The *foam* comes out at the nozzle and when directed on to the fire, puts it out, as carbon dioxide does not allow substances to burn in it. The foam settles round the burning material and prevents it flaring up again. Foam continues to flow until the extinguisher is empty, and is messy to clean up afterwards. The extinguisher is heavy to lift when directing the nozzle at the fire. These disadvantages make this type of extinguisher less suitable for the salon.

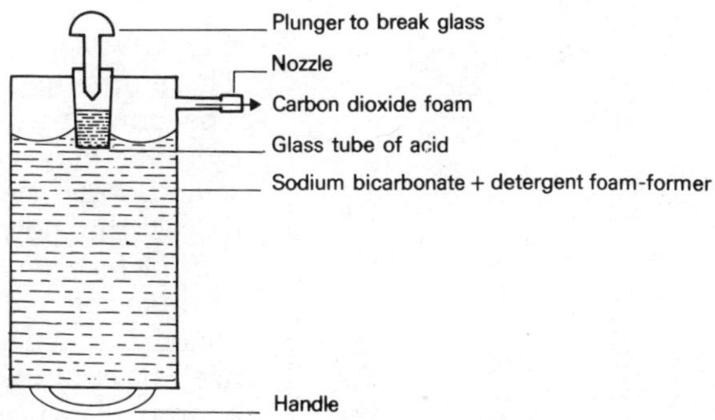

Cross section of carbon dioxide fire extinguisher

CARBON TETRACHLORIDE EXTINGUISHERS

Carbon tetrachloride is one of the few organic compounds which are not inflammable. It also has a low boiling point (77° C) volatilizing when sprayed on to a fire. As the vapour is heavy, it settles over the flames, excluding air. The danger in using this type of extinguisher is that in contact with hot metal, carbon tetrachloride forms the poisonous gas *phosgene*, and so should be used only in the open air.

BROMOCHLORODIFLUOROMETHANE EXTINGUISHERS (BCF)

These extinguishers contain an organic compound related to carbon tetrachloride. The vapour is heavy and prevents oxygen from reaching the fire. It does not allow combustion, has a cooling effect, and does not conduct electricity. The liquid is under pressure in a metal container, and vapour is released by pressing a button to open a valve. When the button is released no more vapour escapes so the extinguisher does not empty automatically. The vapour is not poisonous, but the resulting smoke after putting out a fire is, so the salon must be well *ventilated* after using this type of extinguisher. It causes no mess or damage to furniture. It can be checked to ensure that it will work.

17.2 BCF extinguisher

17.3 Dry powder extinguisher

DRY POWDER EXTINGUISHERS

These produce a dry powder which keeps air away from the fire. The powder is driven out by gas under pressure. The whole cylinder may be pressurized, or there may be a gas cartridge which, when pierced, pressurizes the body of the extinguisher and drives the powder out. The powder they contain is usually *sodium bicarbonate*. Refills can be obtained for some extinguishers of this type, making them more economical. The powder can be cleaned up with a vacuum cleaner after use, which is an advantage. It cannot, however, be checked to see if it is working effectively without emptying it.

Electrical safety precautions

1 Have all electrical appliances serviced regularly.
2 Fit three-pin earthed plugs to all appliances, which should have three-core flex, unless they are all-insulated, when a third or earth wire is not necessary.
3 Switch off at the mains or disconnect the appliance before making repairs, looking for faults, or changing lamps.
4 Report any faulty appliance (it may smoke or smell), switch or plug which is broken, or gets hot, as the insulation may be damaged.
5 Replace damaged or frayed flex.
6 Do not place flexes under carpets where damage cannot be seen.
7 In each plug fit a fuse which is the correct size for the appliance.
8 Never handle an electric appliance, or touch switches, with wet hands, as water may conduct electricity, giving an electric shock. Have pull-cord switches fitted where wet hands might be a danger.
9 Never pull plugs from sockets by tugging at the flex, or you may pull the earth wire away from its terminal inside the plug. The appliance would then not be earthed.

17.4 Magnetic door fastener

10 Do not use a light socket for power appliances or you may overload the lighting circuit.
11 Do not overload an electric power point by plugging in too many appliances so that the maximum wattage of the power point is exceeded.
12 Do not knock nails into walls where they might penentrate the insulation round wiring in the plaster.
13 Make sure that all equipment is switched off and the plugs removed from the sockets before leaving the salon at night.

Preventing accidents in the salon

As the hairdressing salon frequently contains a good deal of equipment in a small space, and as people are moving about all the time, care must be taken with the placing of equipment and furniture, so that people will not fall over it or bruise themselves on it. The salon and any staircases must be uniformly *well-lit*. The floor should be made of *non-slip* materials, and unpolished. Any spilt liquids should be wiped up straight away to prevent falls. Furniture should have rounded corners and recessed handles. Wall fittings should be fixed well above head-height. Door hinges and fastenings should be well-maintained. Doors that swing open are a frequent cause of accidental injury, so *magnetic fasteners* which ensure they remain closed, are advisable. A magnetic fastener utilizes a magnetic force. Certain metals such as iron and steel are magnetic being attracted towards magnets. *Magnetism* is a property of a naturally occurring substance called *lodestone*. Pieces of hard steel can be converted into magnets by stroking them with an existing magnet several times, and always in the same direction. Even very brief contact with a magnet can make pieces of steel magnetic. The attractive power of a magnet acts in the space surrounding it for some distance and thus sets up a *magnetic field*. A magnetic fastener consists of a *magnet* attached to the door frame, and a strip of *soft iron* attached to the door at the same level. As the door is closed the soft iron strip approaches the magnet. The magnetic force pulls the strip to make contact with the magnet and holds it there. To open the door a pulling force greater than the magnetic force must be exerted.

First-Aid equipment

The first-aid box should contain the following equipment, which should be frequently *checked*, making replacements where necessary:

Several sizes of sterile non-medicated dressings
Sterile eye pads
Sterile adhesive dressings
Bandage and adhesive tape
3-inch crepe bandage and a triangular bandage
Small packets of cotton wool
1% solution of cetrimide antiseptic
Soluble aspirin tablets B.P.
Bottle of smelling salts
Scissors, safety-pins, and tweezers.

Near the first-aid box a blanket, hot-water bottle, cup, and small jug should be stored.

First-aid treatment

First-aid involves immediate treatment of minor accidental injuries, or of more serious ones before they are seen by a doctor. It is designed to prevent death or further damage to injured persons.

BURNS

Skin burns may be caused by caustic chemicals, contact with hot metals or liquids, steam, or electricity. For extensive burns it is necessary to treat for *shock* (see Shock). *Chemical* burns should immediately be held under cold running water from the tap, and any clothing affected by the chemical should be taken off. The cold water dilutes the chemical, so a lot of water should be used. The cold water will also reduce the pain from the burn. The burn should then be covered with a sterile dressing and treated by a doctor, unless it is very minor, as burns readily go septic. Chemical burns may be caused by ammonium hydroxide solution and other alkalis, or by acids. Strong solutions of hydrogen peroxide will also produce skin burns. *Hot metal* or liquid burns if extensive, or if the skin is blistered, should be covered at once with a sterile dressing, and the patient taken for medical treatment. A small burn where the skin does not blister should immediately be held under a running cold water tap when the lowering of the skin temperature will reduce the pain. It can then be covered with an adhesive dressing or dabbed with cetrimide solution. *Scalds* are severe burns, as steam, which causes them, is not only at a high temperature (100°C), but also gives out latent heat when it condenses on the skin. Scalds should be treated in the same way as severe burns from hot metal.

CONCUSSION

This is unconsciousness or a dazed condition following a blow on the head. Lay the patient down, keep her quiet, but remain with her until a doctor is available and give nothing to drink. It is usually necessary to X-ray the skull to see if a fracture has occurred, and patients are usually kept in hospital. Concussion may produce delayed effects if not treated.

ELECTRIC SHOCK

If someone receives a paralysing electric shock from a faulty appliance, it is necessary to make sure that you do not electrocute yourself while helping, as electricity will still be passing through the victim, and will pass through you if you touch her. Switch off the current at the mains first. If this is impossible, wear *rubber* gloves and stand on rubber, wood, or dry magazines to insulate yourself from the earth. Use a wooden brush handle or wooden chair to separate the victim from the appliance. It may be necessary to give *artificial respiration* by the mouth-to-mouth method, and to start the heart beating again by placing the hands one on top of the other over the breast-bone, and pressing down with your full weight. If the patient's heart and breathing have stopped, alternate one breath into the patient's lungs with six to eight presses over the heart at a rate of one press a second. (See Visual Aids for Chapter 17). Get medical help. There may also be burns which need treating as for hot metal burns.

EPILEPTIC FIT

A person having an epileptic fit becomes unconscious and falls. The muscles contract, causing the limbs to jerk convulsively. Remove all furniture away so that they do not bruise themselves, but leave them lying on the floor. Place a pencil between the person's teeth to prevent their tongue being bitten. The patient regains consciousness in a few minutes, but may need to rest afterwards.

EYE-INJURIES

Chemicals which splash into the eye may be very painful. As well as caustic liquids such as acids and alkalis which burn the eye, some hairdressing lotions (e.g. cold wave lotion, cetrimide conditioners, selenium sulphide dandruff treatments, bleaches, and shampoo) may cause irritation of the conjunctiva. Any painful chemical must be washed out of the eye with cold water, either by pouring water on to the eye from a small jug, or directly from the tap. The unaffected eye should be protected to keep the contaminated water out of it. *Scratches* on the eyeball from long nails or scissors must be treated by a doctor at once. Cover the eye with a sterile eye pad until the patient reaches the doctor or hospital. *Foreign bodies*, e.g. grit or eye-lashes, can be removed from the eye with a twist of damp cotton-wool if they are visible when the eyelid is lifted. Where the foreign body cannot be seen or removed, cover the eye with a sterile eye pad, and take the patient to a doctor or hospital. Pulling the upper lid down over the lower lid and blinking, will often remove a foreign body from the eye.

FAINTING

If a client feels faint push her head down between her knees. Improving the ventilation by opening a window may help, and so may holding smelling salts to her nose. Once the patient has recovered, a hot drink can be given, or sips of cold water. If the client loses consciousness lay her down on the floor raising up her feet on a support. Fainting is caused by an inadequate blood supply to the brain, so lowering the head and raising the feet will increase the blood supply to the brain.

FRACTURES

A fracture is a break in a bone. Pain, swelling, or distortion may occur. Do not move the patient, but cover her with a blanket to keep her warm, and send for a doctor. Do not give anything to drink as an anaesthetic will be given so that the bone can be set. Treat the patient for shock.

HEART ATTACK

A heart attack is often preceded by a tight strangling sensation or pain in the chest, and the person may become unconscious. Get medical help quickly, and if the patient is conscious sit her down and watch for loss of consciousness. If the patient is unconscious, listen with your ear to her chest for the heart beat. If you are certain that the heart has stopped, alternate pressure on the heart with mouth-to-mouth *artificial respiration* (see Electric Shock), while waiting for medical help. The brain survives undamaged for only four minutes without oxygen.

HYSTERIA

This is a loss of control in which the person may laugh, cry, shout, or move about wildly. Take the person away on her own, as the presence of others will prolong the attack. Speak firmly and do not be sympathetic. Encourage her to wash her face, and reapply her make-up once she has quietened down.

NOSE BLEED

If the nose starts to bleed the person should remain sitting up, with the head held forward to prevent blood being swallowed, or entering the lungs. The soft part of the nose round the nostrils should be pinched together, and held for five minutes. This will cause the blood to clot. The nose should not be blown roughly for sometime afterwards, so that blood clots are not disturbed.

POISONING

Burning poisons such as acids and alkalis should be diluted by drinking plenty of water immediately. The bottle which contained the poison should be kept, and a doctor sent for. Do not make the patient sick.

Non-burning poisons such as aspirin or sleeping tablets may be taken. If the patient is unconscious and not breathing, apply mouth-to-mouth artificial respiration. If the patient is unconscious but breathing, turn them on to their side with the upper leg and arm extended at right angles to the body. This is known as the *coma position*, and prevents the patient from rolling on to her back again, and choking if saliva or vomit should block up the air passages. Never attempt to give an unconscious person anything to drink, as it may choke them. If the patient is conscious make her sick by tickling the back of her throat using a finger and keep her moving about if possible, otherwise lying on one side in the coma position. Send for a doctor as it will be necessary to pump the poison out of the stomach. Keep the bottle which contained the poison.

Carbon monoxide poisoning may be caused by unburned town gas, and can occur when either town or natural gas is burned in a faulty appliance. It is also caused by carbon monoxide present in car exhaust gases. The carbon monoxide combines irreversibly with the red blood pigment, and prevents it from carrying oxygen. Unconsciousness occurs rapidly because no oxygen reaches the brain. White skin may appear bright pink. Take a deep breath outside, then drag the person out of the gas-filled room if possible. If not, turn off the source of the gas, open all doors and windows, and then attempt to bring the patient out into the fresh air. If they are not breathing give artificial respiration by the mouth-to-mouth method, and get medical help.

SHOCK

Shock is a state of collapse which can cause death. It may occur as a result of severe bleeding, extensive burns, a fracture, or a heart attack. The surface blood vessels contract so that the skin goes very pale, and the blood goes to the internal organs. The patient may break into a cold clammy sweat, and may gasp for breath. Lie the patient down and reassure her. Remain with the patient and send for medical help. Cover the patient with a blanket, but do not give a hot-water bottle or any stimulant. Do not overheat the patient.

SPRAINS

A sprain is damage to a tendon or ligament connected with a joint. Ankle, wrist, and knee joints are the ones most commonly sprained. The damaged region is usually painful, and swells. A cloth soaked in cold water should be wrapped round the joint after removing any constricting object quickly before the swelling starts, e.g. shoes, stockings, bracelets, wrist watch. The joint should then be bandaged firmly with a crepe bandage to support it, and the patient taken to hospital for an X-ray, in case bones are fractured.

WOUNDS

In any injury where the skin is broken the important procedures are to keep the wound clean, and stop the bleeding. The wound should be held under running cold water to clean it or it can be sponged with 1% cetrimide solution. It should then be covered with a *sterile* dressing to prevent further infection. Where wounds are bleeding freely *finger pressure* should be applied to the wound on top of the sterile dressing. Scissor or razor cuts on the ear lobe may be covered with cotton wool, and the edges of the cut pressed together to stop the bleeding. Wounds on the head often bleed freely because of the rich blood supply, and the gaping of the cut blood vessels, which slows clotting. Unless wounds are trivial they should be treated by a doctor, as stitching may be required.

Practical work

1 CARBON DIOXIDE

(*a*) *Preparation* Into a flat-bottomed flask place some calcium carbonate in the form of marble chippings. Place a stopper carrying a thistle funnel and a delivery tube into the neck of the flask, and put the other end of the delivery tube into a gas jar. Place a glass plate over the top of the gas jar to cover as much of the opening as possible. Pour dilute hydrochloric acid down the thistle funnel. The gas produced will pass through the delivery tube into the gas jar, displacing air. When the production of gas in the flask slows down, remove the gas jar, and cover the top with the glass plate.

(*b*) *Fire-extinguishing properties* After removing the glass plate from the top of the gas jar, punge a lighted taper into the carbon dioxide.

17.5 Preparation of carbon dioxide

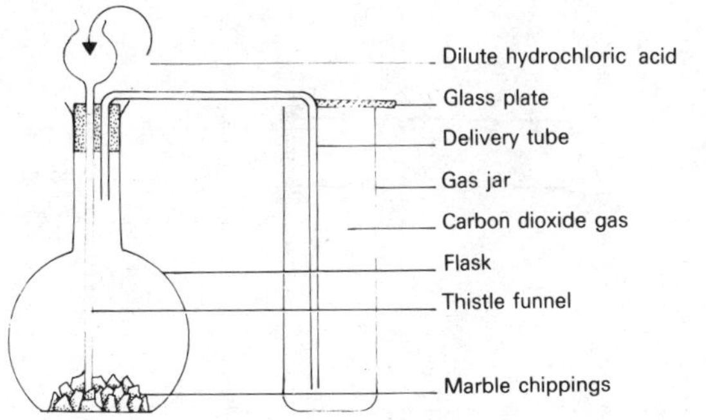

2 FIRE EXTINGUISHERS

Look at fire extinguishers of the various types and read the instructions for their use.

3 MAGNETISM EXPERIMENTS

(*a*) *Making a magnet* Take a steel knitting needle and a long soft iron nail, and stroke each in turn several times from the same end with the same pole of a bar magnet. Place a few iron filings on a piece of scrap paper, and hold the needle and nail above them to test their magnetism. If they do not attract iron filings, stroke them with the magnet again in the same way, until they become magnetic.

(*b*) *Showing magnetic force* Suspend a bar magnet by cotton from a stand, then bring a second magnet, which you are holding, towards the suspended magnet. Bring the north pole of the magnet you hold towards the north and south poles of the suspended magnet in turn. Then bring the south pole of the magnet you hold towards each pole of the suspended magnet. In what way do the poles attract or repel one another?

(*c*) *Showing the magnetic field of a magnet* Take a bar magnet and place it underneath a large sheet of white paper. Sprinkle fine iron filings on the top of the paper and gently tap the edges. You will notice that the iron filings become arranged in a pattern relating to the magnet, as they are in its magnetic field. The iron filings lie along the lines of force of the magnetic field.

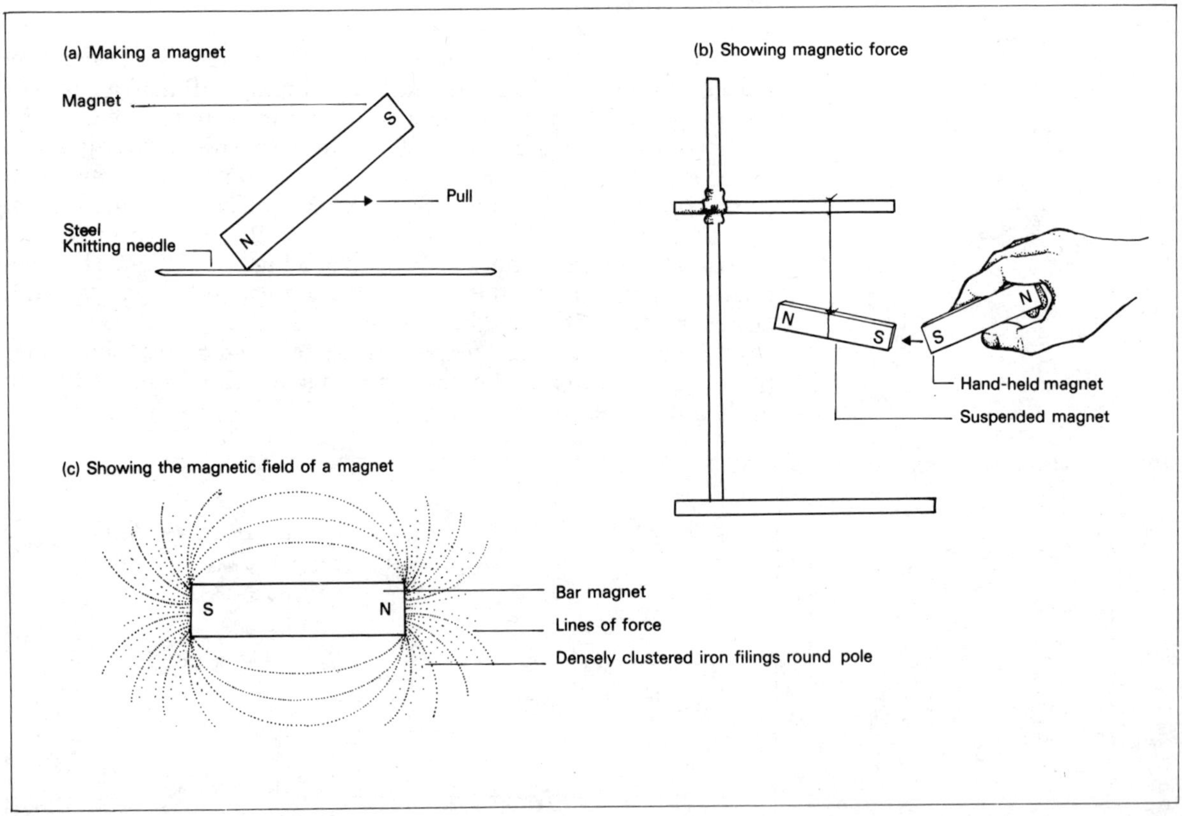

17.6 Magnetism experiments

Multiple choice questions

1 An aerosol hair lacquer can may explode if placed on a hot surface because the
a lacquer liquifies *b* solvent condenses
c volatile solvent expands *d* metal can expands

2 A hot drink may be given to a patient who
a is in a coma *b* has concussion
c has recovered from a faint *d* has broken a limb bone

3 If cold wave perming lotion runs into a client's eye you should
a pour cold water over the eye *b* tell her to blink rapidly
c bathe her eye with neutralizer
d wipe her eye with a tissue

4 If a client who is under a hairdryer appears about to faint you should
a cover her with a rug *b* switch down the dryer thermostat
c give her a drink of water
d push her head down on to her knees

5 Fire extinguishers containing sodium bicarbonate and an acid produce a gas called
a carbon dioxide *b* carbon disulphide
c carbon tetrachloride *d* carbon monoxide

6 If the plug to a hairdryer gets hot when the dryer is in use a likely cause of the fault is
a a disconnected earth *b* a blown fuse
c damaged insulation *d* reduced voltage

7 If a fire starts in the salon and it cannot be controlled you must first
a switch off the electricity *b* contact the Fire Service
c open the windows to remove smoke
d send everyone outside

8 A slight burn from hot metal should be treated with
a olive oil *b* cold running water *c* antiseptic ointment
d petroleum jelly

9 Polystyrene ceiling tiles become a fire hazard if they are
a unpainted *b* emulsion painted *c* distempered
d gloss painted

10 The region over which the lines of force of a magnet act is a
a polar cap *b* attractive force *c* magnetic field
d north pole

Appendix 1

Table of chemicals used in hairdressing and skin preparations etc.

NAME	CLASS OF SUBSTANCE	USES
Acetic acid	Organic acid	Acid rinse (vinegar)
Acetone	Lacquer solvent	Nail varnish remover
Agar	Gum	In brushless shaving creams
Alkylolamide	Organic compound	Foam stabilizer in soapless detergents
Almond oil	Vegetable oil	Antiwrinkle and muscle oils
Aluminium chlorhydrate	Salt	Antiperspirants
Ambergris	Animal secretion	Fixing odour in perfumes
Ammonium carbonate	Inorganic salt	Catalyst for hydrogen peroxide bleach
Ammonium hydroxide	Alkali	Making cold wave perming lotion Catalyst for hydrogen peroxide bleach
Ammonium thioglycollate	Reducing agent	Cold wave perming lotion
Amyl acetate	Ester	Nail varnish solvent
Arachis oil	Vegetable oil	Cheaper antiwrinkle and muscle oil
Barium sulphide	Inorganic salt	Depilatories
Beeswax	Wax	Waxing thread in boardwork. Polishes
Benzyl alcohol	Organic base	Solvent for nitro-dyes
Brilliant green	Water-soluble dye	Colouring shampoo and hand cream
Bromochlorodifluoromethane	Organic compound	Fire extinguisher
Calcium carbonate (chalk)	Inorganic salt	In talcum powder
Calcium oxide (lime)	Inorganic base	In exothermic pads
Calcium thioglycollate	Organic salt	Depilatories
Camomile	Vegetable dye	In colour shampoo
Carbon tetrachloride	Fat solvent	Dry cleaning wigs and hairpieces
Carnauba wax	Wax	Making mascara
Castor oil	Vegetable oil	In lipstick. Sulphonated, in shampoo
Cetrimide	Organic base	Antiseptic and hair conditioner
Cetyl alcohol	Organic base	Making cosmetic creams
Chlorine	Non-metallic element	Purifying water. Disinfecting lavatories
Citric acid	Organic acid	Acid rinse (lemon). Setting lotion
Civet	Animal secretion	Fixing odour in perfumes
Coconut oil	Vegetable oil	Making soap and surfactants
Essential oils	Vegetable oils	As perfumes and mild antiseptics
Ethanol (alcohol)	Organic base (alcohol)	Solvent for resins. Antiseptic
Formaldehyde (formalin)	Organic compound	In sterilizing cabinets
Formaldehyde resin	Synthetic resin	Hair lacquer. Plasticizer in nail varnish
Glycerol	Organic base	Emollient in skin creams
Hexachlorophene	Organic compound	Antiseptic in medicated shampoo
Hydrogen peroxide	Oxidizing agent	Bleach. Perm neutralizer. With para-dyes
Isopropanol	Organic base (alcohol)	Hair lacquer solvent. Cleaning mirrors
Isopropyl myristate	Ester	Plasticizer in hair lacquer
Karaya	Gum	Setting lotion
Lanette wax	Synthetic wax	Emulsifying agent in cosmetic creams
Lanolin	Wax	Super-fatting soap. Conditioners. In hand cream
Lard	Animal fat	Soap making. Pomade
Lauryl alcohol	Organic base	Making soapless shampoo
Lavender oil	Essential oil	Perfume

Lawsone (Henna)	Vegetable dye	Permanent hair dye
Liquid paraffin	Mineral oil	In protective skin and hair creams
Magnesium carbonate	Inorganic salt	In talcum powder and bleaching paste
Magnesium silicate (talc)	Inorganic salt	In foot powders
Magnesium stearate	Organic salt	In talcum powder
Methanol	Organic base (alcohol)	Perfume solvent. Methylating ethanol
Methylated spirit	Resin solvent and fat solvent	Hair lacquer solvent. Cleaning mirrors
Musk	Animal secretion	Fixing odour in perfumes
Nipagin	Ester	Preservative in hairdressing preparations
Nitrocellulose	Organic compound	Film-former in nail lacquer
Nitro-dyes	Organic base	Semi-permanent tints. Colour shampoo
Olive oil	Vegetable oil	Making soap and surfactants. Hot oil treatment
Palm oil	Vegetable oil	Making soap and surfactants
Para-aminobenzoic acid	Organic acid	Suntan preparations
Paraffin wax	Mineral oil	Depilatory wax
Para-phenylenediamine	Organic base	Permanent oxidation tint
Para-toluenediamine	Organic base	Permanent oxidation tint
Persulphates	Salts	Boosters in bleaching paste
Petroleum jelly	Mineral oil	Skin creams and brilliantine
Phosphoric acid	Inorganic acid	Stabilizer for hydrogen peroxide
Phthalates	Esters	Plasticizers in nail lacquer
Polyvinyl acetate	Synthetic resin	Hair lacquer and plastic setting lotion
Polyvinyl pyrrolidone	Synthetic resin	Hair lacquer and plastic setting lotion
Potassium aluminium sulphate (alum)	Inorganic salt	Astringent and styptic
Potassium hydroxide	Alkali	Making soft soap. Cuticle remover
Potassium palmitate	Organic salt	Soft soap shampoo
Quaternary ammonium compounds	Organic bases	Antiseptics and conditioners
Rosewater	Essential oil solution	Perfume and astringent
Salicylic acid	Organic acid	Preservative. Stabilizer for peroxide
Selenium sulphide	Inorganic salt	Dandruff treatment
Shellac	Resin	Film-former in hair lacquer
Sodium bicarbonate	Inorganic salt	Tooth powder. In fire extinguishers
Sodium bisulphite	Reducing agent	Heat wave perming lotion
Sodium borate (borax)	Inorganic salt	Water softener. Emulsifying agent
Sodium bromate	Oxidizing agent	Cold wave 'neutralizer'
Sodium carbonate (washing soda)	Inorganic salt	Water softener. Cleaning drains
Sodium chloride (common salt)	Inorganic salt	Recharging zeolite water softeners
Sodium hexametaphosphate	Inorganic salt	Water softener (Calgon)
Sodium hydroxide (caustic soda)	Alkali	Making soap and soapless detergents Cuticle remover
Sodium lauryl sulphate	Organic salt	Surfactant in soapless shampoo
Sodium perborate	Oxidizing agent	'Neutralizer' in Home perms
Sodium sesqui-carbonate	Inorganic salt	Water softening bath crystals
Sodium stearate	Organic salt	Toilet soap and soap washing powders
Spermaceti	Wax	Making cosmetic creams
Stearic acid	Fatty acid	Making cosmetic and hair creams
Sulphuric acid	Inorganic acid	Sulphonating oils in making surfactants
Tallow	Animal fat	Making soap
Tartaric acid	Organic acid	Making acid dyes stick to hair

Thioglycollic acid	Organic acid	Making cold wave perming lotion
Tragacanth	Gum	Setting lotion
Triethanolamine	Organic base	Making soapless detergents and mascara
Triethanolamine lauryl sulphate	Organic salt	Surfactant in soapless shampoo
Turtle oil	Animal oil	Super-fatting soap
Witch-hazel	Vegetable product	Astringent
Zeolite	Complex salt	In water softening cylinders (Permutit)
Zinc carbonate (calamine)	Inorganic salt	Anti-sunburn lotion
Zinc oxide	Inorganic base	In sunscreen preparations
Zinc pyrithione	Organic salt	Medicating agent in shampoo

Appendix 2

Visual aids

Chapter 1

Films: Your skin, Your hair and scalp, Unilever
8 mm Film Loop: Human skin, SB/D/2, Macmillan & Co. Ltd.
Models: Head showing muscles and blood vessels, Griffin L03.090; Adam, Rouilly MC6
Hair follicle, Adam, Rouilly
Skin section, Adam, Rouilly MS4
Human skull
Micro-Slides: VS Human scalp, H9-1, Phillip Harris
Human plantar skin, H9-2, Phillip Harris
Skin showing elastic fibres, H9-23, Phillip Harris

Chapter 3

Films: Water, I.C.I.; Hard Water, Outline of Detergency, What is Soap?, Chemistry of Soapless Detergents, Unilever

Chapter 5

Film strip: Understanding Electricity Electricity Council—England and Wales. 8 parts
Pamphlets: For safety learn the new wiring colours, H.M. Stationery Office

Chapter 6

Inclined mirrors, concave and convex mirrors, dry cell cut in half vertically, filament bulb (clear glass)—single coil and coiled coil types, fluorescent tube.

Chapter 8

Film: Your hair and scalp, Unilever

Chapter 9

Colour triangle, Newton's disc.

Chapter 10

Film: Your hair and scalp, Unilever
Model: Hair follicle structure

Chapter 12

Film: Your Feet, Unilever

Chapter 13

Films: Your digestion, Nothing to eat but food, Let's keep our teeth, Your feet, Your mouth, Unilever; Respiration in Man, Fundamentals of the nervous system, Encyclopedia Britannica International Ltd.
8 mm Film loop: Human skin, SB/D/2, Macmillan & Co. Ltd.
Model: Skeletorso B 5200, Phillip Harris
Human skeleton

Chapter 14

Film: Air, I.C.I.
Mercury and anaeroid barometers, Hair hygrometer (Edney), Regnault's hygrometer, Wet-and-dry bulb hygrometer

Chapter 15

Films: Room for hygiene, Unilever; Point of new departure (man-made fibres), I.C.I.; A world of difference. Unilever
Film strip: Good grooming and skin care, C6880, E.P. Productions.

Chapter 16

Films: The Griseofulvin Story, Guild Sound and Vision Ltd.; War to the last itch, London School of Hygiene and Tropical Medicine

Chapter 17

Films: If only I knew what to do, Burn's best friend, Coma, 240 volts, Only 10 pints, Please don't move me, The St. John Ambulance Association

Film loops: Eothen Cinette, Emergency resuscitation, Mouth to mouth, CEM/N/A/E1
External cardiac massage. CEM/N/A/E3.

Bibliography

Bennet, G. A. G., *Electricity and Modern Physics* Edward Arnold

Burnet, F. M., *Viruses and Man* Penguin Books

Gostelow, J., *Cosmetics in the School Laboratory* Shell

Gostelow, J. & Dean, P., *Experiments in Detergency* Shell

Harris, *Handbook of Textile Fibres* Harris Research Laboratories

Hibbott, *Handbook of Cosmetic Science* Pergamon Press

Hodgson, G., *Hazards of Beauty Culture* 'The Practitioner', Nov. 1962, Vol. 189, 667-673; Dec. 1962, Vol. 189, 778-787

Isaacs, A., *Introducing Science* Penguin Books

Jarrett, A., *Science and the Skin* English Universities Press

Kilgour & McGarry, *An Introduction to Science and Hygiene for Hairdressers* Heinemann

Lapage, G., *Animals Parasitic in Man* Penguin Books

Lee, C. M. & Inglis, J. K., *Science for Hairdressing Students* Pergamon Press

Lewis, H. E. *et al.*, *Aerodynamics of the Human Micro-environment* 'The Lancet', 28 June 1969, 1273-1277

Mackey, H. O., *A Handbook of Diseases of the Skin* Macmillan

McIntyre, J. E., *The Chemistry of Fibres* Edward Arnold

Marples, M. J., *Life on the Human Skin* 'Scientific American', Jan. 1969, 108

Montagna, W., *The Structure and Function of Skin* Academic Press

Montagna, W. & Ellis, R. A., *The Biology of Hair Growth* Academic Press

Moore, E., *Vegetable Oils & Fats* Unilever

Nuffield Biology Texts Longman/Penguin Books

Savill, A., *The Hair and Scalp* Edward Arnold

Sinclair, R., *Essential Oils* Unilever

Sinclair, R., *Soap-making* Unilever

Young, A., *Practical Cosmetic Science* Mills & Boon Ltd.

British Man-made Fibres Federation *Facts About Man-made Fibres*

Consumer's Association *Electricity Supply and Safety*

Journal of the Society of Cosmetic Chemists, 22, 839-850 (Dec. 1971); 23, 447-470 (July 1972)

St. John Ambulance Association, The *Digest of First-aid*

Index